Professional Home Inspection Results

A Complete Source of Reference for Aspiring and Practicing Home Inspectors

by Richard Lee Burgess
with contributions by Phillip Stojanik

PROCOR EDISON PUBLICATIONS
Houston, Texas

Copyright © 2003 by Richard Lee Burgess.
All rights reserved

Procor Edison Publications

Library of Congress Cataloging-in-Publication:
International Standard Book Number: 0 9713610 0 2

Professional Home Inspection Results
A Complete Source of Reference for Aspiring and Practicing Home Inspectors

Printed in the USA

Warning and Disclaimer:
Although every reasonable effort has been made to ensure the accuracy of the information herein, no guarantee of any sort is implied. Applicable federal, state, and local regulations must always be obeyed. This book is not a substitute for legal counsel. Readers are expressly advised to seek competent legal counsel regarding any points of law discussed herein. The author, publisher, and other contributors to this book take no liability nor responsibility to any person or entity with respect to loss or damage arising from the use of, or reliance upon, the information contained in this book.

Trademarks:
The use of any term in this book should not be regarded as affecting the validity of any trademark or service mark.

author	Richard L. Burgess
technical consultant and editorial contributor	Phillip Stojanik
pest control consultant	Frank Mena of North America Pest Control
publisher	Procor Edison Publications
publishing facilitator	Brockton Publishing Company
printing & binding	Printed in the USA
photographs & illustrations	Procor Edison Publications
special illustrations	Creative Publishing international, *The Complete Photo Guide to Home Repair*
cover design	Procor Edison Publications and Brockton Publishing Company

DEDICATION

To my father, a man of vast kindness, patience, and wisdom, and an inspiration to all who have known him.

ACKNOWLEDGMENTS

The author would like to thank all those who had a hand in the development of this book. The skills of technical consultant and editorial contributor **Phillip Stojanik** have proven to be invaluable in the quest for technical excellence. Publishing facilitator **Brockton Brown** of Brockton Publishing has displayed the highest levels of expertise and cooperation directing and formatting the finished product you see here.

Very special thanks go out to **Bryan Trandem**, Executive Editor at Creative Publishing iqnternational, who so generously granted permission to reproduce some of the extraordinary copyrighted images which grace these pages.

The real estate industry's foremost instruction and inspection leaders who gave so liberally of their valuable time cannot know the depth of the respect and appreciation I hold for them. They include:

Richard J. Baudry, Director, Accu-spect Home Inspector Institute

Michael Cothran, CIO, MLC Inspections, TREC Instructor

Stephen L. Crawford, CPM, CCIM, RPA. Senior TAR Instructor

Michael Crow, US Inspect

Scott Funk, Attorney at law

James Hime, National real estate author, lecturer, consultant

Gloria Isackson, Executive Director, National Association of Home Inspectors

Dr. Valerie C. Lamont, Director, Real Estate Institute, University of Southern Maine

L.J. Meyer, Attorney at law

R.H. Proctor, P.E.

Weldon Sikes, President, National Association of Home Inspectors

George Szontagh, President, American Society of Construction Analysts

Ralph Tamper, DREI, GRI, CBR, President, The Real Estate School

To *all* of you, for your efforts and encouragement, thank you.

FOREWORD

Today's home inspector must deliver to the client a comprehensive report resulting from a thorough examination of virtually all structural and mechanical systems found in the home.

It is, therefore, incumbent upon the home inspector to be familiar with a vast constellation of ever-changing industry standards, building codes, manufacturers' specifications, and legal issues which surround the home construction and inspection fields.

The variety of potential defects to be found in modern homes is infinite, and it would be unimaginable that any single book could address every last one. Richard Burgess, however, has thoroughly compiled, analyzed, and distilled an enormous wealth of the most pertinent data available, and has delivered it in this clear and comprehensive book.

This volume belongs on every inspector's reference shelf. It is an extraordinarily valuable resource, not just for those entering the profession, but for the seasoned inspector as well. I often consult it myself.

Mr. Burgess is to be commended for his relentless research efforts and his carefully structured writing style. Home inspectors everywhere will certainly find this book immensely useful.

George Szontagh
TX PREI 2212
American Society of Construction Analysts, Houston
Past President

PREFACE

An abundance of information and educational materials related to the home inspection field are readily available. Much of it is hidden within the pages of sources intended for reference by students of *related* disciplines, such as framing, plumbing, heating and air conditioning, appliance repair, and electrical wiring.

Home inspection is unique in the depth and breadth of the skill requirements of its practitioners. Inspectors are not required to have the same level of expertise in any one of these disciplines as the tradesmen whose careers are based upon them. Instead, competent home inspectors must have knowledge of *all* such disciplines, but only to the extent that a largely visual inspection and performance evaluation can be satisfactorily performed.

Students of home inspection will find that the study of those materials intended for individuals pursuing one of the related trades can be arduous. Identifying the information pertinent to inspector training from within a vast body of mostly unnecessary data can often frustrate the learning effort. Inspectors must be broad-based generalists, not specialists in any single field of technical discipline.

This book is intended to provide practicing or aspiring home inspectors with a uniquely complete source of reference. It includes everything inspectors require for excellence,

while omitting the in-depth details needed only for the specific related trades.

A wealth of technical data, government regulations, trade association tenets, expert opinions, and an array of writings related to the subject of home inspection were assembled, compared, and meticulously scrutinized for points of commonality. It became apparent that the most progressive home inspection authorities have come to significant agreement on many subjects, with minor exceptions. Language that best conveys those common points of view was chosen for this book.

In those instances where important philosophies were found to hold disagreement, an effort was made to express and explain those differences. Except for the careful translation of language used within the research sources, very few of this author's opinions are reflected herein.

During the 40-month period in which this book was written, the home inspection industry saw a host of evolutionary changes. To the extent possible, the impact of those changes were incorporated into *Professional Home Inspection Results* by this author, right up to the time of our print deadline.

I am confident that readers will find this book to be accurate, complete, and as easy to understand as the subject matter permits.

Best of luck to all,
Richard Burgess

CONTENTS

Professional Home Inspection Results
A Complete Source of Reference for Aspiring and Practicing Home Inspectors

1. Primary Inspections

STRUCTURAL SYSTEMS 13

Foundations 13
- Pier and Beam Foundations 13
- Basement Foundations 15
- Slab-On-Grade Foundations 16
- Screeded slabs 18
- General performance of all foundation types 18

Grading and Drainage 21
Roof Coverings 24
- Wood Shingles and Shakes 26
- Asphalt Composition Roofing 27
- Tile, Slate, and Mineral Fiber Shingles 28
- Built-Up Roofing 28
- Metal Roofing 29

Roof Structure and Attic 30
Walls (Interior and Exterior) 33
Ceilings and Floors (Including Stairways) 36
Doors (Interior and Exterior) 37
Windows 39
Fireplaces and Chimneys 40
Attached Porches, Decks and Carports 43
Review Questions - Structural Systems 44

ELECTRICAL SYSTEMS 49

Service Entrance and Panels 51
Branch Circuits, Connected Devices and Fixtures 54
- Wall and Appliance Switches 59
- Fixtures, Lighting Devices and Fans 59

Review Questions - Electrical Systems 61

HEATING, VENTILATION AND AIR CONDITIONING SYSTEMS 65

Heating Equipment 65
- Forced Air Heating 66
- Gas Furnaces 67
- Condensing Furnaces and Boilers 71
- Electric Furnaces and Electric Baseboard Heating 72
- Electronic Air Cleaners 73
- Hot Water Space Heating 74
- Steam Heating 75
- Oil Heating 76

Cooling Equipment and Heat Pumps 77
- Heat Pumps 81

Evaporative Coolers 82
Ducts and Vents (HVAC) 83
Review Questions - Heating, Ventilation & Air Conditioning Systems 86

PLUMBING SYSTEMS 91
   Water Supply System and Fixtures 91
      Sinks 92
      Bathtubs and Showers 94
      Commodes 96
      Hosebibs 96
      Laundry Supply 97
   Drains, Wastes, and Vents 97
   Water Heating Equipment 99
      Gas Fired Water Heaters 103
      Electric Water Heaters 105
   Hydro-Therapy Equipment 106
   Review Questions - Plumbing Systems 108

APPLIANCES 111
   Built-in Dishwashers 111
   Food Waste Disposers 113
   Range Hoods 113
   Ranges/Ovens/Cooktops 114
   Built-in Microwave Cooking Equipment 115
   Trash Compactors 115
   Bathroom Exhaust Fans and Heaters 116
   Whole-House Vacuum Systems 116
   Garage Door Operators 117
   Doorbell and Chimes 118
   Dryer Vents 118
   Review Questions - Appliances 119

2. Optional Inspections

SWIMMING POOLS AND EQUIPMENT 121
   Water Quality 121
   Pool Safety 122
   Pool Construction 122
      Interior Surfaces 122
      Lights, Steps and Ladders 123
      Level 124
      Diving Boards and Slides 124
      Walking Surfaces 125
   Mechanical Equipment 126
      Drains, Skimmers and Returns 128
   Pool Area Electrical Systems 131
   Barriers 133
   Review Questions - Swimming Pools And Equipment 136

WOOD DESTROYING INSECTS 141
   Termites 142
   Wood-Boring Beetles 144
   Carpenter Ants 144
   Wood Wasps and Carpenter Bees 145
   Review Questions - Wood Destroying Insects 146
   Private Well Water Pumps 148

PRIVATE WATER WELLS & SEPTIC SYSTEMS 149
   Water Wells 149
   Septic Systems 151
   Review Questions - Private Water Wells & Septic Systems ... 153

3. Miscellaneous Optional Inspections

Lawn Sprinklers 155
Outbuildings 156
Outdoor Cooking Equipment 156
Gas Lines 157
Security Systems 158
Fire Protection Equipment 159
Review Questions - Miscellaneous Optional Inspections 160

4. Professional Conduct, Ethics, and Standards of Practice

STANDARDS OF PRACTICE 161
Structural Systems 164
Electrical Systems 166
Heating and Cooling Systems 167
Plumbing Systems 169
Appliances 171
Optional Inspections 174
Review Questions - Professional Conduct, Ethics, and Standards of Practice 177

5. Forms, Marketing and Contracts

THE HOME INSPECTION FIELD FORM 183
SAMPLE REPORT FORM 199
MARKETING AND OTHER BUSINESS 211
CONSULTING CONTRACTS 215
REPORTING LANGUAGE SAMPLES 219

6. Glossary 241

References 248
Procor Edison Publication's Contact Information 249
    Book Ordering
    Answer Keys
    Final Examinations
    CE Course Licensing Agreements
About the Author 250
Reader Survey and Contribution 251

INTRODUCTION

Home inspection is a fast growing industry, and one that is following a trend toward increased regulation and inspector licensing. In Texas, for example (the first state to license real estate inspectors), the stringent rules of the Texas Real Estate Commission have evolved into a model of comprehensive regulatory excellence, prescribing apprenticeship, specialized training, rigorous examination, promulgated reporting formats, and adherence to strict operating and ethical standards.

Millions of homes change hands each year in the United States, and inspection reports have become pivotal negotiating tools, especially in those states where inspection contingency language is written into standard home-purchase agreements.

There now begins to emerge a common thread through the fabric of the regulatory parameters established by those states where regulation is already in place. As the trend toward licensing grows, both practicing and aspiring inspectors will be required to comply with mandated standards of practice.

Professional Home Inspection Results is intended to fill the need for a complete and practical reference book, wherein students and practicing inspectors can learn the basics of residential construction, mechanical systems, and reliable inspection techniques.

Readers will find that the inspection checklist, developed by this author, serves not only as a comprehensive source of reference in the field, but also as an indispensable learning tool. Its importance cannot be overstated.

Knowledgeable home inspectors enjoy satisfying and high-paying careers. Their skills are in considerable demand, and their work calendars are often full. This book offers the student a complete and exciting journey into the world of home inspection, and an opportunity to travel straight to the top of the field.

Typical American Home

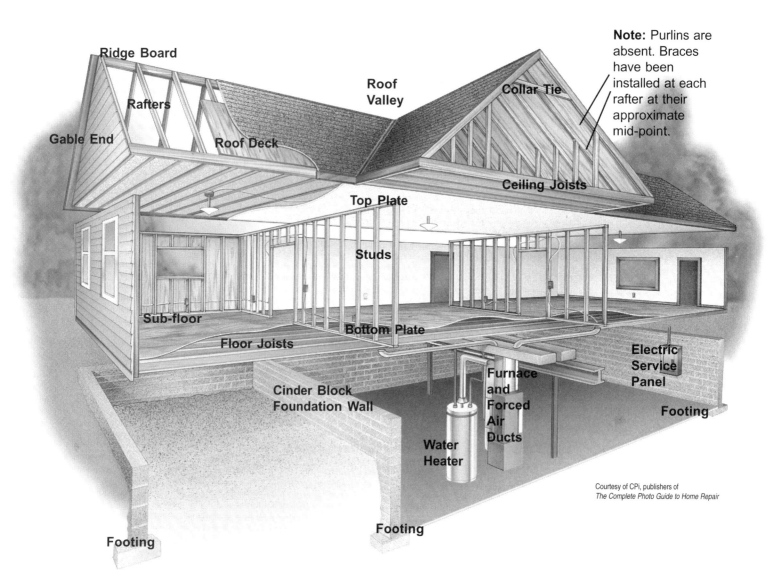

1
Primary Inspections
STRUCTURAL SYSTEMS

Learning Objectives

1. Learn the basics of residential construction methods and principles.
2. Be able to identify the causes of structural defects commonly found in homes.
3. Know what evidence of adverse conditions to look for during structural-systems inspection.
4. Be aware of the obligations borne by inspectors regarding the scope of structural inspection and reporting.
5. Become familiar with the significance of interrelated structural defects.

Foundations

Foundation design is an exacting science practiced only by those with specialized expertise in architectural or structural engineering. The inspector's job is not to assess design adequacy or enforce building codes, but to report to the client any conditions that are suspected of requiring repair in order to provide safe, sound, and sanitary living within the structure.

All soils compress, and foundations of all types are subject to the resultant settlement. When settlement is slight, uniform, or antipicated in the foundation design, it is of little concern. When a foundation settles unevenly (differential settlement), it introduces stresses that can weaken the building.

This stair-step pattern of brick/mortar cracks is a condition normally associated with foundation movement. When cracks in this pattern are found in a brick wall greater than 20 feet in horizontal length, it may be due, at least in part, to expansion of the brick veneer (if no expansion joint is installed). Look for loss of monolithic integrity at the foundation's vertical perimeter grade beam faces below such brick cracks.

Pier and Beam Foundations

Pier and beam foundations may be constructed with or without a continuous vertical outside wall of concrete, block, brick or other material. Such a continuous perimeter grade beam lends strength and resistance to heaving, but the cost of such construction is often prohibitive. Simpler, and less costly is the use of piers installed at carefully calculated perimeter and interior load-bearing locations. Girders or beams are then installed across the supporting piers, and level adjustment is fine-tuned with the installation of shims at appropriate places. A decorative skirt of wood, lattice, or other material is usually installed around the perimeter to keep animals from entering the crawlspace.

The mortar joints in this brick support are badly deteriorated. Repairs will be needed if this pier-and-beam foundation is to continue to perform satisfactorily.

If all crawl space areas are not accessed during inspection, an explanation is required. There are some conditions that might prevent complete inspection. If, in the judgment of the inspector, there is inadequate accessibility, where the access opening is less than the code-required 18 x 24 inches, or if under-floor height is less than 18 inches, the inspector may find entry for inspection impossible. If hazardous conditions exist, such as the presence of construction debris, or active rodents or wasps, the inspector may choose to inspect the crawl space only from the access locations. Even in these cases, the inspector must make every effort to observe and report all adverse conditions present.

Moisture is the main enemy of the wood girders, beams, joists, and sub-floors commonly found in pier and beam foundations, so crawl space areas require specific minimum ventilation provisions and positive drainage conditions. Ventilation area should be at least 1/150th of the total area, or footprint, of the foundation. For example, a 2300 square foot foundation needs at least 15.3 total square feet of ventilation openings. Ventilation openings should be found not more than 3 feet distant from each main foundation corner. It is, however, generally acceptable to omit openings at the front or most visible face of the home (a common practice where aesthetics are a priority). An exception to the 1/150th rule is in the presence of a vapor barrier ground cover, where at least 1/1500th of the total footprint is acceptable ventilation area. Perimeter grade beam walls should extend at least 3 inches above finished grade to preclude water penetration into the crawl space. If underfloor grading appears inadequate for proper runoff, look for a sump pump, or recommend one, if necessary. Inadequate drainage conditions, even in the absence of resultant damage, is reportable.

Access to the crawl space should be at least 18 x 24 inches, unless mechanical equipment (such as a furnace) is installed there. This requires a larger access opening, at least 30 x 30 inches, but in all cases, large enough to remove the equipment. Minimum crawl space headroom required by current code is 18 inches.

Crawl spaces are breeding grounds for pests and molds, so it is highly advisable for inspectors to take the proper measures to protect both skin and lungs. Some cases of hospitalization have been reported by inspectors and house movers who have been unfortunate enough to experience severe insect bites or the inhalation of microscopic organisms found under a house. Protective gear is recommended.

Check to see that girders and joists are properly supported, that there is no evidence of wood damage caused by splitting, rotting, or wood-destroying-organisms (especially at the beam pockets, under bath, kitchen, and laundry rooms, and where floor joists attach to sill plates). Metal flashings, called termite shields, are often found atop the piers in an effort block a termite's logical path to the wood girders or beams they can destroy. See that such shields, if present, are not torn or otherwise compromised.

This floor joist is not properly resting on the support beam.

Crawl spaces should be free of debris and the musty odors that are indicative of excessive moisture conditions. Also, observe the condition of any moisture barrier on the ground, usually of polyethylene sheeting. Look for voids, tears, or low spots that are vulnerable to the accumulation of standing water.

Is there insulation between the floor joists? If not, report it. If so, inspect for tears and other flaws. If insulation below the floor has a vapor barrier (of paper or foil), the *barrier should face the heated side* so that moisture is not trapped in the insulation within the floor joist cavities. The presence of such a vapor barrier may not be apparent to the inspector if it is well tucked up into the cavities, as it would be covered from view by the insulation. Electrical wiring must be properly secured, and any visible plumbing, dryer vents, or other mechanical components should be inspected for leaks and other flaws.

Are there cracks in any of the beam walls? Are any concrete elements crumbling? Are piers tipping or sinking? The piers should properly support girders at all points of intersection, and any notches in the girders should fit well into their mating elements. Cinder block or brick piers are not as robust as concrete, and are more likely to show signs of deterioration, so always look for crumbling mortar joints, especially at stress points. Shims should be solid and secure. Additionally, joists and girders must not rest on the ground, nor should they appear to twist or sag.

Basement Foundations

Basement foundations can be thought of as pier-and-beam construction, and are inspected in much the same way. Questions of ventilation, access, headroom, and debris do not apply, of course, but the basement is really little more than a large crawl space. It is important to determine whether the basement foundation is of the poured concrete type or of block construction. Blocks may be of concrete, cinder, brick, or other

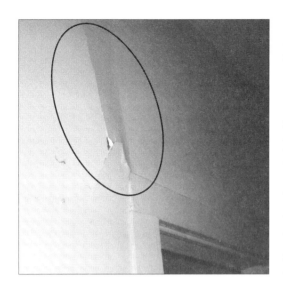

Stress deflection at interior door header areas is a condition normally associated with foundation movement.

materials. Since block walls do not have the strength of poured-in-place concrete, visible cracks and other flaws in block foundations are quite common.

Whether monolithic or block, minor flaws can be easily repaired with mortar or caulk to prevent water and insect penetration. Differential settlement is a larger problem that can affect all foundation types. When encountered, its severity must be carefully assessed by a variety of observations. Visible cracks in foundation walls may or may not be indicative of total foundation failure. Since all soils compress, all footings that are not resting on bedrock are subject to settlement. Slight or uniform settlement is normal, and is no cause for alarm. If, however, differential settlement has caused severe cracks in foundation or brick walls, or obvious stress deflection in the interior walls and ceilings, the foundation has lost its integrity, and is not satisfactorily performing.

Other signs of foundation failure may include floors which are out of level, ill-fitting windows and doors, and structural members which have cracked or pulled their nails loose (especially roof rafters which have pulled away from their attachment points at the ridge beam). Some of these conditions can be caused by other factors, such as the drying and shrinking of wet (or "green"), framing lumber. The installation of a perfectly level foundation is uncommon, so level measurements, if taken, must be reported as only one component of the foundation performance analysis. The inspector must be capable of analyzing all the different foundation stress factors as they relate to one another.

Efflorescence at this tile floor is indicative of a high moisture condition.

Look for evidence of water penetration through basement walls, especially around window and door frames. Make certain that gutters, downsputs, and other drainage conditions positively carry water well away from the foundation walls. Check the operation of any sump pumps, and look for white stains called *efflorescence*, a deposit of soluble salts found in masonry components, often brought to the surface by excess moisture. If such deposits create a visible ring around the entire basement, at any level, it indicates a flooding condition. Its presence and implications would be reported.

Slab-On-Grade Foundations

According to The Department of Housing and Urban Development (HUD), slab-on-grade foundations should have at least 6 inches of exposure above finished grade for homes with brick siding, and at least 8

Primary Inspections — Structural Systems

inches of exposure above finished grade for homes with wood siding. The purpose of this is twofold. First, adequate slab exposure helps prevent rainwater or ground moisture from entering the structure (if proper grading and drainage are maintained). Secondly, foundation fractures and insect activity can be more readily observed. (Note that locally accepted standards for minimum slab exposure can vary, allowing as little as 2 inches in some locales, so inspectors should contact a local Building Official if there is any doubt).

Inspect for any evidence of water penetration into the structure. Stains, peeling paint, or other evidence of conditions which might be caused by high moisture content will alert the inspector to investigate potential water sources. Such conditions might be found at the interior sill and baseboard areas of the inside walls behind gardens or other high soil locations, or at entry door thresholds where outdoor grading is too high or improperly sloped for proper drainage.

This rafter appears to have pulled away from the ridge board at its nailing attachment point, a condition which may be indicative of foundation movement.

A moisture meter is useful to help determine the severity of water problems when stains or discoloration are found, or if conditions suggest vulnerability to water penetration. Moisture content of over 19% (by weight) in building products is not acceptable. According to Haag Engineering of Dallas/Houston, 30% moisture content is normally required for wood rot and decay. All such rot, decay, mildew, and other deterioration will be reported, as well as any wet or high moisture conditions conducive to their occurrence.

Look for evidence of differential settlement or previous slab repair. Holes drilled through any portion of the slab, and filled with epoxy or concrete can be evidence of mud-jacking or pier installation. Mud-jacking is the process of pumping under-slab voids full with cement grout or polyurethane foam through small holes drilled into the portions of the slab that are settling. Alternatively, pre-cast piers are generally installed in larger holes, dug as deep as would be required to find soils capable of bearing the load. Piers are generally placed at six to eight foot intervals along the perimeter grade beam, and sometimes in the interior portions of a slab, where breaking through the floor or tunneling is required. Known or suspected slab repairs must be reported to the client. Use caution identifying the foundation repairs. Some termite treatments that include the drilling of holes at perimeter foundation locations (and even the tendon anchor ports associated with post tensioning), might be confused by the inexperienced inspector with some types of foundation repair.

This concrete patch is evidence of pier installation, intended to stabilize a slab foundation.

This cable anchor in a post-tensioned slab foundation is not adequately sealed.

Most newer slab-on-grade foundations are of the post-tensioned type, where sheathed steel cables or tendons are installed in a grid pattern before the concrete is placed. These cables are mechanically pulled tight after the concrete has cured for several days, increasing the foundation's strength. The cable anchors or "ports" around the perimeter of the foundation are easily visible, and should be sealed. No cable ends should be exposed.

HVAC ducts should not be routed inside the slab. The porous nature of concrete can cause the introduction of unwanted ground moisture, and ground-temperature conditions will encourage the formation of condensation. The accumulation of this moisture can cause the formation of mold or mildew, a known health risk, and may also prematurely deteriorate both insulation and ductwork.

Screeded slabs

A screeded slab is similar to a slab-on-grade foundation, but has floor joists or sleepers laid and attached over its surface. These joists support the sub-floor, creating an air space between slab and floor. These cavities must not be vented outdoors. Also, since the under-floor spaces are often used as a return air duct for heating and air conditioning, it is unsafe to treat this area chemically for termites. The condition of wood members and plumbing components under a screeded slab floor is impossible to determine without removing the flooring, which is beyond the scope of a non-invasive, visual inspection.

Shower tiles cracked in this patterned manner may be indicative of foundation movement or unusually high stresses in the shower-enclosure framing components.

Inspect for signs of water leaks at plumbing supply and drain lines, the tile/grout surfaces and the shower pan.

Just as in other slab types, screeded slab perimeter foundation wall exposure above finished grade must be adequate to preclude water penetration and direct soil contact with siding materials. Look for evidence of water penetration, and take moisture content measurements if necessary. Again, floors should be level, and visible cracks in the perimeter grade beam or evidence of previous repair should be reported.

General performance of all foundation types

There are additional factors to consider when analyzing total foundation performance. Some imperfect conditions will be found in every home, and it is the manner in which all factors interrelate that will guide the inspector to conclusions regarding foundation performance. Since the inspector's observations are factors from which his conclusions are drawn, all relevant factors must be reported to the client.

Soil should not be shrinking away from foundation walls. This condition is an indication of severe loss of soil moisture. Loss of moisture means loss of volume, and foundations can fail when the volume of soil supporting them is so reduced. In parts of the country with highly cohesive clay soils, it is common practice to water foundations during dry spells to prevent this from occurring. Some homeowners have even installed automatic watering systems just for this purpose. A uniform moisture content around the perimeter of a building will help to minimize the danger of foundation failure due to soil shrinkage resulting in differential settlement.

Trees located close to the foundation can cause enough moisture depletion (or transpiration), and resultant soil shrinkage, to seriously affect foundation performance. Additionally, large tree roots are strong enough to damage any foundation components in their growth path. For these reasons, the Federal Housing Administration (FHA) requires a minimum distance of 5 feet between trees and foundation components. Local authorities sometimes will overlook this Federal standard, relying instead on the judgment of inspectors to permit shorter distances if trees are deemed small enough to present minimal near-term danger. According to the University of Texas at Arlington, though, no tree should be planted as close to the foundation as its ultimate height at maturity. It is impractical to expect trees to be so distant from residential structures in most cases, but this knowledge will help the inspector fully assess foundation performance. Remember, too, that soil shrinkage can also be caused by the drying affect of the sun, especially at a south-facing wall (which gets the most sun in North America). This condition is most pronounced in expansive clay soils.

Look at the roof's ridge to determine if it is level. (Bring a good level when you access the roof, and check both ends as well as the middle of the ridge.) An out-of-level or sagging condition at the ridge may be indicative of differential foundation settlement. Damaged rafters can present a similar condition, so remember to support your conclusions with observations from the attic space.

Observation of brick veneer siding can help an inspector analyze the condition of the foundation. A stairstep pattern of cracking which follows mortar joints can be caused by settlement. If, for example, the perimeter of the foundation settles, the brick veneer resting on the foundation's brick ledge is forced by its own weight to conform to the changing shape of the foundation. The stresses created cause mortar joints to fail in a predictable pattern. If settlement is minor, re-pointing the mortar joints will restore the facade to a weatherproof condition (although filling mortar joints with cementitious material may encourage additional or repeated cracking). Use of an elastomeric caulking material will permit the foundation to continue its flexure without compromising weather tightness.

In severe cases of differential settlement, even the bricks themselves may break along the highest stress points. This is usually indicative of excessive foundation movement. Vertical expansion joints, which are cut from top to bottom in masonry walls running horizontally longer than 20 feet, should be filled with caulk for weather tightness. These expansion joints will show spreading (or, occasionally, closing), if the supporting foundation settles unevenly, providing further clues to foundation movement.

Inspectors should look carefully for signs of previous brick or mortar repair, especially if the brick has been freshly painted. Sellers naturally go to great lengths to make their homes presentable, and cosmetic repairs can obscure evidence of larger problems. Window and door frames are almost always forced out of square by excessive foundation movement. When the frames are racked in this way, window sashes and doors may not close fully, latch correctly, or operate without binding. Window panes can actually break under the stress of severe foundation movement. (Look for the realignment of striker plates at latch jambs intended to restore proper latch function.) This kind of maintenance can make the inspector's job more difficult, but the experienced professional will be alert to the signs of recent repairs, as well as the significance of the conditions found.

The exterior trim around windows and doors should not be separating or freshly caulked in a way that indicates racking or unusual movement. This also holds true for the frieze or rake boards at gable ends. Remember that less-than-perfect trim carpentry is common, and these factors are just pieces of the puzzle inspectors regularly see.

Many homes have had additions to their original structures. Be sure that addition foundations are not pulling or dropping away from the main structure. The resulting potential for damage to structural elements is the same as that described for differential settlement of the original foundation. Water penetration at foundation joinery, and damage to the original foundation components are additional concerns. Look at any concrete steps or porches for the same conditions. Masonry fireplaces will often settle differently from the rest of the structure, too, but settlement of a heavy fireplace is anticipated in good design. Unless its settlement has caused structural damage to the fireplace, chimney, or to adjacent components of the building, the concern is water penetration where the fireplace and chimney meet the wall. Caulking is normally the remedy.

The twisting or bowing of framing members inside the walls due to differential foundation settlement will reveal itself by a pattern of cracking, wrinkling, buckling, or puckering in the wallboard or plaster. This is especially pronounced at window and door openings. The visible patterns representing evidence of settlement are different from typical construction imperfections, and are easily identified. Also look for corner beads and tape joints that appear to be under the stress of excess movement. Gaps at ceiling-to-wall intersections, and countertops or cabinets that have separated from walls are further evidence of foundation movement.

Relatively new on the scene are various mechanical and electronic tools which allow the inspector to easily measure the foundation's departure from dead level. Foundations may have been installed out of level, but other factors (cracked foundation beam walls or floor surfaces, window and door frames which are out of square, interior or exterior wall materials which display signs of stress deflection, and roof rafters detaching from ridge boards), are evidence of differential settlement. With these new tools, the inspector takes a reference or "zero" reading near the center of the structure's ground floor, then subsequent readings around the perimeter, noting each reading and its location on a diagram of the foundation. Readings that indicate sudden changes or large departures from level can support or dispute the preliminary conclusions drawn from other factors. Departure from level greater than 1 inch over 30 horizontal feet (or any ratio thereof) is excessive.

Any area of stone or ceramic floor tile (installed over a slab foundation) that displays a patterned cracking condition is also suspect. Any level measurements taken will provide supporting evidence of differential settlement. The poured concrete floor of any garage is intentionally sloped toward the overhead door to provide proper drainage, but visible cracks, especially those which reach into the vertical face of the perimeter grade beam, are valid evidence of foundation movement. Slight hairline cracks, caused primarily by the shrinkage associated with curing concrete, are common, and may be of little structural significance in the absence of other clear evidence of excessive foundation movement.

Evaluating the foundation requires careful observation, knowledge of the performance characteristics of building materials, experience, and analytical skills. The inspector's job is to determine, and report in plain language, whether the foundation is satisfactorily performing its intended function. This responsibility includes divulging to the client all conditions found which impact the inspector's conclusions.

Grading and Drainage

All foundation materials are affected by the excessive accumulation of water. The inevitable foundation movement caused by the swelling and shrinking of soil as moisture content changes is, by far, the single largest

This soil is too high on the foundation wall, providing less than the FHA minimum required 8 inches of slab exposure. Here, soil in direct contact with the wood-product siding creates a vulnerability to water and insect penetration.

cause of foundation failure. Drainage considerations are, therefore, very important to foundation performance, especially in areas of highly cohesive clay soils, where swelling and shrinking are most pronounced. When soil shrinks away from foundation walls during dry seasons, the voids can cause unsupported portions of the foundation components to break or sink under the weight of the building. When this condition is severe, a foundation-watering program is often recommended. Clay soils expand and contract significantly with changing moisture content. Large voids within their tiny grains can absorb large amounts of moisture. By contrast, sandy soils, with larger grains and smaller voids, drain well, and thus maintain a more stable volume than clay.

Finished grading should have a gentle, even slope to carry surface water away from the structure. At least 1-inch drop in 8 feet is required. A drop of 4 or 5 inches in 8 feet will freely flow surface water, but grading steeper than that (over 5%), creates a vulnerability to erosion, a washing away of the soil. Reverse grading, sloped to create a vulnerability to the accumulation of standing water at the foundation wall, will cause soil at the ponding location to swell excessively, endangering the integrity of the foundation. Severe ponding can result in water penetration into the structure. Flower beds are often landscaped with walls intended to contain special soil mixtures and mulch, but they can trap water, too. Garden walls should be low enough to preclude ponding problems, and should include drains at appropriate intervals if materials are not sufficiently porous.

In locations where the accumulation of water is excessive, special accommodations must be made for its removal. Look for drain inlets and catch basins at low spots or swales around the structure, and try to determine whether their discharge locations are sufficiently low to provide proper gravity drainage.

Most homes will have gutters and downspouts attached to the fascia to collect and drain away rainwater. Some homes have gutters installed only for the protection of entry doors. Some homes have no gutters at all, and allow roof runoff to fall directly to the ground. Look for erosion or ponding where gutters are absent, since this condition can cause damage to the foundation. Downspouts which discharge too close to foundation walls can also cause erosion, creating, in turn, a vulnerability to the accumulation of standing water. The installation of splashblocks at downspout discharge locations should be recommended where they are absent.

Gutters should be installed with some degree of slope to carry rain-water to the downspouts. Gutters will often look crooked or bowed (high in the center), toward this purpose. If gutters are not installed in this way, water that accumulates at low points can back up into fascia, soffits, and rafters, and can cause considerable damage. Leaves, pine needles, and the loose granules from composition shingles can clog gutter outlets, blocking the free flow of roof water, with the same results. Clients should be warned of this.

Galvanized steel gutters require frequent painting and cleaning to prevent premature rust-through. They will usually have seams or splices at 10-foot intervals, and this is where corrosion is likely to begin. Wood gutters also require extra care, and the inspector should look for signs of rotting. Scratch suspected areas of rot with a fingernail or screwdriver if unsure.

Other common gutter materials are aluminum, vinyl, and copper. Aluminum can be seamed or seamless. Vinyl will almost always have seams, as will copper. Observe these seams for integrity and water tightness. In all cases, check that gutters are securely affixed to the structure, with no undue sagging, and that the fascia boards have not sustained water damage.

Homeowners on a budget will often attempt to install their own gutters. The use of obviously inferior grade plastic gutters and leaders, available to consumers at home centers, should be pointed out to the client. These products have a short service life, and perform inadequately under harsh conditions.

Leaders (or downspouts), should also be inspected for deterioration, and should be securely fastened to the gutter outlet, as well as the house. Where downspouts discharge to any roof plane below them, take special care to determine whether any nearby intersection of wall and roof are properly flashed and watertight. Observation should be made from both inside and outside at suspect locations.

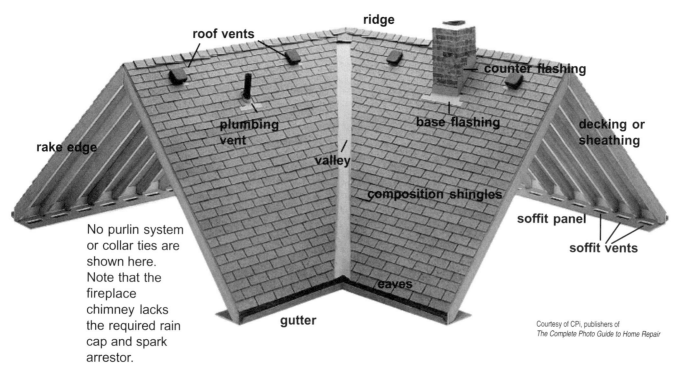

Courtesy of CPi, publishers of *The Complete Photo Guide to Home Repair*

Roof Coverings

Whenever possible, inspectors should access and walk on the roof to best observe its covering, plumbing vents, flue terminations, chimney caps and saddles (or crickets), attic area vents, flashings, and gutter supports. Conditions sometimes exist which make this practice hazardous or impossible, and each inspector should use his judgment to determine whether it is safe. The roof may be wet, too steep, too high, too fragile, or in a dangerously deteriorated condition. In some cases, it may be a good idea to check the condition of the rafters and decking from the attic area before accessing the roof.

When, in the inspector's judgment, conditions preclude roof access, inspection should be made from laddertop, and supported with ground-level observations. In these situations, the ladder will be utilized at logical vantage points selected from all around the structure. From the ground, a good pair of binoculars is essential, and should be a part of every inspector's tool kit. The method used to inspect the roof should always be reported to the client. Some inspection items, such as chimney caps, vent skirts, or flashings, may be unobservable if the roof cannot be accessed.

Walking a roof will allow the inspector to observe the degree and uniformity of "bounce" or, especially, sagging underfoot. Make a mental note to observe any suspect areas for wood damage from the attic space below when you are there, looking for stains and delamination of the roof decking material caused by water penetration or the absence of proper bracing. Often, homeowners will defer the replacement of the roof covering until leaks appear. The inspector must try to determine whether any evidence of water penetration is the result of a problem that has already been cured.

Roof valleys and penetrations accommodating flues, turbines, vents, skylights, and chimneys are vulnerable to water penetration. Observe that rain skirts, flashings, and counter flashings are in good condition, with unbroken caulking or roof cement in appropriate locations. Look for signs of fresh caulking, which may be indicative of recent repairs. Check skylights and roof windows for cracked or broken glazing, and for proper seals. Be certain that turbine ventilators spin freely. Check all roof ventilators for damage and proper installation.

Television antennas are often found strapped to a chimney. The inspector should report whether any damage has been caused to mortar joints or other structural components by the effect of wind loads on the antenna. Any guy wires present must be inspected at their anchor points to be sure no compromise of roof integrity has occurred. Guy wires can be subject to considerable loads, and must not, therefore, be anchored to plumbing vents, appliance flues, or other elements vulnerable to physical damage. Antennas should be fitted with a grounding wire to provide a measure of protection in the event of a lightning strike. The client should always be informed of the potential for damage by any adverse conditions, whether or not damage is in evidence.

A chimney with a dimension larger than 30 inches facing the ridge of a sloped roof should have a cricket. A cricket is a saddle shaped projection on a sloping roof, installed to divert the flow of water. Without a cricket, the valley created by the horizontal intersection of the chimney and the roof plane becomes a trap for rainwater and debris. The likelihood that standing water at this location will eventually find its way into the structure is high.

Tree branches that make direct contact with the structure, especially at roof or cornice areas, can quickly damage building materials. Even without continual or direct contact, leaves, sap, twigs, insects, and animal droppings from above can cause premature deterioration of roof coverings, or clog gutters. Large, overhanging branches, especially

Would you think that these low hanging tree limbs present a hazard?

dead ones, could fall through the roof during a storm. Make your client aware of any such conditions that, in your judgment, represent cause for concern. The inspector will choose the most appropriate place in his report to make such comments, as it is best to report any specific adverse condition only once in the report document.

Wood Shingles and Shakes

Wood shingles differ from wood shakes. The shingles have a sawn, smooth surface, while shakes are split, and have a textured surface. Installation methods are different, too. Shakes are installed over felt, which is visible from the attic area (from which location no shakes or daylight should be visible). Shingles are installed with no felt beneath them, and indirect daylight can sometimes be seen from the attic space. *Indirect* daylight does not necessarily compromise the integrity of the roof covering in regard to water penetration, and, unless evidence of water is present from below, no mention of it is required. *Direct* daylight visible from below indicates that damage is present, and this will permit water to enter the attic area. Repairs are needed any time direct daylight is visible beneath a wood shingled roof.

How many roof layers are visible here?

A wood shingled roof must be of a 4-in-12 pitch or greater. Look for missing, loose, split, curled, weather worn, cracked, soft, or otherwise damaged shingles. Seams must be effectively staggered, and no nails should be exposed. If, from below, evidence of water penetration is present, be sure to check whether repairs have already been made to cure the problem.

Signs of the deterioration of wood shakes are similar to those of wood shingles, so, again, inspect for loose, split, curled, weather worn, cracked, soft, and otherwise damaged shakes. Check for effective seam staggering, and that no nails are exposed. Remember, though, that no daylight should be visible from below, and no felt should be visible from above a wood shake roof. Always check for evidence of water penetration.

When replacing roof coverings, it may be an acceptable practice to install an asphalt composition material over wood shakes or shingles. (Some lenders and insurers find this unacceptable, however, a fact of which the client should be made aware.) When asphalt-composition covering is installed over wood shingles or shakes, the overall thickness of the roof covering creates a drip edge at gable ends and eaves which is unusually thick, and thus vulnerable to water penetration. The installation of a good drip flashing of appropriate dimension is especially important here. For the same reason, it is important to recognize the need for proper sealing at the intersection of roof planes and any vertical walls extending above them.

Asphalt Composition Roofing

Composition shingles are the most common roof covering. They have a base material made of fiberglass or organic felt, which is saturated with asphalt. This, in turn, is covered with a layer of mineral granules. The saturated base material, or mat, provides the necessary weather resistance. The primary purpose of the granular coating is to protect the asphaltic mat from damage caused by the ultra-violet rays of the sun. The mineral granules also provide the desired color. There is a strip or pattern of self-sealing adhesive on the underside of most composition shingles, which serves to seal each shingle to the one below it, improving water and wind resistance.

Investigate the underside of the roof in areas where a wavy or springy condition is observed. It might be caused by water penetration and the resultant deterioration of the roof decking or rafters, but this is not always the case. In areas where snow loads are not encountered, the decking is often of lesser thickness and strength.

"H" clips installed between decking panels are often used in newer construction to strengthen the roof deck. Where they are in use, look for missing clips, especially at locations where the roof sags or displays excessive "bounce" underfoot.

Missing or broken composition shingles, or those shingles with nail heads breaking through, are in need of repair. A composition roof covering with excessive loss of granules should be described as being in need of repair or as having a limited remaining service life. The same is true whenever a puffy, curled, or brittle condition exists.

This composition shingle roof covering displays considerable deterioration. Note torn, curling edges, and the loss of the granular surface coating.

Asphalt roll roofing, found on either pitched or flat roofs, is often coated with mineral granules, just like asphalt composition shingles. It should be inspected for any signs of blistering, cracking, tearing, loss of granules, or curling at the edges. Sometimes, roll roofing is manufactured with the granular surface left off, and may be found to have had a hot tar applied after installation to help seal it. Walking on blistered portions of this type of roof can easily cause tears or openings in its surface, so care should be taken.

As always, inspect the drip edge or flashing, especially at gable ends, and be sure to identify any physical damage caused by hail, golf balls, tree limbs, and such. It is not only the existing damage that must be reported, but also conditions that present extraordinary risk for such damage.

Tile, Slate, and Mineral Fiber Shingles

Tiles for roofing are usually made of either concrete or kiln-dried clay. Although they are long-lasting, they are also brittle, so walking on them is a practice best left to the roofing professional. The same holds true for slate, and also for mineral fiber, once known best as asbestos shingles. All of these materials are good low-maintenance roof coverings, but occasional replacement of damaged pieces should be anticipated. Look for cracked, loose, chipped, or missing tiles. Rust streaks usually mean deteriorating nail heads, a clue to the inspector that maintenance may be necessary. Check for proper flashings at roof penetrations and drip edges. When barrel shaped or mission tiles are present, the bottom course openings should be covered with well fitted bird-stops. Pay particular attention to hips and ridges for weather tightness, and confirm your observations from the attic area below.

If tile or slate is installed as a replacement for composition, wood, or other relatively lightweight materials, it is important to determine whether the original structure was designed for such loads. If clearly new, retrofitted structural bracing is absent in such a roof, the inspector might recommend analysis by a structural engineer to assure adequate strength.

Built-Up Roofing

A built-up roof covering (BUR), is common on flat roofs, and consists of alternate layers of roofing felt and bitumen, which is usually covered with some sort of aggregate to protect the top layer from the damaging effects of the sun. When the aggregate covering is absent, a fresh coating of asphalt emulsion is required every four or five years to maintain water tightness. A metal flange around the perimeter of a built-up roof is installed to prevent any loose aggregate from washing off.

Walking on blistered portions of this type of roof surface can cause the surface to crack. Blistering occurs as a result of air pockets that become trapped between felt layers, increasing the potential for water penetration. Also watch for ponding or water stain patterns, which indicate that water is not draining well. This might be found at any portion of the roof that appears to be sagging. Any vegetation that takes root in these roof ponds can cause considerable damage.

A condition called *fishmouth* may be found where felt layers overlap, one of which is wrinkled, causing an opening in the surface. Seams should not be visible. They should be well covered by the sealing emulsion or aggregate, and deterioration of the surface must be reported as in need of repair. Any built up roof showing movement of the semi-liquid bitumen will also require attention. A surface that looks like alligator skin (displaying a patchwork of small, random shapes, caused by drying and shrinking of the emulsion) is also indicative of the need for repair.

Be sure that interior drains, if present, are not clogged, and that attic ventilation is adequate. Carefully identify any vertical pipes that have rain caps, and are intended for attic ventilation. They must not be confused with the plumbing vent stacks. Inspection of a built up roof will include especially close attention to all roof penetrations and their sealing materials.

Metal Roofing

Galvanized steel, copper, and aluminum are common roof covering materials. Steel roofs are in the form of panels or sheets, and require only occasional applications of paint (or asphalt cement), to keep them from rusting. Copper and aluminum can be sheets, panels, or shingles, and although they are long lasting, the metal is soft. Copper and aluminum are best inspected only from laddertop or ground level (with binoculars), to avoid damage from foot traffic.

Inspect at seams and joints for proper sealing and water tightness, as well as at capflashing locations for integrity of nails and caulking. The joinery at gables, hips, valleys, and ridges must be intact. Weep holes should be provided at the lower edge of three-dimensional aluminum shingles above vent pipes and other penetrations, to allow the escape of any water which has made its way under the shingles before it reaches the leading edge of under-shingle flashings. Report bent or dented sections, as well as evidence of rust or leaks.

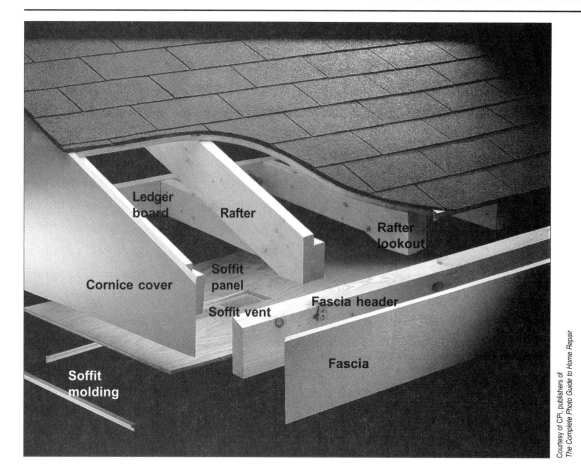

Fascia and soffits close off the eaves area beneath the roof overhang. The fascia covers the ends of rafters and rafter lookouts, and provides a surface for attaching gutters. Soffits are protective panels that span the area between the fascia and the side of the house. Some soffit types attach to fascia headers (above), while others fit into grooves cut in the back sides of the fascia. Soffit moldings and ledger boards are used to mount the soffit panels at the side of the house.

Roof Structure and Attic

Access to the area below the roof is important in every home. This allows inspection, maintenance, and repair of structural members, plumbing and electrical components, vents, firestops, and mechanical equipment. The minimum access opening required by current building codes is 22 inches x 30 inches. If mechanical equipment is installed in the attic space, an access opening large enough to accommodate its removal must be provided.

If the inspector cannot enter the attic space due to insufficient access provisions or conditions deemed hazardous (such as the presence of construction debris or rodents), he must report the method used to inspect. When a property with no attic access is encountered, the inspector should recommend its installation.

Observe and report the depth (or absence), of insulation between floor joists in the attic space and on vertical wall sections behind conditioned spaces. Also check that attic ventilation is adequate. Look for at least 1/150 of the floor's square footage (or 1/300 if 50% to 80% of venting is located at least 3 feet above the eaves, or if a vapor barrier is known to be installed at the attic floor).

Primary Inspections — Structural Systems

Excess moisture in attic areas can cause the weakening of wood structural components, reduction in the effectiveness of attic insulation, and formation of mold or mildew. Such moisture may be introduced by bathroom and kitchen fans, or even dryer vents that terminate in the attic. (Such venting must exhaust, of course, to the outdoors.) A high moisture condition in the attic space can be aggravated by inadequate provisions for attic ventilation, or vent turbines deliberately covered in a misguided effort to reduce heating costs.

The inspector will likely exercise his experience and judgment in his assessment of attic ventilation adequacy, rather than attempt actual measurements. The importance of adequate attic ventilation cannot be overstated, however, and the client is best served by the inspector who stresses this.

Familiarity with the functional purpose of each framing member is important to effectively inspect residential roof structures. Ridgeboards, ridge braces, rafters, collar beams, purlins, purlin braces, strongbacks, and joists are visible in most residential construction. (See illustration)

All visible framing members are inspected for cracking, sagging, splitting, wood rot, or other flaws. Mating components should be nailed or otherwise attached securely. Rafters found detaching from the ridgeboard may indicate that the foundation's perimeter wall is sinking into shrinking or settling soil, but roofing materials that are too heavy for the roofing structure can cause a similar condition (especially where purlins or collar ties are damaged or absent).

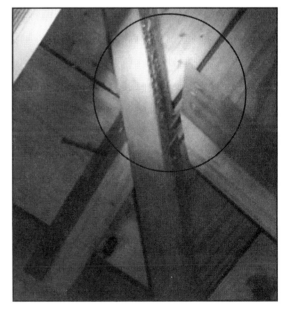

This hip rafter was cut too short at the time of its installation.

Frequently, framing members will be cut, notched, drilled, or even removed to accommodate installation of attic fans, access doors, vents, furnaces, or other items. Where visible, it must be determined if such compromises have created significant weakening of the structure. When visible, load-bearing wall studs should be notched no more than 25% of their width, bored no more than 40%. Non-bearing wall studs may be notched up to 40% of their width, bored a maximum of 60%. These specifications (along with conditions and exceptions) are in accordance with the building codes normally enforced by local Building Officials at the time of construction.

In contrast to roof structures built on-site, truss roof structures have no ridgeboard. They have upper chords functioning as rafters, lower chords functioning as joists, and reinforcing web members performing the same duty as purlin braces and collar beams. Trusses are generally engineered and manufactured off-site, and are assembled with gusset plates or scabs instead of nails. Gusset plates can loosen over time, and should be inspected for tightness. Look for cut or missing web members, which will significantly weaken the truss.

The use of engineered joists is becoming more common. These joists are manufactured with top and bottom flanges of dimensional or laminated lumber glued to a center web of plywood or OSB (oriented strand board). Their manufacture reduces the harvest of mature trees needed for the production of standard framing members, and is therefore friendly to the environment. Properly installed, engineered joists essentially match the functionality of their more traditional counterparts. Installation, though, requires special considerations. First, proper end bearing support is essential for the retention of intended design strength. Second, the thin center webs are not appropriate nailing surfaces for joist hangers or other attachments. When improper installation of engineered joists is encountered, the inspector may recommend consultation with one of the joist manufacturer's representatives for installation instructions. Inspections performed at the post-rough-in stage of construction afford the best opportunity to evaluate a builder's handling of this relatively new product.

This sheet-metal fire-stopping panel does not fit tightly to the fireplace flue.

Roof sheathing or decking is nailed over rafters, creating the nailing surface for roof covering materials. Often, 4 foot x 8 foot panels of plywood or OSB are nailed in a staggered-seam pattern, adding strength. In no case should a vertical seam be installed unsupported by a rafter. "H" clips are commonly used between each rafter, connecting the panels, adding rigidity, and providing the necessary expansion room. In other cases, tongue and groove roofing boards will be found. Spaced battens are used for installation of slate, wood, or clay tile shingles.

Damage or deterioration of the decking material is most often caused by water penetration. Wet decking material is, of course, reliable evidence of water penetration, but staining, rotting, delamination of plies or strands, sagging, or cracking could be caused by a leak which has been repaired. Any of these conditions found will be reported, along with conclusions regarding their causes.

Primary Inspections — Structural Systems

Fireblocking (sometimes called firestopping), is any material installed in open wood-framed spaces at floors, ceilings, soffits, vents, pipes, chimneys, stairs, and other concealed spaces to inhibit the spread of flames. Most firestops are concealed by finished walls or insulation, but the visible and accessible openings, like those which serve to route furnace, boiler, water heater, and chimney flues must be inspected. Such appliance flues require specified clearance to combustible material, so the firestops will be of sheetmetal or other non-combustible material. Clearance to combustibles from fireplace chimneys must be at least 2 inches. Minimum allowable clearance to combustibles from appliance flues is 1 inch. Firestops which are absent, ill-fitting, loose, rusted through, or otherwise not performing their intended function must be described in the report document as in need of repair.

Walls (Interior and Exterior)

This brick wall displays obvious evidence of water penetration. The most likely water sources include a leaky plumbing supply or drain line, a damaged shower pan or enclosure, roof water penetrating into the structure, or errant condensation from an attic-located A/C evaporator and its condensate drain system.

Imperfect workmanship or the occasional wall stud which has twisted or warped with age will cause interior wall surfaces to show wrinkles, buckling, bowing, split seams, or popping nail heads. These common flaws are usually cosmetic, and are easily repaired. Obvious cosmetic flaws of this nature may, at the discretion of the inspector, be omitted from his report. These flaws should not be confused with specifically characteristic foundation related damage.

Evidence of water penetration, accumulation, or damage is of primary concern. Non-destructive visual inspection may not always be sufficient to determine the source of unwanted water, but a practical working knowledge of plumbing, roofing, and air conditioning systems will usually narrow the field of possibilities. Wind-driven rain can migrate through exterior siding as well as roof openings, and can find its way, undetected, to emerge even several floors below. Look for plumbing or shower stall leaks, and condensation from water pipes, air conditioning suction lines and condensate drain lines, and poorly insulated ductwork. Confirm the integrity of flashing and other weather sealing components at roof penetrations, as already inspected from rooftop and attic. Gutters filled with debris or ice can cause dams that allow rainwater to back up under the lower courses of roof covering, and create another opportunity for water to enter. These conditions can present quite a puzzle. If the source of a leak is in doubt, the inspector should call out suspected points of water entry, and recommend attention by the appropriate specialists.

In shower areas, cracked tiles or failure of the grouted joints between them are not always obvious. Shower water that penetrates through to the backer board will cause a gypsum substrate to deteriorate. This can often be detected by pushing with a hand against each tile, feeling for unusual softness, loss of rigidity, and loose tiles. Tapping on the tile surface with a screwdriver will create a relatively dull sound in areas where substrate materials are wet. Water from leaks at tub/shower areas will usually migrate to adjacent walls and floors. The inspector will be especially mindful of this while observing conditions at the baseboard area in rooms adjoining and below tubs and showers.

Where wood paneling is installed, the same pushing and tapping methods can be used to determine whether it has been installed over a rigid wallboard surface. The installation of standard 1/8-inch sheets of wood paneling directly over wall studs is a cost cutting practice, and is evidence of poor-quality construction.

Combustible materials and heat sources are usually found in the garage. An attached garage (one with any wall or ceiling contiguous with the living space), must comply with special safety regulations to protect the home's occupants from any fire that might occur there. One of these measures is the installation of a fire-rated wall covering, usually common gypsum board. Its absence is a hazard to the home's occupants, and must be reported.

Exterior siding materials are many and varied, but their purpose is always the same; to protect the structure from weather and pest infiltration. Inspection for the structural integrity of exterior siding is largely accomplished during the structural systems and foundation performance analysis. Individual elements found to be in need of repair during that portion of the inspection may be noted here. With this in mind, the inspector will be alert for cracked, loose, rotted, missing, or otherwise deteriorated components, as well as flaws in joinery that may admit water or insects.

Brick veneer siding is quite rigid, and minor foundation deflections, which may not be significant from a foundation performance standpoint, can still cause brickwork to crack, especially at mortar joints. Such fractures require re-pointing, or repair of the mortar joints, to maintain weather tightness.

The bottom course of bricks, which rests on the foundation's brick ledge, should be installed with a series of openings called weep holes. Their purpose is to aid in the removal of any moisture that may accumulate in the cavity formed by the brick veneer and the inside wall. High moisture conditions in this cavity, if unable to escape, can reduce the effectiveness of insulation, encourage the formation of mold, mildew (and their attending odor), cause rotting of wood framing members, and attract insects. Look for the presence of weep holes around the entire perimeter of a brick veneered structure, and make note of their absence. Weep holes are often found to be blocked by excess mortar that has fallen on the backside of the brick, defeating their purpose. Inspectors should probe several sample weep holes with a wire or coat hanger to determine their functionality. If several or all are blocked, the report must make this fact known.

Aesthetically pleasing though they may be, ivy or vines that climb up a home's exterior are destructive of wood, mortar joints, and paint. Clients should be advised that the roots grow deep into their hosting structure, disintegrating virtually any material, and the moisture associated with such vegetation promotes wood rot and attracts insects.

Slab exposure standards are intended, in part, to prevent ground moisture and insects from coming in direct contact with siding materials. Wood siding is particularly vulnerable to damage by such conditions. Careful inspection of bottom courses will usually reveal any damage, but recent cosmetic repairs may disguise it. A scratch awl or fingernail will easily penetrate badly deteriorated areas of siding, even if they have been freshly painted. Sections of siding found to have been recently replaced, although in good condition, may also indicate the presence of conditions conducive to water or insect damage.

It should be noted here that a new exterior siding material called Exterior Insulation and Finishing System (EIFS), also known as synthetic stucco, has been shown to cause serious moisture-related problems. This acrylic stucco look-alike is so completely waterproof that any moisture trapped within exterior walls cannot escape, and the resulting buildup very quickly causes framing members to rot. Mildew and fungus will often accompany this condition. The manufacturers of this product have been the target of class-action litigation, and damages may be recovered by owners of homes sided with this product. When in doubt about the stucco-look finish of any wood-framed subject property, inspectors should inform clients of this situation, and recommend that they obtain full disclosure and positive identification of the siding material used. One variation of the EIFS system does incorporate a provision for drainage and ventilation, but the liability borne by an inspector who attempts to identify any siding material as satisfactory is high. It is recommended that all siding suspected of being of the EIFS material be called out for further analysis. Additional information can be found at www.eifsinfo.com

Ceilings and Floors (Including Stairways)

Flaws found in ceilings are very often caused by the presence of water. Always try to determine the source of any water that has caused soft, drooping, sagging, or stained ceilings. Although not usually accessible for inspection, sagging floor and ceiling joists will cause finish surfaces to follow their contours. This will be reported when suspected. Sagging joists may be caused by cracks, rot, insect damage, or oversized holes or notches cut into them as shortcuts during construction or remodeling.

Few floors are built perfectly level, and wood framing can warp, shrink, or settle over time. This is normal, and a slightly out-of-level condition is not structurally significant if it is not caused by excessive foundation settlement or framing flaws. Floors that sag, or feel too springy under foot probably indicate framing performance failure. Floor joists serve as ceiling joists for the floor below, and the usual causes of deterioration are, of course, the same.

An endless variety of floor coverings will be encountered during inspections. Beyond any evidence of tile cracks or an out-of-level condition which could be caused by foundation movement, the inspector must determine whether flooring materials are water-damaged, deteriorated, or otherwise in need of repair. Any conditions which might cause an undue risk of injury are especially important to the client. Such things as loose or lumpy carpet, abrupt transitions between two different materials (such as tile-to-vinyl), or tears in sheet materials (such as linoleum) can be hazardous to the home's occupants. The relatively new laminated flooring panels which are glued or snapped together must be installed to the manufacturer's specifications, with proper expansion gaps at walls and, often, with foam or other underlayment allowing the floor to "float". Evidence of buckling, water damage, or other flaws should be called out for repair.

Stairways are inherently hazardous. A high rise or short run is difficult to negotiate, especially for the elderly or very young. Toddlers face the additional risk of falling through the spaces between handrail balusters. Stairway dimensions set forth by building codes serve to maintain minimum standards of safety. These standards should be compared to conditions found in every inspected home.

Primary Inspections — Structural Systems

Stairways and landings should be at least 36 inches wide, and maintain a minimum 6 feet 8 inches of headroom. Maximum allowable height of each riser is 7 3/4 inches, with a minimum tread depth of 10 inches. No riser or tread can differ in dimension by more than 3/8 inch from the other risers or treads in the staircase. Standards for spiral, winding, and circular stairways differ somewhat.

Handrails are required at stairways with 3 or more risers, and must be 30 inches to 38 inches in height (as measured from tread nosings), except when the handrail is located at the open side of a stairway, where 34 inches is the minimum height. Be certain that handrails are continuous, cover both the bottom and top treads, and are well-secured in place.

Balustrade spacing at this handrail is greater than the maximum permitted 4 inches.

Porches, balconies, and raised flooring surfaces more than 30 inches above the floor or grade require a guardrail at least 36 inches in height.

"Required guardrails on open sides of stairways, raised floor areas, balconies and porches shall have intermediate rails or ornamental closures which do not allow passage of an object 4 inches or more in diameter. Exception: The triangular openings formed by the riser, tread, and bottom rail of a guard at the open side of a stairway may be of such a size that a 6 inch sphere cannot pass through." This language is drawn directly from the *1995 CABO One and Two Family Dwelling Code* @ 315.4. Every professional real estate inspector should have a copy of the current building codes, starting with the new *2000 International Residential Code for One- and Two-Family Dwellings.*.

Doors (Interior and Exterior)

Aside from factors considered in the analysis of foundation performance, doors and doorways are inspected for proper operation, fit, and general condition. Every accessible door in the house should be checked for hinges, handles, locks, latches, and striker plates that are loose, missing, or damaged. Peeling veneer, split, cracked, or rotted wood sections, and damaged glass should also be reported.

No door (excluding screen or storm doors) should be hinged to swing over landings or stairs. Interior doorways requiring a step-down greater than 1½ inch are considered a tripping hazard. (An acceptable *exterior* door step-down is less than 8¼ inches). Weather-stripping at exterior doors should be intact and provide a proper weather seal.

Additionally, all doors and sidelights (windows adjacent to doors), with glass panes must utilize glass of the safety-labeled type unless panes are small enough to restrict passage of a 4 inch sphere. (Leaded or art glass is excluded.) Glass shower or tub enclosures, and their doors, must also be of safety-labeled glass. Doors with glass panes (as well as windows) located at the bottom of staircases or landings, and those located less than 5 feet from a pool-edge walkway also require the safety glass label.

A doorway between living spaces and any attached garage requires a door that is fire-rated, properly sealed, and self-closing. Fire rated doors have no glass, are heavy, and are usually made of metal or solid wood (unlike hollow, lightweight interior doors). No openings, such as pet doors, are permitted. A garage-side step-up or curb, at least 3 inches in height, helps keep noxious or flammable fumes (which tend to settle at the floor), out of the living space. The absence of such a curb is reportable as hazardous.

Another safety concern relating to the attached garage is the potential spread of fire into the attic. It is for this reason that walls and ceiling are covered with a fire-rated wallboard. Additionally, any attic access opening located in the garage must be fitted with a door or access cover, made of a material that meets fire-rating requirements (like gypsum or heavy plywood), to inhibit the spread of flames into the attic space.

Sliding doors, often called patio doors, should roll smoothly in their tracks. The same holds true for their sliding screens. See that locking hardware operates correctly, and that weather sealing is intact around both movable and stationary sections.

The most common overhead garage doors are articulated panels of wood or steel that ride on metal rollers in a pair of tracks. A spring and cable system reduces the effort required to lift the weight of the door, and serves to protect against hard closing. Broken springs of the extension type are easy to spot, but failure of torsion springs, found at the face wall, is not always so obvious. Safety cables (run through extension springs to contain them in the event they should break) must be present. Their absence is a reportable defect. Cam and bar locking systems are checked for proper operation and alignment (except when the locking mechanism is permanently held open by a screw or other device to prevent interference with the operation of an automatic door opener). Hinges and tracks should be securely fastened and free of excessive rust. Wood doors are vulnerable to rot from water damage, especially at the bottom panel that makes contact with the ground and is subjected to rain splash. (With metal doors, rust is the concern here). Wood doors found sagging in the middle are in need of repair. Finger joints at stiles and rails should be checked for deterioration. Note any damage caused by impact, and check for cracked or broken glass panes.

Windows

From outside, windows are inspected for apparent weather sealing flaws (like peeling caulk or damaged glazing bead) and for missing or damaged screens. Once inside, the inspector begins by looking for evidence of water penetration. Water stains at windowsills are not always caused by faulty weather sealing. Condensation can form on the inside of windows and window frames, especially if air conditioning supply ducts are nearby to chill the inside of a pane in humid climates. In other cases, potted plants (which get regular watering) may have been perched there, only to leave water stains. Cracked or broken glass, or windows left open, will, of course, permit water to enter, as well.

Insulated glass windows of double or triple pane construction are filled with a gas intended to prevent the formation of condensation between panes. Failure of the gas-retaining seal will result in obvious fogging between panes. When such fogging is present, replacement is the only remedy.

Windows must be inspected for proper operation. An out-of-square condition, as assessed during the evaluation of foundation performance, can be detected by looking at the sash as it parts from the frame during opening. The sash should glide easily, and present a perfectly parallel departure from the frame when opening. Wood sashes that stick or bind are not necessarily the result of foundation movement, but may simply have swelled due to the presence of moisture. Metal window frames can rust or corrode, causing similar difficulties, and all types of windows are subjected to wind-driven debris that can foul their tracks.

Windows may have been painted shut, or intentionally disabled with nails or other hardware in an effort to deter intruders. This is of particular importance in bedrooms, where operable windows are needed to provide a secondary escape route in case of fire. It is for this same reason that all bedroom window burglar bars should be of the type which are capable of being opened from inside without keys or tools. The size and location of windows intended for emergency egress is spelled out in the building codes. The 1994 Uniform Building Code, for example, requires that the sill height of windows intended for secondary egress be no more than 44 inches from the floor, and that such windows have minimum opening dimensions of 5.7 square feet (including a minimum of 20 inches in width and 24 inches in height). Other codes differ slightly, but if emergency bedroom escape provisions are inadequate for any reason, in the judgment of the inspector, it must be called out in his report, irrespective of code reference.

A window location at the bottom of a stairway creates a hazard unless its sill is high enough from the floor or landing to prevent a person from falling through. Installation of a guardrail should be recommended if such a window has a sill height less than 36 inches from the floor.

Inspectors must look for a label identifying glass used in all hazardous places as being of the safety-glass type. Remember that all door glass, as well as sidelights and windows within 24 inches of a door are required to be of the safety glass type. So, too, does any window that is less than 18 inches from the floor and is greater than 9 square feet in area. Door and window glass 5' or less from pool edge must also carry the safety label. *The absence of safety glass in any location which presents a high risk of injury should always be reported.*

Fireplaces and Chimneys

Masonry fireplaces are constructed of brick or stone, and their fireboxes may be metal or firebrick (a refractory ceramic material resistant to high temperatures). Flue linings are usually smooth terra cotta, but an acceptable alternative is a full firebrick chimney interior.

Prefabricated fireplaces are commonplace. These relatively inexpensive factory assembled metal units are designed to allow installation in close proximity to combustible materials. Their flues are constructed of special double wall metal pipe, designed for the purpose.

Look to see that any exposed brick (or other structural material), at the top surface of a chimney is protected by a cover of concrete, mortar, or a secure metal flashing. This is called a mortar cap, coping, or crown flashing. Its purpose is to prevent rain from entering the chimney structure, causing water damage and accelerating the deterioration of the chimney.

In addition, the flue should terminate with a metal mesh spark arrestor and a rain cap. The spark arrestor is there to prevent burning embers from

PRIMARY INSPECTIONS — STRUCTURAL SYSTEMS 41

escaping, and thus creating a fire hazard. Wood roofing shingles are of particular concern, and have been banned from many communities for this reason. Rain caps are designed to keep rain from entering the flue. This is not just to keep rain from reaching the firebox below, but also to prevent deterioration of the fireplace and chimney structure due to the production of a corrosive acid, created when water mixes with creosote.

The combination of spark arrestor and rain cap will extend the life of the fireplace, discourage attempts at entry by squirrels, birds, and other pests, help to prevent roof fires, inhibit downdrafting, and save occupants of the home from the strong, acrid odor of rain-washed creosote.

Fireplace chimney termination should be at least 2 feet higher than any portion of the structure within a 10-foot horizontal distance, and, in all cases, at least 3 feet above the point where the chimney passes through the roof. This helps to prevent downdrafting, or the downward current of smoke and air in the flue. Structural elements close to the chimney termination can disrupt the flow of air across its top, causing this condition. Inspectors should expect to encounter many chimneys that do not precisely meet this specification.

This vertical wood siding trim board shows excessive deterioration. Gaining access to the roof reduces the chance of overlooking chimney chase damage of this type, especially when such damage is obscured by fresh caulk and paint.

According to the Consumer Product Safety Commission, when a masonry fireplace chimney is responsible for a house fire, the number one cause is "improper construction or deterioration". They list "installation too close to combustible materials" as the first cause where a metal flue is present. High on the danger list for both masonry and metal chimney construction is the buildup of creosote in the flue. Creosote, the condensation of wood combustion by-products, looks like tar, and has an unpleasant odor. Creosote is also highly combustible. A chimney fire fueled by it can burn at a temperature of 2000° F, cracking bricks, melting mortar joints, and radiating enough heat to set nearby wood framing ablaze. The presence of a creosote buildup found in a firebox or flue will be reported as hazardous.

Look at the general condition of visible components, and check for the presence and condition of a lintel supporting any brick or stone. A lintel is the horizontal steel or masonry structural member at the top of, and bridging, the front sides of the firebox opening, supporting the structure above. Be sure that the space between the lintel and the face brick, or breast of the fireplace, is fully sealed with mortar to prevent smoke from entering at the front of the lintel.

Mortar joints within the firebox should be probed with a scratch awl or screwdriver. Cracked or crumbling mortar here can allow heat or smoke to escape. A metal firebox should be free of rust. Visible portions of the flue lining should be inspected for cracks or breaks. Try to determine whether there are any obstructions in the flue, such as a bird's nest. An inspection mirror may help.

Operate the damper to be sure it sets securely in both open and closed positions. Any fireplace equipped with a gas-burning log-set must have a device that permanently secures the damper in the open position. This prevents the introduction of combustion by-products, including carbon monoxide, into the living space in the event a homeowner fails to open the damper for use. Gas fires create essentially no visible smoke that might alert the user to a closed-damper condition. Additionally, with the damper permanently open, any gas left on or leaking from within the firebox can be drawn up the flue by natural convection. A gas shutoff valve must be located within 4 feet of the gas-equipped firebox, and the inspector should check it for gas leaks, using his sense of smell, a spray of soapy water (which will bubble visibly where gas escapes) or a combustible-gas detector.

The installation of a glass firescreen (or glass doors) should always be recommended. Glass doors help to reduce common fireplace dangers, while significantly reducing the living space heating losses inherent in open fireplace use. Also, be certain to warn the client about any hazardous conditions created by the presence of combustibles placed near the fireplace for storage or decoration.

The floor of the firebox is the hearth, and it extends out into the room to protect the floor from burning embers. It should extend at least 16 inches to the front and 8 inches to the sides of any fireplace opening smaller than 6 square feet. Larger fireplace openings require the extension to project into the room 20 inches and 12 inches, respectively. The hearth and its extension must be of non-combustible material, and visually distinguishable from the surrounding floor.

Since 1984, building codes have required fireplace combustion air to be provided from an outside source. Air inlets must be closeable, located at or near the floor of the firebox, and installed in such a way as to prevent burning material from dropping into concealed combustible spaces. The exterior air intake cannot be located within the living space or garage, and requires a corrosion-resistant screen. This is a requirement that has not been met in many homes, especially older ones. Non-compliance should be called out as a condition in need of repair in homes built after 1984. FHA and VA housing construction have included this requirement since 1977.

Attached Porches, Decks and Carports

In this format, observations regarding attached porches, decks, and carports should be noted within this specific category of inspection items for the purpose of final reporting. Inspection parameters are identical to those that apply to the main structure. Visible footings, joists, decking, railings, and attachment points are specifically subject to inspection. Inspection of detached structures, or waterfront structures and equipment (such as docks or piers), is not required to satisfy minimum inspection standards, but it should be understood by the client if these items are to be omitted.

Review Questions - Structural Systems

(circle the letter next to the best answer for each question)

1. *Differential settlement* occurs when:
   a. two or more certified structural experts reach agreement
   b. a foundation settles unevenly
   c. the type of foundation repair required is in dispute
   d. doors and windows show no sign of racking or binding
   e. a. and c.

2. Pier and beam foundations require crawl space ventilation with a total area of at least:
   a. 1/5000 of the foundation footprint in the presence of a vapor barrier ground cover
   b. 1/1500 of the foundation footprint in the presence of a vapor barrier ground cover
   c. 1/150 of the foundation footprint in the absence of a vapor barrier ground cover
   d. 18 inches by 24 inches per 2000 square feet of foundation footprint
   e. b. and c.

3. A condition that is not a sign of differential settlement is:
   a. interior walls which show evidence of stress deflection
   b. rafters which have pulled away from their ridge board
   c. the presence of efflorescence around the perimeter of the foundation
   d. doors which do not fit well in their openings
   e. a. and c.

4. Slab on grade foundations require a minimum slab exposure above finish grade of:
   a. 8 inches to wood siding
   b. 6 inches to wood or brick siding
   c. 8 inches to brick siding
   d. 6 inches to brick siding
   e. a. and d.

5. Common factors that contribute to foundation failure include:
   a. tree roots which deplete moisture from soil close to the foundation
   b. unshaded South-facing walls which give up moisture due to evaporation
   c. downspouts which discharge too close to foundation walls, adding unnecessary moisture
   d. poor grading which allows surface water to accumulate at the foundation wall
   e. all of the above

6. When insulation with a vapor barrier is installed between floor joists in a pier and beam foundation:
   a. the insulation vapor barrier should face the heated side of the structure
   b. all plumbing supply lines should be located between the sub-floor and the insulation
   c. an additional vapor barrier should be installed to cover the ground
   d. plumbing vents are permitted to terminate in the crawl space
   e. clients should be informed about vulnerability to termite infestation

7. Joists that support the sub-floor in a screeded slab foundation:
   a. create an air space unsuitable for use as a heating duct
   b. create an air space which should not be vented to the outdoors
   c. should be regularly treated for insect control
   d. must be spaced at 16 inch (on center) intervals
   e. are shimmed for level at all pier locations

REVIEW QUESTIONS

8. Expansive clay soils consist of:
   a. large grains and small voids, allowing very limited volume variation during extreme moisture conditions
   b. large grains and large voids, allowing very limited volume variation during extreme moisture conditions
   c. large grains and large voids, causing relatively large volume variation during extreme moisture conditions
   d. small grains and large voids, causing relatively large volume variation during extreme moisture conditions
   e. small grains and small voids, causing relatively large volume variation during extreme moisture conditions

9. A fireplace chimney should have:
   a. a rain cap to keep out water and debris
   b. a spark arrestor to keep embers from escaping
   c. a protective crown flashing, coping, or mortar cap to keep moisture out of the structure of the chimney
   d. all of the above
   e. a. and b.

10. Post-tensioned slab-on-grade foundations:
   a. must always be used in post-and-beam structures
   b. have steel cables running through them
   c. utilize pre-stressed concrete components
   d. are considered obsolete
   e. require no excavation

11. Wood roofing shingles:
   a. are split, and have a textured surface
   b. are installed over felt
   c. may permit indirect daylight into attic spaces without compromising weather tightness
   d. are not permitted on roofs of 4-in-12 pitch or greater
   e. should never be covered with composition shingles

12. The primary function of the mineral granules that cover composition-roofing materials is to:
   a. add the desired color or hue
   b. create a traction surface for installation personnel
   c. protect the asphaltic mat from ultra-violet damage
   d. create a proper seal to the shingle below
   e. improve water tightness and wind resistance

13. Inspectors should never walk on a roof which:
   a. could be damaged by foot traffic
   b. is too high or too steep for safe access
   c. can be properly inspected from ground level
   d. a. and b.
   e. none of the above

14. A fireplace chimney should terminate:
    a. at least 2 feet higher than any portion of the structure within a 10 foot horizontal distance
    b. at least 3 feet above the point where the chimney passes through the roof
    c. with a flue opening cross sectional measurement at least 1.5 times that of the damper
    d. a. and c.
    e. a. and b.

15. Framing members normally visible from the attic space include:
    a. purlin braces and collar beams
    b. strongbacks and rafters
    c. studs and sill plates
    d. b. and c.
    e. a. and b.

16. Roof trusses are normally:
    a. invulnerable to wind loads
    b. designed and made up on the job site
    c. designed with narrow ridge boards
    d. assembled with gusset plates or scabs
    e. installed to serve as purlins and collar beams

17. Attic insulation is:
    a. normally installed between roof rafters in colder climates
    b. affected by moisture conditions
    c. required to be at least 6 inches in depth
    d. unnecessary in hotter climates
    e. a. and d.

18. Fireblocking is not required in open, concealed, wood-framed spaces:
    a. wherever flue clearances are greater than 2 inches from combustibles
    b. whenever no fuel burning appliances are present
    c. whenever no fireplace is present
    d. whenever open, wood framed spaces are inaccessible for inspection
    e. none of the above

19. The source of water stains found in a ceiling may be:
    a. water supply or drain pipes
    b. gutters filled with debris
    c. air conditioning ducts
    d. a. and b.
    e. a., b., and c.

20. Fogging between the panes of insulated-glass windows:
    a. is a normal condition during periods of high humidity
    b. can only be cured by a re-charge of the anti condensation gas
    c. is indicative of broken seals
    d. represents a hazardous condition
    e. is caused by high pressure between panes

21. A condition that constitutes an unacceptable hazard in an attached garage is:
    a. gypsum wall board covering the interior walls and ceiling
    b. an attic access door in the garage ceiling with a plywood cover
    c. the absence of a curb at the garage entry door into the living space
    d. an entry door into the living space with a self-closing mechanism installed
    e. a garage floor painted with oil-based paint

22. Except for the spiral, winding, or circular style, stairways should have:
    a. a handrail, if 1 or more risers are present
    b. a riser dimension differential of not more than 3/4 inch
    c. baluster spacing or ornamental closures not greater than 6 inches apart
    d. tread depth of at least 10 inches
    e. a width of at least 30 inches

23. Key-operated burglar bars at bedroom window locations are hazardous because:
    a. they may impede emergency escape
    b. burglars can pick a lock with simple tools
    c. a key is easily stolen
    d. metal keys can get too hot to touch in a fire
    e. inconvenience may cause homeowners to neglect window caulk maintenance

24. A non-combustible fireplace hearth extension must be:
    a. 16 inches to the front and 8 inches to the sides of a fireplace opening less than 6 square feet
    b. 20 inches to the front and 12 inches to the sides of a fireplace opening less than 6 square feet
    c. painted or otherwise coated with a non-combustible surface
    d. raised at least 3 inches off the floor
    e. made of the same material as the firebox

25. According to the Consumer Products Safety Commission, a common cause of house fires attributed to a fireplace is:
    a. improper construction
    b. deterioration
    c. installation too close to combustible materials
    d. a buildup of creosote
    e. all of the above

Typical Home Electrical System

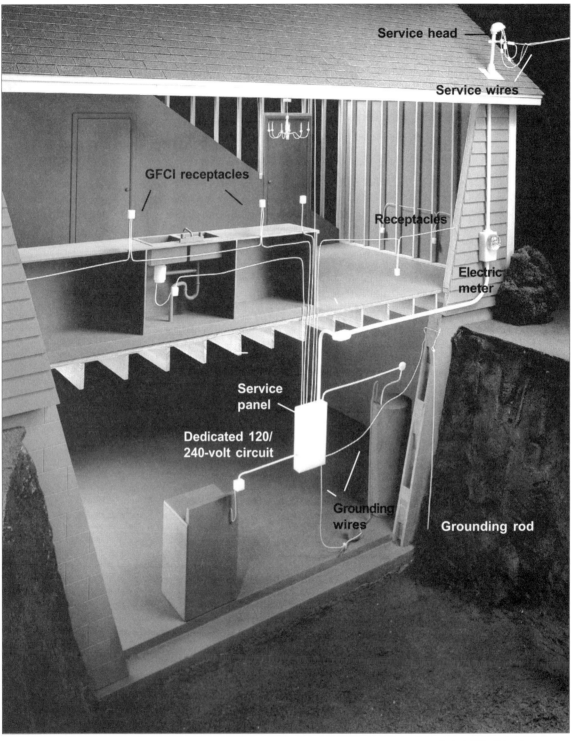

Courtesy of CPi, publishers of
The Complete Photo Guide to Home Repair

ELECTRICAL SYSTEMS

Learning Objectives

1. Learn the basic principles behind residential electrical system design.
2. Identify evidence of hazardous and other adverse conditions related to electrical systems in the home.
3. Be aware of the obligations borne by inspectors in regard to reporting unsafe electrical system conditions.
4. Recognize the importance of electrical safety in the home.

The electrical system serving a home consists of two basic categories. (1) The *service entrance and service panel* (sometimes called the panel box, fuse or breaker box, or fuse or breaker panel), are fed from the utility company's power grid through overhead or underground cables. (2) Individual *branch circuits* are breaker- or fuse-protected at the service panel, and are run throughout the structure to deliver electric power to various outlets and connected devices.

There should be a 3-wire or 4-wire electrical service entrance to any residential structure. No 2-wire service can provide 240 volts, and is therefore inadequate. A safe minimum, where less than 6 branch circuits are present, is 60-amp / 240-volt service. Where the number of branch circuits is 6 or more, a main breaker or disconnect is required, and 100-amp/240-volt service is the minimum allowable. The main breaker or fuse should be labeled with its amperage rating, and its compatibility with the service entrance cables must be verified.

The size of the conductors in use is printed on the cable insulation, but cannot always be found. A set of caliper type measuring gauges, designed for determining wire size, will help to identify the size of conductor in use, which must be compared to a chart indicating minimum conductor sizes permitted for specific main breaker or fuse ratings. Aluminum and copper conductors of the same size have different maximum ampacity ratings. (The same holds true for aluminum and copper branch circuit wiring).

Fuses and circuit breakers are heat sensitive devices designed to open a circuit in the event of an overcurrent condition. It is important to understand that the ability of a conductor to safely carry a specific current load is determined by its size, or gauge. Wire size (as defined by the American Wire Gauge standard, or AWG), and circuit protector ratings must be compatible for safe operation. Fuses and circuit breakers are permanently marked with ampacity ratings. The chart below shows aluminum and copper wire sizes, and their corresponding ampacity ratings, as used for service entrance and branch circuit conductors.

In dedicated circuits (those serving a single outlet or appliance) circuit conductors may be "overfused" by the equivalent of 5 amps when breakers are rated at or below 50 amps. For example, the 45 amp breaker found serving a (dedicated) air conditioner circuit may be wired with #8 AWG copper conductors, although the chart indicates conductors of this gauge are permitted only with breakers rated up through 40 amps. Conductors used in dedicated circuits of 50 to 125 amps may be "overfused" by the equivalent of 10 amps. This means that a breaker (or fuse) serving a dedicated appliance circuit rated at 70 amps may be wired with a #6 AWG copper conductor, despite the fact that the chart shows #6 AWG copper conductors to be compatible only with breakers rated up through 60 amps. This breaker/conductor compatibility exception is found in the *1999 National Electric Code.*

Conductor size and compatible breaker/fuse ratings

AWG	Service entrance copper / aluminum	Branch circuit copper / aluminum
14		15 A
12		20 A / 15 A
10		30 A / 25 A
8		40 A / 30 A
6		55-60 A / 40 A
4	100 A	70 A / 55-60 A
2	125 A / 100 A	95-100 A / 75-80 A
1	150 A / 110 A	110 A / 85-90 A
1/0	175 A / 125 A	125 A / 100 A
2/0	200 A / 150 A	145-150 A / 115-125 A
3/0	225 A / 175 A	165-175 A / 130-150 A
4/0	250 A / 200 A	195-200 A / 150 A
250 kcmil	300 A / 225 A	
300 kcmil	/ 250 A	
350 kcmil	350 A / 300 A	

Each branch circuit is protected from overcurrent damage by its fuse or circuit breaker, designed to match the electrical capacity of the circuit wiring. An overcurrent condition may be caused by the use of connected devices and fixtures that draw a larger load than the ampacity rating of the circuit (commonly called overload). An abnormal and faulty connection is called a "short" circuit when power is drawn from a "hot" wire, through an unintended low-resistance path, back to the neutral wire or other ground.

One of the many requirements set forth by building and electric codes is strict adherence to color-coding standards. Black, red or blue insulation designates a "hot" wire in any circuit. White is neutral, *except* when used as a leg in a 3-way switch loop or unless serving a 240 volt circuit.

Green insulation, with or without a yellow stripe, is used for grounding conductors, as is bare, (uninsulated) wire. This knowledge is important to the inspector for the proper assessment of conditions at the service panel, and sometimes at receptacles or connected devices where junction boxes are absent or opened.

Service Entrance and Panels

The condition of insulation covering any overhead cables should be observed. Look for physical damage caused by aging, weathering, pests, or falling branches. Any overhead cables should be configured into a drip loop at the weatherhead to prevent rainwater from running down the cables into the weatherhead, and each individual conductor must be physically separated from the others.

Minimum allowable overhead clearance between service entrance cables and walkways is 10 feet. This clearance must be maintained in all cases, and includes the point of attachment of service drop conductors to the structure. Private driveways require at least 12 feet of overhead clearance, and public roadways, alleys, and parking lot surfaces must measure over 18 feet to cable height.

Where a service mast is used for the support of service drop conductors, it must be of adequate strength to support the weight of the cables. Bracing or guy wires are required if it extends freely upwards more than 3 feet from its mounting point. Service entrance cables and their required drip loops must remain a safe distance from roof surfaces. The *1995 CABO One and Two Family Dwelling Code* at 4104.2.1 prescribes a distance of "…not less than 8 feet above the roof surface"… unless …"the roof has a slope of not less than 4 inches in 12 inches", where "the minimum clearance shall be 3 feet". Additionally, "The minimum clearance above only the overhanging portion of the roof shall not be less than 18 inches…".

Inspectors should assess the potential for damage to service drop conductors caused by falling tree limbs, and recommend that any limbs that present an unacceptable risk be removed.

Indoor service panels will often be found located in clothes closets. Although this is a violation of current code, such a location was, at one time, approved. Existing homes with panels so located may not present an unacceptable hazard if conditions are otherwise acceptable. Some inspector-licensing authorities require service panels located in clothes closets to be reported as in need of repair, regardless of other safety con-

This is typical of what is found behind the cover plate of a service panel. Inspectors must determine if the breakers are compatible with the conductors in use.

Are there any double-wired breakers here?

Are the neutral bus bar and grounding bus bar electrically bonded?

Do the conductors enter the panel box with protective grommets in place? Be sure the cover-plate securing screws, (when in place), don't make contact with any of the conductors inside the panel.

Is there any evidence of burning, arcing, damaged or loose conductors?

What about excessive oxidation, (especially at the neutral conductors where they connect to the bus bar)?

Is there a visible, uncompromised grounding electrode? Panels must be securely fastened to the wall and free of excessive rust. All knockouts must be filled, and breakers must be clearly and permanently labeled for ampacity.

siderations. Bathroom panel locations, however, also prohibited by current code, present an unacceptable degree of danger due to the water sources inevitably found there. Clients may choose not to demand changes in any such service panel locations, but they should be made aware of any potential hazards that so exist. Building officials have also concluded that outdoor service panels located less than 3 feet from balconies or openable windows and doors also create and unnecessary risk.

Service panels (and sub panels, if present) should be securely mounted and, where outdoors and unprotected, weather-tight. Before opening the service panel, it is a good idea to touch it with the back of the hand to see if it is warm to the touch. Once open, exposing the overcurrent devices and the cover plate (or dead-front), check to see that all breakers or fuses are permanently labeled with their ampacity rating. There should be no odor of burnt plastic, no heat coming from the breakers or fuses, no evidence of water penetration or corrosion, and no open knock-out spaces. Knock-out spaces are provided in the cover plate to accommodate the installation of fuses or breakers, and should never be left unfilled. The absence of a cover plate, exposing all wiring and connections, obviously represents a very hazardous condition and must be reported.

Before the cover plate is removed, a few safety precautions and a basic knowledge of residential electrical systems will help prevent accidents. "Hot" wires inside the service panels, (always those with black, blue, or red insulation, and some with white insulation in 240 volt branch circuits), must not be allowed to make inadvertent connection to ground. Neutral branch circuit wires (those with white insulation, except some in 240 volt circuits), are grounded. The service panel should be grounded, as well. In the event an inspector probes a "hot" wire or other energized component with a metal tool, unless he is electrically insulated from grounded components and the earth, he may become the shortest path to ground, and a potentially fatal electric shock can occur. This danger can be reduced by wearing rubber-soled shoes (or standing on a dry board, especially if the ground is wet), and keeping metal tools away from the interior of the service panel. Only tools specifically designed to isolate the user from electric current should be used at the service panel.

In addition to the grounded neutral conductor provided by the utility company, the electrical system of every home should have a system ground. Its main purpose is to protect the system from dangerously high voltage, as might be caused by lightning strikes. System grounding is accomplished by connection of metal system components to either the metal water sup-

PRIMARY INSPECTIONS — ELECTRICAL SYSTEMS

ply pipes, or to a metal electrode driven into the ground. Where visible, the system ground should be inspected for use of approved connection clamps. Be sure they are tight, and free of corrosion that might compromise performance. Ground connections, when made to the water inlet pipes located at the house side of the water meter, must maintain continuity past the meter, to the street side, by use of a jumper wire. Modern, prudent practice is to use the grounding rod method, as plastic (non-conductive) water entrances are becoming more and more common.

Be certain all service panels are grounded, with bonding screws electrically connecting the neutral and grounding bus bars. Bus bars are the heavy, rigid conductors of aluminum, copper, or steel, which provide a point of interconnection between the service entrance conductors and the branch circuits. Some installations will utilize one large bus bar to serve as both neutral bus bar and grounding bus bar. Look for evidence of scorching or arcing at the bus bars. Service entrance and branch circuit conductors should not be burned, damaged, loose, disconnected, or oxidized. Check to see that all conductors entering the panel box are protected from unnecessary vulnerability to chafing at metal passthrough ports by vinyl or rubber grommets or electrical clamps designed for this purpose.

No circuit breaker or fuse should serve more than one individual circuit. This happens when two wires are secured to one side of a circuit breaker or fuse lug, and is called double wiring. This practice is an invitation to an overload, and should be reported as a hazardous condition.

Just as in the inspection of service entrance conductors, branch circuit conductors must also be checked for compatibility of overcurrent protectors with the wire size in use (see previous chart). This is especially important where plug-type fuses are present, because replacement fuses of differing ampacity ratings install easily in any circuit, leaving open the possibility of "overfusing". S-type or T-amps fuses are threaded to fit special adapters correlating to their ratings, and their installation should be recommended. Coins or other improper inserts that defeat the overcurrent protection of the system are not acceptable. Another type of fuse is the cartridge fuse, either with or without knife-blade contacts. These are generally found on higher amperage circuits, and must also be checked for compatibility with the wire size used.

Circuits of 240 volts, generally required for air conditioners, cooktops, clothes dryers, ovens, water heaters, and central electric heat systems, utilize double circuit breakers. In essence, they provide two 120-volt circuits to the load. These double breakers must be mechanically bridged, so that either 120-volt leg which overloads, opening (or "tripping") its breaker, will simultaneously trip the other leg via the mechanical bridge, opening both halves of the circuit. Double breakers with no visible physical bridge may have an internal common trip, and will be so marked. The absence of a bridging mechanism in a 240-volt circuit protected by a double breaker is a hazard, and should be reported as such.

Some electrical equipment will be served by dedicated circuits. When amperage ratings of such equipment are identifiable, a comparison of the equipment and its overcurrent protector should be made. A water heater with a manufacturer's label prescribing a maximum breaker rating of 30 amps, for example, must not be served by a breaker or fuse rated higher than 30 amps. The following chart shows appliances requiring dedicated circuits, as well as their typical maximum breaker ratings.

Appliances Requiring Dedicated Circuits

kitchen range . . .	240v	50A	built-in oven	240v	40A
cook top	240v	40A	water heater	240v	30A
clothes dryer	240v	40A	food freezer	120v	20A
built-in dishwasher	120v	20A	garb disposal . . .	120v	20A
trash compactor .	120v	20A	bthrm heater	120/240v	20A
furnace motor . . .	120v	20A	well pump	120v	20A
a/c condenser . . .	240v	(varies-see mfr's label)			

Service entrance wiring is often aluminum, easily identified by its bright, silvery appearance. Aluminum is a good conductor, and is inexpensive compared to copper. The use of this material for service entrance installation, where proper installation and performance are easily monitored, is quite safe. Special considerations apply to aluminum branch circuit wiring, however, due to its rate of expansion under heat, and its susceptibility to corrosion when insulation is removed to make connections.

Branch Circuits, Connected Devices and Fixtures

The expansion and contraction of aluminum, caused by the range of temperatures encountered in typical house wiring installations, can loosen connection screws in branch circuit devices. Compounding this problem, oxide of aluminum is a poor conductor. A faulty connection as a result of a loose wire, especially when aggravated by aluminum oxide corrosion, becomes a fire hazard.

When aluminum branch circuit wiring became allowable in 1965, the National Electric Code required the use of special receptacles, switches, and breakers whenever it was used. Those approved devices, intended to improve the performance of aluminum connections, were labeled CU/AL (for use with copper or aluminum). Those intended for use with copper (or copper-clad aluminum), were not labeled.

By 1971 it became apparent that these CU/AL-labeled 15-amp and 20-amp switch and receptacle devices (those appropriately served by #12 AWG and #10 AWG monofilament aluminum conductors), were not performing as well as expected. In 1971, the NEC banned the use of 15- and 20-amp devices labeled CU/AL (breakers excepted), with aluminum wiring. Those devices were replaced with an improved version, labeled CO/ALR. Breakers labeled CU/AL remain acceptable for use with aluminum wiring.

If branch circuit wiring has been identified as aluminum, a sampling of cover plates should be removed to determine whether switch and receptacle devices are marked CO/ALR. Except when monofilament aluminum wiring has been spliced with copper wire ends for connection to all 15 and 20 amp switch and receptacle devices (a practice called pigtailing, which requires special tools to obtain the high pressure crimp necessary for safe and secure splices), *only those new 15 and 20 amp switch and receptacle devices marked CO/ALR are acceptable for aluminum wiring.* No push-in (or stab-back) devices are marked CO/ALR, as they are not suitable for use with aluminum wiring. With aluminum wiring, expect to frequently find evidence of burned, loose, or oxidized wires, as well as the (improper) use of aluminum wire with stab-back devices.

It is imperative that inspectors inform clients when aluminum branch circuit wiring is found, regardless of the presence or absence of the CO/ALR devices or the "pigtailing" of aluminum with copper ends for use with CU/AL, CO/ALR, or unlabeled devices. Aluminum branch circuit wiring is known to be less safe than copper branch circuit wiring in all cases. It is the absolute obligation of the inspector to report recognized hazards and potentially unsafe conditions to their clients, using the most factual language possible.

Ground Fault Circuit Interruptors

A ground fault occurs when any current from the energized conductor in a circuit returns to ground through any route other than the intended neutral conductor. A ground fault circuit interrupter (GFCI), is a device designed to quickly open (or "trip"), a circuit, much like a fuse or circuit breaker, when even a very small errant current to ground is detected. This

Typical GFCI receptacle device with "test" and "reset" buttons

works by comparing current levels in hot and neutral conductors, instantly opening the circuit when even a very small difference occurs. When hot and neutral current levels are not essentially equal, a fault to ground must be present, either through the grounding conductor, or some other source of ground (such as a sink and its user in contact with a faulty appliance). Under such circumstances, properly functioning GFCI devices will open the circuit before injury can occur. GFCIs react instantly to current differentials of just several thousandths of an ampere (milliamps, or MA), well below the level of electrocution danger to humans, which is about 750 MA, or 3/4 ampere.

Any location that is of particular danger to humans must be protected by a GFCI device. Such danger exists where water can help a person's body complete a circuit from an electrically charged component to ground. The National Electric Code requires that GFCI protection be provided at the following locations:

All receptacles serving kitchen countertops
All receptacles within 6 feet of any sink
All outdoor receptacles which can be reached from the ground
All bathroom receptacles
All garage receptacles (except those located in a protected niche and intended for use by a permanently installed appliance, like a freezer)
All receptacles in an unfinished basement
All crawl space receptacles (except those intended for sump pump use)
All spa-tub pump motor circuits
All swimming pool equipment
All pool-area lighting circuits and receptacles

Installation of GFCI devices can be either at the service panel, in the form of a special circuit breaker, or at receptacle and other point-of-use locations, in the form of special devices with "test" and "reset" buttons. GFCI receptacles can be installed to protect all receptacles in the branch circuit they serve, so GFCI protection in required locations is not always readily apparent. For this reason, an electronic circuit analyzer with GFCI trip mechanism will be required to ascertain the presence of GFCI protection at all required locations. Furthermore, test buttons on receptacle-type GFCIs cannot always be relied upon if and when a branch circuit grounding wire is improperly secured, so the trip function of the analyzer should always be used. Those GFCI devices located in the service panel must be tested by operating the "test" button. Failure to trip, or inability to reset any GFCI device indicates improper functioning. The absence, improper installation, or improper operation of GFCI devices at required locations must be reported as a "recognized hazard".

Primary Inspections — Electrical Systems

Knob and tube wiring was sometimes used in homes built before 1950. This wiring system uses porcelain knobs and tubes to insulate and support the individual hot and neutral conductors, which are run separately, a few inches apart. The typical installation is 60-amp service, #12 AWG copper wire in 15-amp branch circuits. No junction boxes were used, opting for a system of twisting, soldering, and wrapping all splices. Some knob and tube wiring circuits fuse the hot and neutral side separately, leaving the hot side energized if only the neutral side fuse opens (or "blows"). This is known as a fused neutral, and can be hazardous to the uninitiated.

There is no circuit-grounding conductor in the knob and tube system, so receptacles are of the two-slot variety. With this (and other ungrounded wiring, identified by the two-slot receptacles), the inspector should suspect the lack of system grounding as well.

Since knob and tube conductors are mostly buried inside walls and ceilings, visible and accessible components will only be found in attic or basement locations, and they should be inspected for cracked, dry, brittle, or damaged insulation. Knob and tube wiring has its critics, with good reason, but with proper maintenance and monitoring, it can be safe. All service and repairs to such wiring must be performed by a qualified electrician.

All accessible receptacles must be checked for the presence of power, correct polarity, functional grounding, and, where applicable, proper installation and operation of GFCI devices. The simple plug-in circuit analyzer required for this is inexpensive, simple to use, and available at most home centers and hardware stores. Plugged into a receptacle, circuit analyzers display warnings when hot, neutral, or grounding connections are faulty, when polarity is reversed (a condition which can cause damage or improper operation in some modern electrical equipment and appliances), and when GFCI devices are malfunctioning. Any such conditions are reportable defects.

Homes built before the common use of grounded electrical circuits will have 2-slot (ungrounded), receptacles. GFCI devices may have been retro-fitted, and they can provide some protection, even without a grounding conductor. The fault conductor (such as a person), becomes the missing ground, tripping the device. Because there is no circuit ground conductor, though, the test button (and the inspector's analyzer/tester) may not trip the device. The use of GFCI devices in ungrounded circuits is not ideal, but at least some protection is afforded.

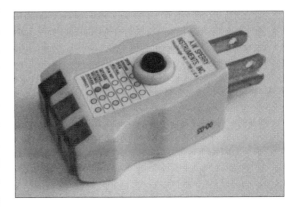

A circuit analyzer with GFCI trip button is an essential part of every inspector's toolbox.

Two-slot (ungrounded), receptacles located in a kitchen, bathroom, crawl space, garage, or outdoor location without GFCI protection present a particular shock hazard. Three-slot receptacles installed without a circuit-grounding conductor will be easily identified with a circuit analyzer. This is a hazardous condition, and will be reported as such. The proper and permanent installation of a three-slot adapter with grounding wire will eliminate the hazard if a positive circuit grounding connection can be verified.

Look for the installation of a receptacle near the heating and cooling equipment in attics and crawlspaces. This requirement is to make the use of lights and power tools convenient for service personnel. Absence of this outlet is reportable. Aside from the GFCI requirement, receptacles at outdoor locations, installed under a porch roof or other cover, should be of the type which protects them from the weather while not in use. Outdoor receptacles installed without permanent overhead cover must be of the type which are weather-protected, whether in use or not.

If an undersink disposal cord of the plug-in type is used, its length must be between 18 and 36 inches. (Allowable cord length for dishwashers and trash compactors is 36 to 48 inches). Cords in these tight spaces and/or adjacent to a water source should be of a length intended to limit inadvertent disconnection or physical damage, and subsequent shock hazards. These cord-length rules do not apply to wired-in appliances. Additionally, extension and appliance cords should not be permanently installed under rugs, or through walls, ceilings, or doorways.

Pendant style lighting fixtures, including hanging and cord-connected lights, present a hazard if installed within reach by the occupant of a bathtub. These fixtures may only be installed outside of a zone 3 feet horizontally distant and 8 feet higher than the flood rim of any tub.

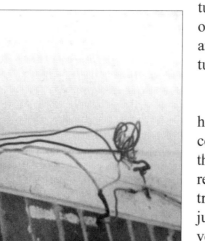

This homeowner's special wiring arrangement is dangerous. How many hazardous conditions are shown?

Most homeowners are unaware of the hazards inherent in substandard electrical configurations, and unknowingly endanger themselves with makeshift modifications and repairs. In many homes where amateur electrical modifications have been made, the junction boxes required to safely house high voltage wire splices will be omitted. In other cases, junction boxes are left open, exposing the splices. Electrical junction boxes

Primary Inspections — Electrical Systems

must have cover plates. The absence of a cover plate is a reportable defect. Also, look to see that house wiring routed within 6 feet of attic access doors, or other locations where it is vulnerable to physical damage, is protected by conduit or raceway.

Wall and Appliance Switches

Wall switches serving room lights and appliances must all be inspected for proper operation, and for evidence of arcing or excessive heat. Dimmer switches, in particular, normally produce some heat, but any which become too hot to lay a palm comfortably across should be called out for attention. Typical dimmer switches for residential lighting are rated at 600 watts per circuit, or less. Dimmer ratings are printed or embossed on the device housing, and can be found beneath the cover plate. When bulbs in the dimmer circuit are of a total wattage greater than the dimmer rating, excessive heat is produced at the dimmer, a hazardous condition.

Only incandescent light bulb circuits should use dimmers. In no case should a ceiling fan motor be wired to a dimmer. Varitrol switches, specifically intended for controlling ceiling fan speed, are the only acceptable devices for this purpose. Ceiling fans wired to a dimmer create a fire hazard.

Be sure that switches are securely fastened in place, that cover plates are present and undamaged, and that switches are "on" when in the up position. Three-way (or multi-way) switches (those that typically operate a light fixture from two or more locations) will not follow the "on" when up rule. Light switches are sometimes connected to receptacles instead of ceiling fixtures, and are intended to be used with lamps. Some electricians install such switched receptacles "upside down" (with grounding slot to the top) for easy identification. Switches or receptacles that at first appear to be non-functional may be so wired. Often, only one receptacle in a duplex device is wired this way, the other remaining unswitched. A droplight or radio plugged into a "dead" receptacle will come alive when its wall switch is turned "on" by the inspector. Remember that only incandescent bulbs should be used for this test if the switch is of the dimmer type.

Fixtures, Lighting Devices and Fans

Built-in lighting fixtures, ceiling fans, and other electrical devices must be properly secured to their mounting points. No fixture should be hanging from or supported by its electrical wires (unless they are of the type designed by the manufacturer to do so). Also, look for signs of exposed or improper wiring, poorly balanced fan blades, or missing pieces. Be sure to operate fans at all speeds, and report any unusual noise or other irregularities.

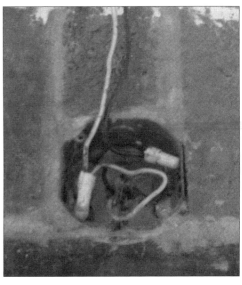

Exposed wirenut connections in an open junction box

Recessed light fixtures must be installed in accordance with their manufacturer's instructions. Unless they are specifically labeled and listed for direct contact, clearance to combustibles must be at least ½ inch, and clearance to insulation, often visible at attic spaces, must be no less than 3 inches. If any scorching or other evidence of heat related damage is visible, it must be reported. Where lighting brightness is suspiciously intense, bulbs in use should be compared to the fixture's label describing the maximum wattage allowable. Recommend replacement of any bulbs that do no comply.

Lighting fixtures found inside closets are often economy grade fixtures, installed with little regard for proper placement. Inspectors must be concerned with the safety of such installations, and can look to the building codes to guide them. All fixtures of the fluorescent type, and incandescent fixtures recessed into the ceiling, should be installed at least 6 inches (measured laterally), from shelves *or shelf space which could be occupied by items likely to be stored there.* Surface mounted incandescent fixtures require 12 inches of such clearance. All bulbs installed in closet fixtures must be enclosed within a protective globe or cover.

Some structures will have a portion of their electric wiring run through conduit or gutters that are surface mounted to walls or ceilings. Where so installed, conduit should be adequately secured to the structure, especially at termination points. Rigid gutters must be secured along their entire run, with no open gaps that might permit conductors to escape their enclosure. Metal electrical gutters should be bonded with the system ground by means of a grounding wire or bonding screw.

For safety while servicing, electrical disconnects are required at air conditioning condenser units, furnace motors, electric water heaters, hydromassage tubs, and any motor or device which is rated at 1/8 horsepower or more. The disconnect switch serving (outdoor) air conditioning condensers should be readily visible from the unit, allowing a technician to observe anyone who might inadvertently turn power on while service is in progress. An electrical service panel (breaker or fuse box), within a sight line from the equipment fulfills this need. When the electrical panel location does not fulfill this need, a separate disconnect switch is installed very near the condenser. The disconnect method for fueling burning furnaces is usually a standard wall switch, mounted close to the furnace. Hydromassage equipment may be directly wired into its electrical circuit, or simply plugged into a receptacle within its base. Here, too, some form of electric service disconnect must be provided nearby, whether by way of a shutoff switch, or simply an accessible plug connection. The inspector should note the absence of disconnection devices as hazardous.

Review Questions - Electrical Systems

(circle the letter next to the best answer for each question)

1. Minimum residential electrical service, providing 120- and 240-volt service, requires:
   a. 2, 3, or 4 wire service entrance
   b. 60-amp / 240-volt service
   c. a minimum of 6 branch circuits
   d. a main breaker or fuse
   e. copper service entrance conductors

2. A service panel with a main breaker rated at 150 amps must have:
   a. service entrance conductors, if aluminum, of at least #2/0 AWG cable
   b. service entrance conductors, if copper, of at least #1 AWG cable
   c. service entrance conductors, if aluminum, of at least #4/0 AWG cable
   d. service entrance conductors, if copper, of at least #2/0 AWG cable
   e. a. and b.

3. A 20-amp circuit breaker serving a branch circuit is safe and compatible with:
   a. #14 AWG copper wire
   b. #12 AWG copper wire
   c. #14 AWG aluminum wire
   d. #12 AWG aluminum wire
   e. b. and d.

4. Service entrance cables marked #3/0 AWG AL are safe for use with main breakers labeled:
   a. 100 amps
   b. 125 amps
   c. 150 amps
   d. 175 amps
   e. all of the above

5. Overhead clearance between service entrance cables and private driveways must be at least
   a. 10 feet
   b. 12 feet
   c. 14 feet
   d. 16 feet
   e. 18 feet

6. Overhead service entrance conductors must:
   a. have minimum clearance above only the overhanging portion of a roof of at least 18 inches
   b. be configured into an effective drip loop at the weatherhead
   c. not be unduly vulnerable to physical damage by overhanging tree branches
   d. be physically separated from each other at the weatherhead
   e. all of the above

7. System grounding conductors:
   a. must be electrically isolated from the neutral bus bar
   b. must be electrically isolated from the service panel and components
   c. are connected to a grounding rod or metal water supply line
   d. afford no protection from dangerously high voltage, as might be caused by lightning strikes
   e. must be covered in insulation

8. Double wired breakers:
   a. are required to provide 240 volt service
   b. are identified by the presence of 2 branch circuit conductors connected to one side of a circuit breaker or fuse lug
   c. reduce the danger of overload
   d. must be used for dedicated circuits, such as those serving an electric range or spa-tub
   e. must be of the GFCI type

9. The use of bare or uninsulated wire for branch circuit grounding conductors is:
   a. safe
   b. uncommon
   c. prohibited
   d. required
   e. none of the above

10. Ground fault circuit interrupters:
    a. open a circuit when the serving circuit breaker malfunctions
    b. can only protect the receptacle where the GFCI device is located
    c. are not required at receptacles in an unfinished basement
    d. are not required at garage receptacles intended for use by a freezer
    e. are hazardous if installed near water sources

11. Aluminum branch circuit wiring:
    a. expands less than copper wiring when heated
    b. creates oxide of aluminum, a good conductor, when it corrodes
    c. must be used when outlet devices are labeled CU/AL
    d. can cause faulty connections at light switches
    e. a. and d.

12. Knob-and-tube wiring:
    a. provides no circuit grounding conductor
    b. was not installed in homes after 1950
    c. uses porcelain knobs to insulate and support individual conductors
    d. often provides fuses at both hot and neutral sides of a circuit
    e. all of the above

13. Reversed polarity in an AC (alternating current) circuit:
    a. is not important
    b. cannot be easily identified by using a simple circuit analyzer
    c. is required for safe use by some modern equipment and appliances
    d. can be reversed by using a simple 3-prong adapter
    e. none of the above

14. 3-slot receptacles that register a faulty ground connection with a circuit analyzer:
    a. should be reported as in need of repair
    b. should only be used with appliances rated at less than 4 amps
    c. should be re-tested with a simple 2-slot analyzer
    d. alert the inspector to the use of knob-and-tube wiring
    e. all of the above

REVIEW QUESTIONS   63

15. Hazardous conditions commonly found in electrical systems include:
    a. evidence of a drip loop at a service entrance weatherhead
    b. hanging or cord connected lights too close to an entry door
    c. exposed 120 volt wire connections outside of a junction box
    d. all of the above
    e. a. and c.

16. Electrical junction boxes:
    a. are not required at all high voltage wire splice locations
    b. are typically found at knob-and-tube wire splice locations
    c. must have cover plates
    d. are designed to dissipate heat
    e. are not required at ceiling fan or light fixture attachment locations

17. Wall switches should be inspected for
    a. excessive heat
    b. proper operation
    c. secure attachment to mounting surfaces
    d. damage
    e. all of the above

18. Lighting fixtures inside clothes closets:
    a. must be physically supported by their electrical wires
    b. require a wall switch within 6 feet of the fixture
    c. should not be too close to useable shelf space
    d. must use only incandescent bulbs
    e. must not be covered

19. Electrical disconnects are required (for the safety of service personnel) near:
    a. electric water heater locations
    b. furnace motor locations
    c. (outdoor) air conditioner condenser locations
    d. hydromassage tub locations
    e. all of the above

20. A 3-way light switch:
    a. is always on when in the up position
    b. controls 3 (or fewer) lights
    c. controls one fixture from 2 locations
    d. has 3 switch locations
    e. a. and d.

Typical Gas-Fired Forced Air Furnace

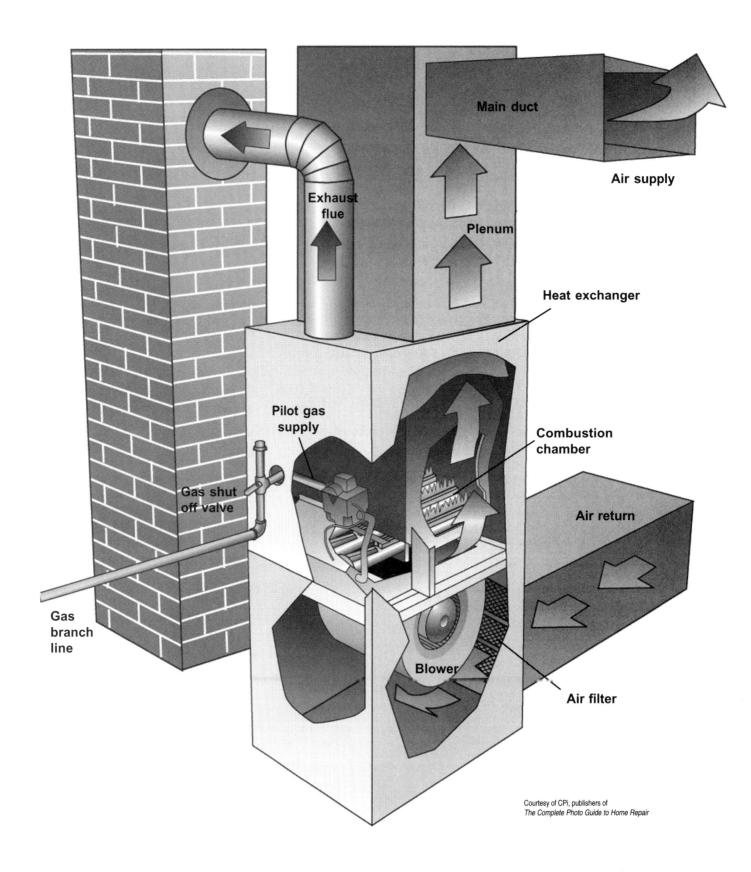

Heating, Ventilation and Air Conditioning Systems

Learning Objectives

1. Learn how the various types of heating and cooling systems found within residential structures are intended to work.
2. Understand the causes of residential heating and cooling system malfunction.
3. Be able to recognize those visible conditions which represent evidence of malfunction in heating and cooling systems.
4. Be aware of the obligations borne by inspectors regarding the reporting of improper installation and operation of residential heating and cooling systems.
5. Become familiar with the potential hazards posed by residential heating and cooling systems.

Heating Equipment

In residential heating, there are many system configurations, employing a broad array of fuels and methods of distribution. Inspectors will discover countless variations, including unlikely combinations of equipment that can only be properly evaluated by heating specialists. It is the function of the inspector to apprise the client of the conditions found *to the best of his ability*. The best home inspectors will readily report the presence of equipment or conditions which are outside his field of expertise, and, in such cases, recommend the services of professional specialists.

Every heating system, regardless of type, requires an array of controls to properly orchestrate the safe production and distribution of heat. Master fuel and electric service shutoffs should be present at each heating unit. Every thermostat, master shutoff, gas valve, relief valve, pressure or level gauge, and other control device should be inspected for general condition and proper operation. Visible wiring should be secure and intact, with no evidence of damage, arcing or charring. In addition, the inspector will look for corrosion, rust, stains, broken or missing control knobs, leaks, poor mounting, and any other condition that might indicate the need for repair. Heat producing surfaces must be located with enough clearance to framing members, stored items, and any other combustible material to maintain fire safety.

Thermostats should be level, properly secured in place, and undamaged. With the thermostat cover removed, look for dust or dirt that can interfere with the delicate electrical contacts inside. This is a common occurrence when the thermostat for a ducted system is mounted on a wall that serves as a return air chase. Such placement puts the thermostat in the direct path of dust-carrying air, where its wiring enters the plenum wall. If a mercury switch (a glass bulb with electrical contacts inside of it), is visible, inspect it for cracks and evidence of leaking. It will be mounted on a bi-metallic coil or strip, which reacts to temperature fluctuations by uncoiling or bending, causing the mercury in the bulb to bridge the contacts, and thus energize, the proper control circuits.

Forced Air Heating

The most common type of heating system is forced air. It can be fueled by natural gas, liquid propane, oil, or electricity. Except where electricity is the heat source, such as in electric furnaces and heat pumps, heat is produced by the combustion of fuel and air in the burner compartment of a furnace, where it is transferred to the conditioned air through a heat exchanger. The combustion products are then exhausted out through a flue vent. The heat exchanger must not allow any combustion products to mix with the conditioned air, which is circulated throughout the living space by a blower. The heated air is distributed through a network of air ducts. The presence of ductwork for supply and return air, along with a contained blower, or air handler, is what identifies the system as a forced air type.

Blowers and belts in a forced air system should be clean, secure, and quiet when operating. The blower compartment should be effectively airtight to prevent unconditioned air from entering under the negative pressure created upstream during blower operation. Similarly, the pressure created in the plenum downstream of the blower compartment will permit escape of the conditioned air in the absence of an airtight seal. Ticking or knocking sounds, indicative of a poorly balanced blower (or "squirrel cage"), are often the result of an accumulation of dust, grease, or soot on the blades. Look for a filter provision in the return air plenum, and the presence of a clean filter element. Inspectors should listen for improperly balanced blowers, damaged or misaligned blower belts, loose blower assembly mounts, and deteriorated blower motor bearings. All are common sources of unusual noise.

Gravity convection hot air heating is similar to a forced air system, but without any powered means of air distribution. Air, heated by the heat exchanger in a furnace, rises through ductwork and enters the living space at ceiling level. As the air gives up heat to its surroundings, it becomes cooler and denser, returning by force of gravity to floor level, where it returns to the furnace for re-heating. Since this system relies solely on convection for distribution of heated air, it requires large temperature differentials to function properly, and produces too little air movement to force its way through a filter. This relatively inefficient system is now obsolete, but can be retrofitted with a blower to extend its useful life.

Gas Furnaces

A gas furnace will be fitted with either a standing gas pilot flame or an electronic ignition device designed to light a pilot flame, which in turn ignites the burners. A thermocouple is engulfed in the pilot flame to prove heat, and gas is thereafter supplied to the burners through an automatic gas valve. In the absence of a pilot flame, no gas is delivered. If the pilot and thermocouple are readily accessible, the inspector should determine whether the thermocouple is properly positioned, directly in the path of the pilot flame. Some newer furnaces have no pilot flame at all, but utilize electronic "Hot Surface Ignition" (HSI), to directly ignite the burners, after which the hot surface igniter is disengaged by a flame sensor. With circuit breaker, master power switch, fuel supply, and any pilot lights on, the thermostat should be set to call for heat.

Inspection panels or covers should be removed from the furnace housing to see as much of the burner compartment as possible. For this, a long-handled inspection mirror is useful. Color, intensity, and other flame characteristics are assessed to confirm a proper fuel-air mixture. *A clearly defined soft blue flame with a bright blue inner cone, resting directly on the burner ports* indicates a proper mix of fuel and air. Proper burning of natural gas requires both primary combustion air (to be mixed with the gas before the point of primary ignition), and secondary combustion air (which mixes with the burning primary flame for complete secondary combustion). Primary combustion air is controlled by adjusting a gate or shutter upstream of the burner head. A yellow flame (or one with a yellow outer envelope or yellow tips), or a flame which floats or lifts steadily off the burner, would indicate the need for mixture adjustment. So, too, would a lazy flame with undefined tips. Dust particles in the combustion air may cause red or orange streaks in the flame, and are not significant unless excessive. Flashback occurs when gas burns inside the burner port or orifice, and may be indicative of either an improper gas mixture or low gas pressure. The accumulation of soot at the flue termination is an additional clue to an improper mixture.

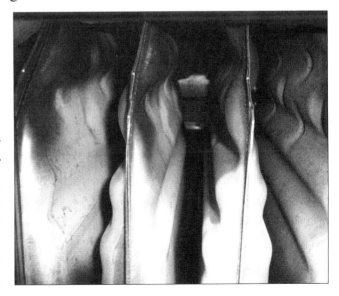

A good view of a typical gas furnace heat exchanger.

The condition of the burner flame must be carefully assessed during inspection, not only for evaluation of the fuel-air mixture, but also to identify evidence of possible heat exchanger failure. Along with poisonous carbon monoxide (CO), by-products of gas combustion include sulfur and water vapor, which combine to create sulfuric acid. The acid promotes rusting, scaling, or corrosion of the heat exchanger, which, over time, can rust completely through. (Improper mixture,

This gas-fired water heater is located within the return air plenum that houses the central heating and cooling system. The negative pressure within this equipment room (created during blower operation) will draw combustion gasses from the water heater and deliver them into the stream of conditioned air. Carbon monoxide (CO), a by-product of gas combustion, is poisonous.

creating hot spots in the metal of the exchanger, can also accelerate exchanger failure by simply burning through it).

Holes in the exchanger will allow combustion products to pass through, which then mix with the conditioned air intended for heating the structure. Flames at the burner may "dance" when this occurs as they are blown around in the burner compartment by the force of the leaking air passing over the outside wall of the exchanger. The holes are not always obvious, and may be actually visible only by dismantling the furnace.

Sticky black soot in the blower compartment of a fuel-burning furnace usually indicates failure of a heat exchanger. When this happens, soot may also be found building up at the supply registers. Great care should be taken in the evaluation of heat exchanger integrity. The human body has an absorptive affinity for inhaled carbon monoxide many times greater than that of the oxygen it replaces, and can therefore cause death by asphyxiation even in very low concentrations. Whenever the heat exchanger integrity is in question, complete evaluation by a qualified heating system technician must be recommended.

Openings, cracks or holes on the leeward side of the heat exchanger may not cause the flame to dance, but can draw the flame into the air stream, along with by-products of combustion. The effect on the flame pattern often goes undetected under these circumstances.

If no dancing, lifting, or draw down of the burner flame is present, if no sticky black soot accumulation appears at supply registers, if no holes or heavy scaling or rust are evident at visible portions of the heat exchanger or burner area, and if no headaches are reported by occupants during the heating season, only then can the inspector feel reasonably confident that heat exchanger failure has not occurred.

Utility suppliers always add a distinctive odorant to natural gas so that leaks can be easily detected. It is normal to detect the faint smell of gas for a few seconds after ignition of a pilot or burner, but a continuing odor of gas, even though slight, is not acceptable. Home inspectors typically advise their clients that gas supply pipes and components are only inspected at points of use, where they are readily accessible. Comprehensive system-wide gas leak detection is a professional specialty beyond the scope of a standard home inspection. When small gas leaks are detected, they should be noted in the inspection report. Larger gas leaks, especially in confined spaces where there is a danger of accumulation, must be dealt with immediately.

Gas leaks can occur anywhere, but are most often found at connection fittings or appliance gas valves, where the supply is distributed to a series of controls; a pressure regulator, a manual valve, a pilot filter, a reset plunger, and the pilot and burner gas outlets. The main gas meter serving the dwelling is another common source of leaks. Sense of smell is usually a reliable detection method. Soap-solution bath and electronic combustible-gas detectors are also good. The practice of holding a lighted match to suspected gas leak locations to purposely ignite errant gas, although common, is not advisable.

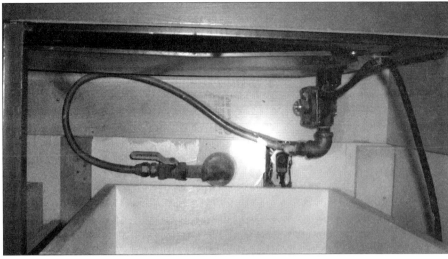

The use of copper gas connectors will be called out as a hazardous condition. Only epoxy-coated or stainless steel connectors are permitted.

Gas burning furnaces should be connected to their fuel supply with either rigid black iron or galvanized steel piping. Flexible connectors are permitted when of approved material. Flexible gas connectors should be epoxy coated brass or corrugated stainless steel. Hydrogen sulfide, an element within natural gas, has a corrosive effect on copper and brass, rendering both materials inappropriate for gas service where concentrations of this element are greater than .3 grains per 100 cubic feet. In any case, copper gas supply lines, when used, and flexible connectors must never be routed through walls, floors, or ceilings. A gas branch shutoff valve should be installed no further than 6 feet from the point of gas use at each furnace, and only epoxy coated or stainless steel gas connectors are acceptably safe. Gas connectors serving furnace equipment must be no more than 3 feet in length. Some older flexible brass gas connectors are still in use, and when they are encountered, inspectors should recommend their replacement with an approved connector.

This furnace flue provides less than the minimum required 1 inch of clearance to the combustible roof deck.

Proper venting of flue gasses must be accomplished by the methods dictated within the building codes. It is essential for combustion products to exhaust safely to the outdoors in a way that prevents the release of poisonous gasses or vapors within the structure. The flue must also be designed to prevent the transfer of heat to combustible materials. B-class flue vent materials and installation must be in precise compliance with code for safe operation. Flue pipes used with gas appliances must be of double wall construction. Single wall vent connectors, sometimes used at the flue collar for connection to the flue, must not be used in concealed, unoccupied, or attic spaces, nor should they pass through walls or ceilings. Vent pipes must be a minimum of 3 inches in diameter, and installed with at least 1 inch of clearance to combustible materials. Unless flue gasses are powered by a fan (as with induced draft or power vent systems), the minimum vertical distance from the exhaust collar of the appliance to vent termination is 5 feet, and, in all cases, the flue must terminate with an approved vent cap to help prevent downdrafting and rain penetration. Vent pipes must be installed in accordance with their exhaust flow-direction labeling and without screws or rivets (which are only permitted at the furnace connection).

Where a flue passes through a pitched roof, its termination must be at least 2 feet higher than the roof surface, and 8 feet distant from any vertical surface, such as a chimney or side wall. Where a roof is pitched less than 6-in-12 inches, flue termination may be as little as 1 foot higher than the roof surface. A positive slope of at least $\frac{1}{4}$ inch rise per foot of length must be maintained for the entire length of the flue to assure proper evacuation of flue gasses.

An adequate supply of air must be available for both combustion and drafting in vented gas appliances. If a gas-fired furnace is installed in an attic, utility room, or other enclosed space, be sure there is adequate ventilation.

A draft diverter (or draft hood), must be present at the exhaust collar of any gas burning appliance designed to be vented without the aid of a fan. The purpose of the diverter is to allow the free flow of air (draft air), into the flue to aid in evacuation of the exhaust gasses, while dissipating downdrafts, preventing them from entering the burner compartment. If the flow of hot gasses up the flue is interrupted due to improper flue installation, exhaust gasses may spill out of the draft diverter. The accumulation of soot or corrosion at the edges of the diverter is a clue to such spillage. The flame and smoke of a lighted kitchen match held near a properly drafting hood will be drawn inside.

In the case of a gas fired furnace utilizing induced draft or fan driven venting, no draft hood is present. A fan located at the flue collar, either inside or immediately outside of the appliance cabinet, should start up instantly at the time the thermostat creates a heat demand, and it will run for a time after the burner flame is extinguished. This is not to be confused with the main blower, which circulates conditioned air throughout the living space, and will not start until the proper temperature is reached inside the burner compartment or a specified time interval has passed. The main blower will also run after the burner flame is extinguished, until the burner compartment temperature is sufficiently lowered to safely shut down air circulation. An independent timer or heat-sensing circuit is used to control the blower function. The proper operation of these independent fan and blower controls must be confirmed during inspection of all types of furnaces.

With full heating demand, furnace operation should follow a cycle of heat delivery periods consistent with the call for heat from the thermostat. A flame or blower which short-cycles is indicative of faulty limit control devices or an improperly adjusted thermostat heat anticipator, and service by a qualified heating technician should be recommended.

Condensing Furnaces and Boilers

In recent years, the efficiency of gas-fired boilers and furnaces has increased to a point where enough heat can be transferred through the heat exchangers to cause water vapor in the flue gasses to condense. It is for this reason that they are called condensing boilers or condensing furnaces. Their efficiency can reach up to 97%. This is made possible by the use of high efficiency heat exchanger arrangements, usually including a secondary tier exchanger. Some high efficiency units use fuel in a series of short bursts, at the rate of about sixty burns per second. These "pulse" boilers or furnaces are somewhat noisier than conventional units.

Adequate combustion air is especially critical to the proper operation of condensing furnaces and boilers, so most units include some provision for outside air to be ducted directly into the burner compartment. Combustion gasses are cooled enough to preclude the need for a conventional flue or chimney, and can be safely exhausted outdoors through a plastic pipe. Since the cooled gasses do not readily rise by natural convection, a power vent or blower is required. Any condensing furnace or condensing boiler using a masonry chimney for venting must provide enough flue pipe to reach all the way to the top of the chimney. A vent pipe that shows rust at its termination may be an indication of improper combustion, usually caused by inadequate combustion air or improper gas valve adjustment.

The condensate must be removed, usually by connection to the waste-water drain system, or via floor drain. Such floor drains must be properly routed into the drain system, and not simply run into a hole in the foundation floor so as to accumulate there. In any case, the condensate drain must be dedicated for exclusive use by the furnace, and should be fitted with a proper "P" trap to prevent sewer gasses from entering.

Electric Furnaces and Electric Baseboard Heating

When electricity flows through a conductor, resistance causes the production of heat. Conductor materials are chosen to best perform the desired task. Tungsten light bulb filaments maximize light output, albeit with an undesirable heat by-product. Furnace elements of nickel-chromium alloy (ni-chrome), produce maximum heating, with only a small amount of light by-product. Ovens, coffee makers, toasters, and electric water heaters are just a few examples of heat production by electrical resistance. When this principle is employed in space heating system design, it is utilized in one of two ways.

First is the forced air central electric furnace, in which an electric current is run through a bank of heating elements. Usually, there are 2 to 6 elements, which typically begin to receive electric current 20 or 30 seconds after a call for heat from the thermostat. Sequencing controls engage the heating elements one at a time until all elements are on. This may take two or three minutes, depending on the number of heating elements. When the thermostat ends the heat cycle, the elements begin to sequence off, usually in the same order in which they were engaged. A blower circulates air from the living space directly across the heating elements. The blower may be activated immediately with the call for heat, or may be delayed until shortly after the first element is energized, depending on the design of the furnace and the type of thermostat used. The blower is controlled by an independent timer or heat sensing circuit, and will sometimes continue to run for a brief period after the heating elements are disengaged.

A clamp-on amp probe is used for determining whether all elements are operating properly. Access to the high voltage service line can be found either within the furnace, if access panels are provided, or at the electric service panel or breaker box. Each element typically draws between 15 and 22 amps. The blower motor typically draws 4 to 6 amps. Actual maximum amperage drawn should closely equal the number of heating elements x amperage drawn by each element + the amperage drawn by the blower motor. This Full Load Amperage rating (FLA) will be found on the furnace manufacturer's label, affixed to the appliance.

Example: 3 heating elements
         x 20 amps each element
         = 60 amps
         + 6 amps (blower motor)
totals   66 maximum amps drawn

Maximum amp draw measurements significantly higher or lower than the FLA rating listed by the manufacturer indicate malfunction, and the need for repair. When more than one branch circuit supplies power to the furnaces, amp draw values must be added together for an accurate total.

In those instances when furnace access panels and main electric service panels are inaccessible for inspection, a supply/return air temperature differential calculation will help the inspector to determine whether furnace operation is normal. Furnaces with one heat element can be expected to provide heat at the supply registers which measures about 15-20° higher than the return air temperature. Furnaces with 2 heat elements should provide about 25-30° of differential. Furnaces with 3 or more elements will provide 25-40° of differential. These figures are generalities, and some variations will be encountered. Within these general guidelines, a slow, steady rise and fall of temperature will be observed as the thermostat cycles on and off if the heating elements and sequencing circuits are functioning properly. Heat elements which glow a bright red (when observable) are usually a sign of inadequate airflow or malfunctioning blower.

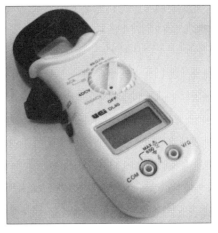

A typical clamp-on multi-meter

In all furnaces, visible wiring should be inspected for improper routing, abrasion, burning, melting, loose or open connections, and other unsafe conditions. Be sure the furnace and its wiring are properly supported or mounted, and not located so as to be unduly vulnerable to physical damage.

The second way in which electric resistance is commonly used for space heating is with baseboard heaters installed in each room. Usually, each unit has its own thermostat, allowing occupants to tailor comfort levels. Electric resistance baseboard heaters have thermal reflectors behind the heating elements to direct the radiated heat toward the living area. Convection takes place, too, as heated air rises in the room, replaced by cooler air at the floor, which is then heated, and so on. Some electric baseboard heaters have fans built into them to aid in the distribution of heat.

Electronic Air Cleaners

Electronic air cleaners are designed to remove particulate matter as small as one thousandth of a millimeter in size, including some bacteria and mold spores. They are usually installed in conjunction with forced air furnaces or air conditioners. A pre-filter removes larger airborne particles. Those that remain are electrically charged, then passed through a fine mesh grille, called the ionizer. There, they are drawn to a collection grid by an opposite electric charge. By design, electronic filters only operate while a furnace or air conditioning blower is forcing airflow.

There is usually a test button at the control panel. When pressed, it discharges the high voltage power pack, emitting a distinct snapping sound, indicating normal functionality. A slight odor usually accompanies normal operation. If an inspection cover is present, it should be removed to reveal the pre-filter, the charging and collection grilles, and the case interior. They should all be clean of dust and debris. Electronic air filters are sensitive to the build-up of dust, and must be cleaned regularly. A slight buzzing sound is normal, but frequent "popping" usually indicates the need for cleaning. Although inspection of electronic air cleaners is beyond the scope of minimum standards set by most regulating authorities, clients will be well served to learn about them from their inspectors.

Hot Water Space Heating

Gas and oil are the most common fuels used for hot water space heating. Heated water is pumped through a network of pipes and radiators, and then returned to the boiler for re-heating. Older, less sophisticated hot water systems may rely on gravity to circulate the heated water throughout the structure. As water heats, expansion causes it to become lighter than the cool, heavier water returning from the radiators (where it has lost some of its heat to the room). This continuous cycle of heating, rising, cooling, and falling back down to the heating source is quite simple. It can be compared to the gravity warm air system, wherein no blower or fan is used to circulate the heated air. Gravity systems require that the heat source be located below the living space. These gravity systems are inefficient compared to those using mechanical means to distribute the heating medium. Gravity systems are now considered obsolete, although they can still be found in older homes. Many gravity hot water systems have been successfully retrofitted with pumps to improve their performance.

Gravity hot water systems can be difficult to discern from steam systems, except that a properly installed steam system will be equipped with a water level gauge. (Steam boilers are only partially filled with water, requiring about a third of the boiler's volume for air). Hot water boilers have no water level gauge, but will be equipped with an expansion tank. Forced hot water systems should have temperature and pressure gauges as well.

In an open system, in which the water is open to the atmosphere, the expansion tank must be located higher than the highest radiator to contain the system water. The attic is the most common location, and expansion tanks located there should be insulated to protect them from freezing. Since its overflow pipe is open to the atmosphere, it should be routed to a safe exhaust location. No pressure relief valve is necessary in an open hot water heating system.

Water supply to a closed system boiler is plumbed in directly from the house supply, with a regulator in place to reduce pressure to around 12 psi. An expansion tank is required to buffer the volume changes created by the expansion and contraction of the water as it heats and cools. In a closed hot water system, an air cushion in a sealed expansion tank absorbs the water's volumetric changes caused by heating and cooling. Closed system expansion tanks are located near the boiler, and a pressure relief valve is required for safety. Forced hot water heating is invariably of the closed system type.

Look carefully for any sign of leaks, while understanding that some condensation at the boiler will usually form during initial startup. Observe the relief valves and gauges for apparent functionality. Circulating pumps will often fail, and are vulnerable to leaks at their shaft seals. Expansion tanks must be properly located and adequately supported, and equipment-room ventilation must be provided. As always, flue drafting and termination, component integrity, materials, installation, and clearance to combustibles must be observed. Finally, check to see that all radiators are warming adequately.

Hot water space heating systems can be equipped to provide domestic hot water (water used for bathing, washing dishes, etc.). When such systems are in place, the thermostat controls only the circulating pump, while the burner is controlled by an aquastat, which regulates water temperature. These devices are used to permit the production of domestic hot water in summer months, without heating the home. Solenoid operated flow control valves will be provided as well, to prevent unwanted space heating by convection.

Steam Heating

In a typical steam heating system, gas or oil is burned to bring water in a boiler to its boiling point. As water is converted to steam, it expands and moves through pipes to radiators, where heat is given off. As it cools, steam condenses back into a liquid state. Simpler steam systems provide for the water to then simply return, by gravity, back down the steam supply piping into the boiler for re-heating. Other steam systems utilize

OIL-FIRED BOILER

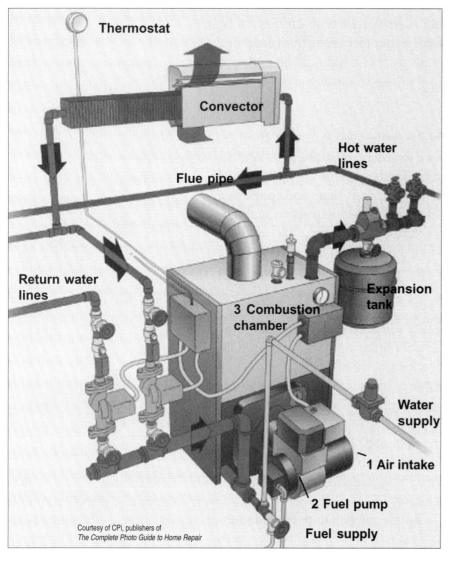

A blower draws in air through the air intake (1) while a fuel pump (2) maintains a constant supply of fuel oil. The mixture is ignited by a high-voltage spark as it enters the combustion chamber (3), heating the water.

two pipes, one to supply steam to the radiators, and the other for return of the condensate.

When water is boiled, producing steam as it changes from liquid to gas, a large volumetric increase occurs, which requires release to avoid pressure buildup. A temperature and pressure relief valve must be provided for safety from overpressure. In the single pipe system, venting valves are installed at each radiator. A malfunctioning air vent (or one painted over), will restrict the flow of steam to the affected radiator, thereby limiting its effectiveness. In a two-pipe system, a steam-trapping air vent is installed in the condensate return pipe. This acts as a system pressure limiter, while allowing the free flow of steam through the radiators for normal operation.

Oil Heating

Oil, like gas, can be burned in a furnace to heat air, or in a boiler for the production of hot water or steam. Since heating oil must be in a gaseous state for combustion to occur, it is pumped through a nozzle in the firebox, causing vaporization. It then mixes with combustion air brought in by a fan, and is ignited by electrodes in a gun assembly. Exhaust gasses escape directly up the flue, without the need for a draft diverter. Draft is regulated by a hinged and weighted door, called a barometric damper, located in the flue. It is designed to open, allowing room air into the chimney, if draft is too great. Be sure the flue is pitched upward, and that the draft regulator has not been defeated by blocking the intake.

With a call for heat from the thermostat, check to see that the oil burner pump motor and combustion air fan operate properly. A safety control shuts off the oil pump if flame cannot be proven, either by a heat switch in the exhaust path or a photocell at the burner.

A visual inspection of the combustion chamber or firebox should reveal no holes or other obvious damage. Cracks or open joints allow excess air into the firebox, affecting proper draft. They should be patched with refractory cement. Look at the tip of the burner head to see if it has burned off, as they will do over time. Visible oil lines must not be loose or damaged, and should include a filter and fuel shutoff valve. Integrity of the heat exchanger in forced air systems should be questioned if holes, excess carbon build-up, or scaling are visible. Look for soot at supply registers, as well.

Any oil tank located indoors must be at least 7 feet distant from any flame, and should have an outdoor fill provision. Report whether a fuel gauge is present. Look for leaks, damage, corrosion, or pitting of the tank, especially at the bottom.

Cleanup of environmental damage caused by leaking outdoor oil tanks will always be the responsibility of the homeowner. Such cleanup is performed under strict governmental guidelines, and can be very expensive. Remember that an oil tank may be buried where an oil heating system has been replaced with some other system. The inspection report should make this point very clear whenever appropriate.

It is important that the inspector familiarize himself with the proper installation and function of the various thermostats, relief valves, pumps, temperature and pressure limit controls, pressure gauges, temperature gauges, and (for steam systems) low-water-level cutoff systems and water level gauges. Proper water level in a steam system is critical for safe operation. For complete inspection, each boiler or furnace should be operated (if it is deemed safe), and allowed to cycle through its full range of functions.

Cooling Equipment and Heat Pumps

The refrigeration process, commonly called air conditioning, moves heat energy "uphill", from a cool space to a warmer space. This is accomplished by controlling refrigerant pressures within a closed loop. Controlled pressure changes cause the refrigerant to undergo phase transitions from gas to liquid, or liquid to gas, as needed. These phase changes are accompanied by the introduction or removal of heat energy. Heat-laden refrigerant vapor is compressed into a high-pressure gas and is delivered to the condenser coil for heat removal.

Typical Split Refrigeration System (Air Conditioner)

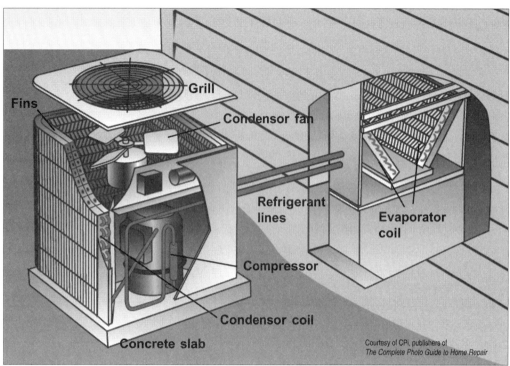

Refrigerant is pressurized and pumped through a condenser coil where it releases heat. It then flows to the evaporator coil. Air from the blower is cooled as it crosses the evaporator. The refrigerant is then pumped back outdoors to be cooled once again. A heat pump operates in much the same manner as an air conditioner during the summer. During the winter, a reversing valve is used to reverse the heat pump's operation so that the refrigerant extracts heat from outdoor air and releases the heat indoors.

In residential systems, heat is released by passing outdoor air over the heat-dissipating surfaces of the condenser coil. The combination of heat removal and high pressure causes the gas to condense into a liquid. Still under high pressure, the cooled liquid is sent to a metering device via the liquid line where it is sprayed into the low-pressure side of the refrigerant loop at the evaporator coil. The dramatic change in pressure causes the liquid refrigerant to start the evaporation process and begin its transition back to a vaporous state. Rapidly expanding refrigerant gas in the evaporator absorbs heat. The transfer of heat energy into the cooled refrigerant, via the surfaces of the evaporator coil, accelerates the evaporation process. The now heat-laden vapor is drawn back into the condenser by the compressor to begin another circuit through the refrigeration loop.

Many factors must be considered when designing a cooling system for a particular application. One such factor is the amount of cooling capacity, known as tonnage, required for proper cooling within the given living space. Generally, proper cooling requires about 1 ton (12000 btu/hr) for each 550 square feet of living space. In newer installations, where SEER (seasonal energy efficiency rating) numbers are higher, 650 to 700 square feet of living space per ton is not uncommon. Use of these very generalized figures must be with caution, but inspectors should be alert to the possibility that a cooling system capacity is simply inadequate, due, perhaps, to a recent room addition for which HVAC capacity improvements were not made. Systems that clearly are undersized, for any reason, should be called out as a condition in need of repair.

Air conditioners can be either of the split type or the single-package type. The split type locates the condenser coil outdoors and the evaporator coil (or cooling coil), indoors. The single-package system puts all operating components in a single location.

When warm air is moved across a cooling coil, the resultant temperature drop causes some of the moisture in the air to condense. (The same occurs when a cold soda can is placed out in a warm room). When the cooling coil is located indoors, a drain is required to carry away the condensate, to prevent any water damage that might be caused to the structure. Such a drain will be found exiting from the side of the evaporator case, at the bottom edge. It is required to be at least 3/4 inch in diameter, and can terminate at an outdoor location, into a properly plumbed floor or fixture drain (always ahead of a trap), a sump, or to a plumbing vent with its own *sealed* trap (where permitted by local building officials).

Any primary condensate drain which discharges into the wastewater plumbing system must be sealed, and must include a trap to prevent sewer gasses from backing into the conditioned air. The drain line should be insulated for the first 12 feet from the evaporator case to prevent condensation from forming in living or attic areas vulnerable to water damage, and proper slope must be continuously maintained to assure reliable gravity flow of the condensate to its point of discharge.

Cooling coils located over any ceiling also require a safety pan and secondary condensate drain system to catch and carry away water in the event of a primary drain line blockage. Safety pans must be permanently installed, with proper slope to pan and drain line, so as to maintain good drainage. The pan should be large enough to catch water which might drip from any part of the evaporator case. The secondary drain line must be at least 3/4 inch in diameter, and should terminate at a conspicuous location, such as over a window, so that a primary drain blockage, which causes the secondary drain to flow, will quickly become obvious to the home's occupants.

Take note of any damage or excess corrosion at the evaporator case, and check for damage, tears, or absence of the insulation required for the entire length of the vapor (or suction), line. Kinks or other damage to either of the two refrigerant lines must be observed and noted.

At the outdoor unit, see that the condenser coil and case are free of fin damage, obstructions, or debris that might restrict air circulation. Also be sure that the unit is level, and located high enough above the soil finish grade to prevent ground moisture or water from causing premature rust at the case bottom. Oily residue at the refrigerant fittings can be caused by leaks or recent charging. Fan blades that are rusty, bent, missing, or otherwise damaged should be reported, as well. Unusual noises at the condensing unit fan motor are often the result of worn bearings or loose motor mounting.

High voltage electric power serving the condensing or outdoor unit must be routed through properly secured conduit. See that the conduit and the low voltage control wiring are connected so as not to be vulnerable to water penetration. High voltage conduit must be well secured at the ends, and installed with a "drip loop", or sag in the middle to help keep rainwater from entering either the condenser case or the wall cavity. An electric service disconnect must be provided within 50 feet of the unit, on the same wall, in a direct line of sight. This requirement is for the safety of service personnel. A main breaker panel so located fulfills this requirement.

Operation of an air conditioner (or the cooling cycle of a heat pump), when outdoor temperatures are below 60° F can cause compressor damage, and must be avoided. Under these circumstances, no supply/return air temperature differential readings can be made. It must be reported to the client whether operation was tested. Normally, these readings are taken with a simple thermometer or infrared temperature-sensing gun at the appropriate return air plenum and supply registers, where 15° to 20° F differential is within normal range. Differentials less than 15° F may simply indicate a low refrigerant charge, if no other malfunction is present. Readings above 20° F may indicate a dirty coil, filter, or other obstruction in the flow of air. Reporting language should include the opinion that the Supply/return air temperature differential was within, below, or above the normal range, as well as the actual readings obtained.

Note that the air conditioning contractor who is called in to service any system the home inspector has called out for repair will most likely take his measurements right across the evaporator coil, where the normal range of temperature differential is slightly higher, 17° to 23° F. The inspector who has reported inadequate supply/return air temperature differential as measured at supply registers and return plenum, and who is subsequently challenged by an air conditioning contractor (based solely on his measurements) should be prepared to point out to the client that, although the coil may well be performing within normal range, some condition (such as hot attic air infiltration somewhere in the duct runs) is causing inadequate differential *in the living space.*

If an air conditioning system fails to respond to the thermostat, check the electric service disconnects at the compressor, evaporator, and service panel. Once operating, note any unusual noises and report them. A suction line or cooling coil that is frosted over at the indoor unit may indicate low refrigerant or an airflow restriction. Short cycling, or too-frequent on-off operation, is abnormal, and indicates the need for repair. Outdoor coils should blow warm air, suction lines should be cool, liquid lines should be slightly warm or at ambient temperature, and any sight glass found at the outdoor liquid line should be bubble-free during operation to indicate proper refrigerant charge.

Heat Pumps

One type of central forced air heating system, called the heat pump, utilizes the same principles of heat transfer as the air conditioner. In a conventional (refrigeration) air conditioning system, heat is forced "up-hill", absorbing heat energy from cooler air within the living space and delivering it to the warmer air outdoors. Run in reverse, the air conditioner will absorb heat energy from the cooler outdoor air and deliver it to the warmer indoor air. Some specialized controls, equipment, and reversing valves are required, but the operating principle is the same, regardless of the direction of the heat transfer.

During the heating mode, ice can form on the outdoor coil when outdoor temperatures are very low. To address this, heat pump designs incorporate a temporary automatic reversal into the cooling mode. This concentrates heat at the outdoor coil to melt the ice. The outdoor condenser fan remains off during this "defrost" cycle to allow maximized concentration of heat at the coil. Defrost cycles are usually controlled by ice sensors, timers, or both. During the defrost cycle, auxiliary electric resistance heating at the indoor coil is provided to counteract the temporary cooling function. The air conditioning and heating are on simultaneously for the duration of the defrost cycle. During normal heating operation of the heat pump system, the vapor line at the indoor unit will be hot to the touch.

Many heat pump thermostats have more than one heat setting. The "heat" setting operates the system in normal heat pump mode, while an "auxiliary" setting controls the indoor electric resistance heating source to augment the heat provided by heat pump operation. Auxiliary heat cycles are sometimes controlled automatically by the thermostat, so there may be no user-selectable "auxiliary" setting. Additionally, an "emergency" heat setting is almost always provided, which completely disengages the heat pump and operates only the indoor heating source. The "emergency" heat setting is used when the outdoor temperature is too low for the heat pump to efficiently absorb heat from the outdoor air.

As used for cooling, heat pumps are subject to the same ambient air temperature operating restriction as standard air conditioners. They must not be operated while outdoor air is below 60° F, as the compressor at the outdoor unit is at risk for damage. Some newer units will include an automatic shunt, and will not operate at such low temperatures. Conversely, the operation of the heat pump in its normal heating mode presents a similar risk to the equipment when outdoor temperatures are above 80° F.

When outdoor temperatures are between 60 and 80° F, both the heating and cooling cycles of a heat pump should be operated for inspection. A cooling check, including the supply/return air temperature differential measurement, will verify the operation of the entire system. The heating cycle, then, need only be operated long enough to observe the proper operation of the reversing valves.

Regardless of outdoor temperatures, the emergency or auxiliary heat strips should be tested by calling for heat at the controlling thermostat using the "emergency heat" setting, and making observation that they are functioning properly. When heat pump thermostats are set to the emergency heat mode, compressor operation is locked out.

Evaporative Coolers

Evaporative coolers are simple and effective in reducing temperatures and increasing comfort levels in high-heat/low-humidity climates. Unlike electric refrigeration (air conditioning), which uses a phase-changing refrigerant to pump heat "uphill" while dehumidifying the conditioned air, evaporative coolers *add* moisture to the conditioned air, and so are suitable only for use where the air is typically too dry for comfort. Evaporative coolers are found mostly in the desert regions of the Southwestern United States for this reason.

Water-carrying pads (continually soaked by means of a spray, drip, or carrying drum immersed in a reservoir) are installed in the path of a fan-induced air stream. The relatively dry air readily absorbs water from the pads in a process of evaporation. Heat from the air is absorbed by the water as it changes from a liquid to a gaseous state. The cooler air with higher relative humidity is then distributed throughout the living space for comfort.

Blowers must be identified and reported as one-speed or two-speed. Rust buildup, corrosion, or deterioration of the blower or fan should be noted. This and the condition of the fan belt are best observed with the unit off. Ducts and registers should be observed for mildew, damage, and secure mounting. Housings, access and inspection panels, trays, and associated equipment must also be observed for evidence of adverse conditions.

Report any unusual sounds, vibrations, leaks, or improper electrical connections (particularly the pigtail connections at the motor terminals). Replacement of any rotted, deteriorated, or mineral-encrusted pads should be recommended. Be sure that water pumps are working, and that spider tubes, clips, connections, and bleeder provisions are intact. Water supply lines and float brackets must be well secured in place, with at least a one-inch air gap between the discharge hose and the water level (for backflow prevention).

Ducts and Vents (HVAC)

Ducts which carry conditioned air throughout living spaces can be of many different types. Sheet metal, formed into a square, rectangular, or round cross section, has been in use for many years, and is still commonly installed. It is expensive, due in large part to the skill and time required to cut, fit, and assemble each section at the job site. It is very strong, and invulnerable to damage by insects or rodents.

Rigid insulated fiberboard is easier to work with than sheet metal, but it, too, must be scored, folded, cut, fit, and pieced together on site. It is assembled with duct tape and staples instead of interlocking clips, and is not as durable or long-lived as sheet metal.

Ducts disconnected at attic spaces will adversely affect HVAC performance.

Lower in cost are the flexible ducts, a coil of wire with interior and exterior skins of polyethylene or similar material, which encapsulate a layer of fiberglass insulation. This tube-like duct material is very easy to install, as its flexibility precludes the need for the straight-run routing required of hard sided materials. The coils are cut to length, and the inner sleeves are connected with tape. The ends are then sealed and strapped to the distribution plenum and register boxes with plastic ties. The outer skin of these snakelike coils is somewhat vulnerable to tears, but they are otherwise quite satisfactory in their performance. Coiled wire ductwork is now used extensively in new construction of standard quality.

Inspection should include a careful look at duct materials and joinery for breaks, damage, or disconnections that allow conditioned air to escape into unintended locations, such as attic, crawlspace, or basement.

Look for kinks or other restrictions to airflow, which are often found at locations where ducts take a sharp bend, or have been damaged.

All ductwork intended for the distribution of refrigerated air must be insulated in unconditioned spaces. This not only prevents unconditioned air from giving up heat to the cooled air intended for distribution into living spaces, but also prevents the formation of condensation on the ducts. Water stains or damage found at ceiling locations, especially near supply registers, are often caused by condensation dripping from breaks or voids in duct insulation. Flexible ducts should not be installed in direct contact with each other. Where they do make contact there is a tendency to form condensation, which can cause water damage to living spaces below. It is for these same reasons that insulation is required on air conditioner suction lines and condensate drain lines.

Air should flow adequately from all supply registers. Low flow volume can be caused by improperly adjusted balance control dampers within the system, leaks, restrictions (including dirty filters), or runs which are simply too long. Although the inspector is usually not expected to determine the accuracy of system balance, significant deficiencies of flow should be reported.

PVC plumbing drain components located inside the HVAC return air plenum present a toxicity hazard in the event a fire.

With return air plenum grates and filters removed, the inspector should look for the improper routing of gas lines, plumbing vents, and electrical wires or junction boxes within the plenum. Such utilities located here may increase the risk of injury in the event of a fire. Due to airflow, the return air plenum tends to draw flames quickly into its cavity. Gas lines and plumbing vents contain combustible gasses. Electrical wiring (which might, incidentally, serve lighting or smoke detector circuits) becomes a fire hazard itself with insulation burned or melted off. Wires which are not rated (and labeled) for plenum use have insulation that can emit toxic gasses when burned. The same is true of plastic plumbing vents. Gas lines, plumbing vents, and electrical wiring or junction boxes found within any return air plenum should be reported as hazardous. An exception is the presence of any electrical wire run through the *short* dimension of a stud or joist cavity that is also used as a plenum. Such wiring runs are permissible under some current codes. Where a stud or joist cavity is used as a plenum, it should be well sealed to prevent unconditioned (and unfiltered) air from within the walls (and attic), from mixing with conditioned air, causing dilution and loss of efficiency.

Although many factors enter into the equation that dictates the minimum cross-sectional area of a return-air plenum serving any forced air system, a general rule is that such area would most likely be adequate if it were about 72 square inches per ton of cooling capacity. (Heat-only systems can be sized somewhat smaller.) Should the inspector find return air plenum cross-sectional area to be obviously inadequate, based on these generalities, it is best to recommend evaluation by a qualified HVAC contractor. Often, a return air grille of adequate size hides a joist- or stud-cavity serving as a return duct run that is far too small for the job.

Review Questions - Heating, Ventilation & Air Conditioning Systems

(circle the letter next to the best answer for each question)

1. Combustion products in fuel fired forced air heating systems:
    a. are transferred to the conditioned air through the heat exchanger
    b. mix with conditioned air, which is circulated throughout the living space
    c. are distributed through a network of air ducts
    d. must always be reported to the client
    e. are vented to the outdoors

2. A gas-fired forced air furnace will be fitted with:
    a. a temperature-and-pressure relief valve
    b. an automatic gas valve
    c. a water level gauge
    d. a pressure gauge
    e. a. and b.

3. For proper combustion, a gas-fired furnace does *not* require:
    a. a proper fuel-air mixture
    b. adequate availability of primary combustion air
    c. adequate availability of secondary combustion air
    d. a flame which lifts steadily off the burner
    e. a., b., and c.

4. By-products of gas combustion include:
    a. water vapor
    b. carbon monoxide, a poisonous gas
    c. sulfur
    d. b. and c.
    e. a., b. and c.

5. Signs of possible loss of heat exchanger integrity in a gas fired furnace do *not* include:
    a. dancing flames
    b. sticky black soot in the blower compartment or supply registers
    c. heavy rust accumulation and scaling at the heat exchanger
    d. burning eyes and itchy skin during the heating season
    e. small openings in the heat exchanger at the burner area

6. Materials unsuitable for gas supply lines installed within a residential structure include:
    a. black iron and galvanized steel
    b. schedule 40 ABS plastic
    c. copper and brass (where hydrogen sulfide concentrations are below .3 grains per 100 cubic feet of gas).
    d. corrugated stainless steel
    e. a., c., and d.

7. The flue serving a gas fired furnace with natural draft venting must:
    a. exhaust at a point 5 feet or more in vertical measurement from the furnace flue collar
    b. vent directly through a side wall
    c. be of single wall metal construction
    d. be fitted with a full bore shutoff valve or atmospheric damper
    e. be a minimum of 5 inches in outside diameter

REVIEW QUESTIONS 87

8. The purpose of a draft diverter at the flue collar of a natural draft gas fired furnace is to:
    a. prevent the downward flow of air into the burner compartment
    b. allow the free flow of draft air into the flue to assist in the evacuation of flue gasses
    c. divert excess heat away from the flue pipe walls
    d. regulate the fuel-air mixture
    e. a. and b.

9. A gas fired furnace with induced draft venting:
    a. has an external draft hood
    b. uses a fan to assist in the evacuation of flue gasses
    c. utilizes a heat sensitive initiator circuit to start the vent fan
    d. requires no flue termination cap
    e. b. and c.

10. Electronic air cleaners:
    a. are not capable of removing any bacteria or mold spores
    b. are normally equipped with single speed blowers
    c. discharge a high voltage power pack when the test button is operated
    d. are in need of repair if a distinct snapping sound is emitted during test button operation
    e. c. and d.

11. Condensing furnaces:
    a. can safely carry away combustion gasses through plastic pipes
    b. are not sensitive to availability of combustion air
    c. can achieve efficiencies as high as 100%
    d. require no draft induction fan
    e. must be fitted with a condensate drain which discharges into an expansion tank

12. The blower in an electric furnace:
    a. forces air directly through the heat exchanger for distribution to living spaces
    b. shuts down just before the heating elements are cycled off
    c. carries combustion gasses to an outdoor location
    d. usually draws from 4 to 6 amps
    e. b. and d.

13. The operation of all heating elements in an electric furnace can best be determined by:
    a. observing the bright red glowing ni-chrome elements
    b. use of an amp probe at the furnace access panel or main electric service panel
    c. listening for the sequencing circuit actuators over several minutes' time
    d. holding a lighted kitchen match near the draft hood, observing proper drafting
    e. none of the above

14. Gravity hot water heating systems:
    a. require that the heat source be located higher than the living space
    b. may be of the open system type
    c. require no expansion tank
    d. should never be converted to a forced water system
    e. are the most efficient of the hot water heating systems

15. Forced hot water heating systems:
    a. must be of the open system type
    b. require no expansion tank
    c. require a pressure relief valve
    d. circulate water with solenoid operated low-pressure pumps
    e. a. and c.

16. Steam heating systems:
    a. require an expansion tank
    b. require a temperature-and-pressure relief valve
    c. require both primary and secondary condensate drain lines
    d. can be either a single pipe or double pipe system
    e. b. and d.

17. Oil fired heating systems:
    a. require an oil pump
    b. deliver compressed gas through a liquification nozzle in the firebox reservoir
    c. must locate the burner at least 12 feet distant from indoor oil tanks
    d. require environmental certification at the time of sale of the property
    e. a. and c.

18. In electric refrigeration air conditioning systems:
    a. heat is released to outdoor air by passing conditioned air over the surfaces of the evaporator coil
    b. the combination of pressure and cooling causes refrigerant to evaporate into a vaporous state
    c. the rapidly expanding refrigerant gas in the evaporator coil gives off heat
    d. all of the above
    e. none of the above

19. When a cooling coil is located above a finished ceiling, the primary condensate drain line:
    a. must be insulated for the first 12 feet of run
    b. must be at least ½ inch in diameter
    c. must be sloped to assure positive gravity drainage
    d. must terminate at an outdoor location
    e. a. and c.

20. Electric service to an outdoor condensing unit:
    a. must include a disconnect within sight of the unit
    b. must enclose high voltage cable within a protective conduit
    c. must be configured into a drip loop
    d. all of the above
    e. a. and c.

21. Operation of an air conditioner (or cooling cycle of a heat pump) when outdoor temperatures are below 60° F:
    a. must be reported to the client
    b. may cause an electrical short in the low voltage control circuit
    c. reduces cooling efficiency
    d. can cause compressor damage
    e. will render the most accurate supply/return air temperature differential measurements

22. The purpose of the sight glass installed in some air conditioning systems at the refrigerant line, near the condenser unit, is to:
    a. check for proper color of the refrigerant
    b. check for debris in the refrigerant
    c. check for proper oil level at the compressor
    d. check for directional flow of the refrigerant
    e. none of the above

REVIEW QUESTIONS

89

23. Ice formation at the outdoor coil of a heat pump during the heating cycle:
    a. is evidence of a condition requiring repairs
    b. causes the system to automatically reverse into the cooling mode
    c. triggers the outdoor condenser fan to run at its highest setting
    d. automatically shuts down indoor auxiliary heating
    e. permits maximum heat transfer to conditioned air

24. An emergency heat setting at the thermostat of a heat pump system:
    a. disengages the heat pump
    b. activates the 4-way reversing valve
    c. is only used when the outdoor temperature rises too quickly for the heat pump to respond
    d. is required when the desired indoor temperature is over 80° F
    e. none of the above

25. Evaporative coolers:
    a. are used mostly in regions with high humidity levels
    b. cool by causing water to evaporate and absorb heat
    c. markedly reduce moisture in conditioned air, improving comfort levels
    d. require both primary and secondary condensate drain lines
    e. b. and d.

26. Inspection of evaporative coolers does not include:
    a. identification of blower motors as one-speed or two-speed
    b. observation of rust, corrosion, or deterioration of blower or fan components
    c. checking for leaks
    d. testing for water softness (or PH levels)
    e. listening to pump operation

27. All ductwork intended for distribution of refrigerated air:
    a. must bear the Good Housekeeping Seal
    b. must permit air flow to all intended supply registers
    c. must be insulated
    d. a. and b.
    e. b. and c.

28. A wall cavity used as a return air plenum:
    a. is not permitted
    b. must be well sealed
    c. requires a 40 micron filter accommodation
    d. must have a properly installed floor drain for condensation removal
    e. b. and d.

29. Wiring which is not rated for plenum use:
    a. may emit toxic fumes when burned
    b. must never be used with electric furnaces
    c. is required at outdoor locations
    d. will only be found in older homes
    e. none of the above

TYPICAL HOME PLUMBING SYSTEM

1. Fresh water source
2. Water meter
3. Branch water line split
4. Water heater
5. Drain trap
6. Vent pipe
7. Roof vent
8. Waste and vent stack
9. Sewer line

A typical home plumbing system includes three fundamental components: the water supply system, the fixtures and appliances, and the drain system. The photograph above identifies each of these parts.

Fresh water enters a home through a main supply line (1). This fresh water source is provided by either a municipal water company or a private well. If the source is a municipal supplier, the water passes through a meter (2) that registers the amount of water used.

Immediately after the main supply enters the house, the branch line (3) splits off and joins the water heater (4). From the water heater, the hot water line runs parallel to the cold water line to supply water to fixtures and appliances throughout the house.

Once the water becomes waste, it flows into a trap (5) and into the drain system. The drain system works entirely by gravity, allowing waste water to flow downhill through a series of large-diameter drain pipes, attached to a system of vent pipes. Vent pipe (6) allow air to enter the system via a roof vent (7). The fresh air prevents suction that would slow or stop drain water from flowing freely.

All sewage eventually reaches the waste and vent stack (8). The waste water flows into the sewer line (9) that exits the house near the foundation and flows either into a municipal sewer system or a septic system. Meanwhile, sewer gases escape through the vent above the roof.

Plumbing Systems

Learning Objectives

1. Learn the basic principles behind residential plumbing system design and function.
2. Be able to identify what visible conditions represent evidence of the need for repair in residential plumbing systems.
3. Be aware of the obligations borne by inspectors regarding the reporting of improper materials, installation, and function of residential plumbing systems.
4. Recognize the health risks posed by improper plumbing materials and configurations found in the home.

Water Supply System and Fixtures

Only visible and accessible water supply (and drain) components within the structure are typically subject to inspection. It should be made clear to the client that underground or hidden portions of the system that are not readily accessible are specifically excluded. Nonetheless, evidence of leaks or malfunction, such as staining, mildew, or odors, must be reported as suspect.

Water supply lines should be identified as copper, plastic, ferrous (galvanized iron or steel), lead, brass, or a combination of materials. A tour of attic, crawlspace, undersink, outdoor, main shutoff, and service access panel areas will reveal the materials used. Copper is the most common material found in modern construction, as it is reliable, long lasting and easy to work with. It is identified by its reddish brown color, bright green oxide at points where leaks or condensation have accelerated oxidation, and the use of "sweated" or soldered fittings, and the frequent use of brass compression fittings at fixture attachments.

The solder used to make modern day copper connections no longer contains significant amounts of lead, but copper lines installed before the change to lead-free solder materials *will* contain lead joinery. Identification of solder material and its lead content falls under the heading of environmental conditions, a specialty requiring training, expertise, and licensing beyond that of most home inspectors. Details regarding such environmental conditions are not a standard component of home inspection unless the client and his qualified inspector specifically agree to include them.

Plastic supply lines of polyvinyl chloride (PVC) will sometimes be found in economy grade construction. This material is somewhat more vulnerable to physical damage than other materials, and its performance reliability can be affected by extremes of heat or pressure. Plastic water supply lines generally deteriorate with age at a faster rate than traditional materials, but they are still considered a practical option. Some building jurisdictions have forbidden the use of PVC water supply lines, but may still permit the use of the offwhite *Chlorinated* polyvinyl chloride (CPVC) material. Inspectors must look for the labeling and report accordingly.

Water supply lines of gray polybutylene have been inarguably determined to provide inferior durability. Their presence should be reported to the client as the use of an inferior material. This would represent a condition which is in need of repair, whether or not evidence of deterioration has been found.

Ferrous metal supply lines (galvanized iron or steel), will be found in older homes of all price ranges. Their bright silver color comes from the protective zinc coating applied by galvanic baths during their manufacture. Steel pipes are stiff and unyielding, and so must be precisely installed in mostly standard lengths, and connected by threaded fittings. A magnet will attract iron or steel (for absolute identification, if necessary). This material has a service life expectancy of about 40 years. Characteristics of galvanized steel water supply lines include corrosion and the buildup of minerals within the walls of the pipe, causing restriction and, eventually, complete blockage. When checking faucets and fixtures for water pressure, keep in mind that any inadequacy found could well be caused by supply lines within the structure which have become blocked in this way. Short of complete replacement of the plumbing supply lines, there is really no adequate solution to this problem.

Occasionally, inspectors will come across the use of supply line fittings or components made of lead. Lead is a soft, heavy, silver-gray metal which is easily bent, scratched, or dented. Lead is non-ferrous, meaning that it contains no iron, and, therefore, does not "rust" like ferrous metals do. It has long been known that lead poses a health risk when ingested, the very reason for its regulatory elimination from the solder used to connect copper water supply components. Only specially licensed individuals are permitted by law to comment on lead (as it relates to environmental hazard) in several states. Where it is legally permissible, though, inspectors must inform clients of any potential health risk of which they are aware.

Sinks

Kitchen, bathroom, bar, and laundry sinks are all inspected in the same manner. The kitchen sink gets the most use, and is likely to display the most wear and tear. Carefully inspect each sink for chips, rust, or other

PRIMARY INSPECTIONS — PLUMBING SYSTEMS 93

damage. Rust stains in a porcelain sink usually imply finish damage, but similar stains can be caused by a metal cooking utensil left overnight in the sink. Sufficient time and care must be taken to completely satisfy the inspector that his conclusions are accurate.

Cultured marble sinks will often be found to have deteriorated portions within the bowl, which show up as splits or cracks. These may be severe enough to leak right through, or may be simply cosmetic in nature. The quality of any repairs encountered will range from masking tape and bubble gum to silicone caulk or epoxy. Each repair is evaluated by the inspector for its appropriateness, and reported in the way which would best serve the client.

The shape of a drain trap and fixture line may resemble the letter "P," and sink traps are sometimes called P-traps.

Engage the drainstops and fill each sink with water, checking the operation of faucets and vegetable sprayer for water pressure, leaks, hose entanglement, or aerator and spray-head obstructions (such as mineral deposits). All faucets should open and close with positive travel limit stops. Also look at the swing spout or faucet stems for leaks or the heavy accumulation of mineral deposits and corrosion that are evidence of leaks. Such corrosion encountered at any supply lines, connectors, fittings, or fixtures are suspect. Leaks may not be present, but evidence found of any leaks, past or present, is reportable. Slight leaks left unrepaired are often only intermittent, as oxidation or mineral accumulation can temporarily plug them. Be especially alert for compression fittings in new construction that have not yet stood the test of time. Many will be found to have been installed carelessly, left untested, and leaking. (The same holds true for drain lines in new construction).

Waterhammer occurs in the water supply pipes when a momentary or intermittent pulse of pressure, usually caused by the closing of faucet valves, creates a vibration in the pipes. This is accompanied by a loud banging noise, which brings little danger of real damage, but is frequently consistent and annoying. Properly securing the offending pipes to their surroundings can often reduce or prevent this phenomenon, and the installation of air chambers, now a standard practice, has proven to be effective. Air chambers are short vertical pipes, installed at various locations in the supply lines, and capped at the top to trap a small amount of cushioning air. The occurrence of waterhammer should be reported to the client as a condition in need of repair.

Undersink shutoff valves are required by building codes. The valves and their associated connections must be carefully inspected for damage or leaks. It is not recommended that the inspector operate the valves for any reason, as a potential exists for leaks to start. Once leaking, repair may appear, to some, to be the responsibility of the inspector. Try to determine the precise location of any and all leaks, for the most accurate reporting. When in doubt about the exact location, say so.

Sink cabinets are usually filled with a ceaseless array of cleaning products, lotions, aerosol cans, pesticides, and such. It is easy to mistake stains caused by leaky product containers for those caused by water supply or drain system leaks. Remember, too, that flux from the sweating of copper supply lines during installation becomes a liquid under the heat of the torch, and invariably drips down to, and stains, whatever is below. Water damage caused by leaks is reportable, and may, of course, be evidence of the need for leak repairs, as well. Previous leaks that have obviously been repaired successfully require no mention in the absence of associated water damage.

All sinks and tubs must have a vertical air gap of at least one inch between the faucet outlets and the flood rim of the fixture. This is to provide a measure of protection from the possibility of backflow due to the siphoning effect caused by changing pressures within the water supply system. Wastewater could potentially be siphoned into the supply lines, contaminating them with soap, cleaning fluids, or other impurities, unless such an air gap exists to break any system vacuum. Any improper plumbing arrangement which permits this kind of contamination is referred to as a cross connection. Some form of anti-siphon measure is required at all vulnerable locations, including tubs, sinks, dishwashers, hose bibs, lawn sprinkler systems, and fill lines for pools, spas, or water features.

At all points of use, hot water supply controls should be to the left side, cold controls to the right. This standard is for both convenience and safety. Hot water coming from a faucet expected to deliver only cold water is always an unwelcome surprise. Faucet manufacturers have recently come up with a variety of safety innovations designed to prevent burns from unwanted concentrations of hot water, especially in shower applications.

Bathtubs and Showers

Cracked tub materials and damaged shower walls are common. Tiles which are cracked, broken, missing, or in need of grout maintenance must be called out. The inspector should push the lower courses of tile with his hand to feel for soft or mushy substrate material, indicative of water penetration and related damage. Further evidence can be found by tapping tiles with a screwdriver, listening for the relatively dull sound of wet substrates. Tiles in the most vulnerable locations that have been replaced are yet another clue to shower water penetration. Walls, floors, and ceilings in rooms below or adjacent to tubs and showers may provide confirmation of leaks, showing stains or high moisture conditions. Building materials suspected of containing excessive moisture should be tested with a moisture meter.

Check to see that plumbing is not loose, and that fixtures are well sealed against walls at vulnerable water penetration points. Handles will often be found damaged or missing, as will strainers and stoppers. Faucet stops should function properly, and no water should leak past the stems while faucets are open. A few moments pause will be required to ascertain that faucets properly close, without dripping when in the fully off position. Any access doors provided for inspection or service of plumbing housed within tub or shower surrounds should be opened. Once inside, look for signs of leaks, excess corrosion, or other defects. Builders often mount a (code compliant) access panel in an appropriate location for this purpose without ever cutting the actual hole through the wall material. This is done with the expectation that service personnel will cut the hole beneath the panel when service is first required. This is not a job for the home inspector. If in-wall plumbing is not readily accessible without cutting or other permanent alteration of the property, it will not be inspected, unless by specific agreement with the client and with permission of the property owner.

If a tub spout is wall mounted, check that the spout reach is adequate to clear fully over the tub deck, to prevent running or splashing onto the tub deck. Also, any tub with no shower head should not have a fill spout fitted with a shower diverter. Proper diverters must be operated to ensure their functionality. Air gaps to prevent cross-connection from waste and drain water to supply lines must be maintained, and flow rate should be adequate.

Separate shower enclosures (those without a bathtub), are required to be at least 990 square inches in floor area, or about 32 inches square. The dam at the entrance to the stall must be between 2 and 9 inches high. If glass doors or enclosure walls are present, they must bear a label describing the glass as being of the tempered or laminated "safety" variety.

Whether tile, plastic, vinyl, stone, cultured marble, or any other material, shower bases are vulnerable to damage and leaks. It can be a puzzle to accurately identify the source of small amounts of water on the floor

Standard Commode

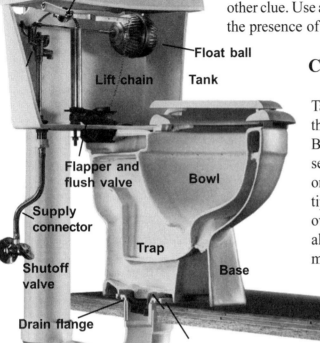

near a shower enclosure, given that wet enclosure doors, shampoo bottles, soap dishes, and people will inevitably leave puddles at shower time. Many inspectors use a rubber drain stop and fill the shower pan with water to check for leaks. Walls and floors in the rooms adjacent to shower stalls will sometimes reveal clues to shower pan failure. Look for stained rugs, baseboards, or wallboard. Rusty wallboard nail heads are another clue. Use a moisture meter, if necessary, at any location where the presence of excess moisture is suspected.

Commodes

Tanks and bowls must be free of cracks and chips. Tanks should be tight to the bowl to prevent leaks at the tank-to-bowl gasket, known as the spud washer. Bowls should be tight to the floor to maintain a proper seal at the wax ring in the floor drain. A bead of caulk or grout is required at the floor to help prevent bowl tipping and drain leaks. This caulk, if found to be overdone, with too much caulk for the purpose, usually means that a makeshift leak-stop effort has been made. Rusted hold-down nuts and bolts are further clues to such a leak. Leaks at the floor indicate the need for replacement of the wax seal, which requires removal and re-installation of the bowl.

Tank operation must be checked for full flush, reasonable recovery time, and complete shutoff. A toilet that runs on, even intermittently, wastes water, and is a reportable defect. The water supply must have a shutoff valve, and all fittings be free of leaks and excess corrosion. A minimum comfort space of 21 inches to the front of the bowl and 15 inches to each side (measured from the center line), are required for code compliance.

Hosebibs

Handles at outdoor faucets that are damaged or missing will be reported, as will any evidence that the stem is leaking while the valve is open. Be sure that faucets do not drip when fully off. Failing faucet stops will often be accompanied by such leaks. The undue accumulation of corrosion at supply line fittings is a clue to connections that may be leaking. Check to see that plumbing is not loose in the wall, and that any wall passthrough accommodation is not so large as to be vulnerable to water or pest penetration. Those hosebibs that are located directly in the ground should be reasonably protected and well secured, so as to minimize vulnerability to physical damage by lawnmowers, automobiles, and people. The presence of low-cost anti-siphon devices at each outdoor faucet will prevent backflow of garden hose water into supply lines. Such devices are now required by building codes in most communities, and their absence is reportable.

Laundry Supply

Again, the inspector looks for damaged or missing handles, evidence of leaks, excess corrosion at fittings, proper functioning of faucet stops, and secure attachment of pipes. The correct arrangement of left and right faucets for hot and cold supply is not usually inspected if washer water hoses are attached. A short length of garden hose will allow the inspector to operate and test the faucets if they are not connected to an appliance. The hose is simply hand-tightened onto the faucet to be checked, and the discharge end is placed into the laundry drain stand pipe. Washers and dryers, as well as other appliances which are not permanently built into the property, such as refrigerators or portable dishwashers, would normally be excluded from inspection.

Drains, Wastes, and Vents

A proper drain system is needed to carry wastewater away from points of use to a private septic or city sewer system. All plumbing fixtures must be served by a water sealing "P" trap to prevent the introduction of sewer gasses into the living space, and outdoor venting must be provided to allow air into the drain system so negative pressures (vacuum) will not interfere with the gravity-induced flow of wastewater.

The lead flashing at the lip of this plumbing vent is damaged, creating vulnerability to water penetration into the attic. Squirrels like to chew on these flashings, frequently to this effect. Unless the roof is accessed for inspection, this type of defect might go unnoticed by the inspector.

In every home, at least one vertical soil pipe directly connects to the building drain and exits above the roof for venting. This is the main stack, and is traditionally made of iron, or in newer homes, PVC. It will be 4 inches or greater in diameter. Additional stacks, called soil stacks, are installed to accommodate the wastewater produced at locations within larger homes that are too distant to be properly served by the main stack. Soil stacks are fed by soil pipes, and are generally referred to as vent stacks from above that point where a soil stack connects to it. These also are vented above the roof. Soil stacks carry the discharge from toilet fixtures, and must therefore be of a larger dimension than drains which carry wastewater from other plumbing fixtures.

Plumbing vents serving other fixtures must be at least 1¼ inch in diameter, and terminate a minimum of 6 inches above the roof passthrough. No plumbing vent should terminate less than 12 horizontal inches from any vertical surface, such as a wall, chimney, or dormer. Any vent less than 2 feet higher than a window must be at least 5 feet distant by hori-

Amateur plumbing repairs have left this sink drain configuration without the required "P" traps. No provision for the prevention of dishwasher discharge hose backflow prevention is present. The large hole in the wallboard creates unnecessary vulnerability to pest entry.

Drum traps like this one found serving a tub in an older home are no longer approved for use.

zontal measure, and no vent termination should be located less than 3 horizontal feet from a property line. Look to see that flanges, boots, or flashings are adequately capable of preventing water penetration into the attic space. Plastic vent pipes must be painted or covered with a lead boot to prevent premature deterioration of the plastic material by the sun's ultraviolet rays. Finally, vents must not terminate in attic or crawl spaces, where sewer gasses and moisture can accumulate.

Materials used in the drain system must be identified and reported. Drain components of plastic, brass, iron, copper, lead, and other materials will be encountered. Very often, a combination of materials is used. Repairs, additions, and remodeling, especially when performed by inexperienced homeowners, can bring with them a variety of plumbing materials, configurations, and, frequently, errors. Any conditions found which are less than safe, sound, or sanitary will be identified in the report document.

Be sure to check for adequate drain flow and proper drain stopper operation at all fixtures. Careful scrutiny of the undersink drain lines with a good flashlight and a dry hand will allow for identification of any leaking connections or components. The connection of a sink drain flange at the drain tailpiece is usually by gasket, plumber's dope, and a cinch nut, and can be prone to loosening. Look here first for drain system leaks. Look for the presence of an overflow safety drain provision at sinks and tubs. Their absence is not a defect, but may be reported to the client as a cautionary note.

In cases where a primary condensate drain line from air conditioning equipment discharges into a plumbing fixture, condensation may form on the outside of the drain trap due to the cold temperature of the condensate. This occurs frequently with the use of economy-grade thin-wall plastic drain components, and can be the cause of drips and puddles inside the fixture cabinet.

All plumbing drains are required to include "P" traps to prevent sewer gasses from entering the living spaces. Tub and shower drain components are not usually accessible for inspection, except where plumbing access panels are provided. Laundry room drains and traps intended for connection to a washing machine are often inaccessible as well, as they are usually enclosed within the wall cavity. A water seal trap is cast right into every porcelain toilet bowl, which then feeds down into the soil pipe at the floor, but all other fixtures require the installing plumber to fashion a proper trap. Bell traps, drum traps, any trap with moving parts or interior partitions, and "S" traps are not permitted. The inspector can expect that the required venting provisions will be absent in most cases where the forbidden drum or "S" traps are found.

The tailpipe, or vertical drainpipe at a fixture drain flange should not be more than 24 inches in length from the fixture outlet to the trap weir. The trap and drainpipe should be level and free from corrosion or evidence of leaks. Makeshift repairs of caulk, epoxy, glue, or tape must be noted. Look for the telltale signs of leaks at sink cabinet floors.

Water Heating Equipment

Standard household appliances for the production and storage of domestic hot water are relatively complex, but standardization of materials and control systems has evolved to a point where their reliability is given little thought by a homeowner, until they fail. Water heaters are pressure vessels, and so each must be equipped with a temperature-and-pressure relief valve (T&P valve, also known as a pop-off valve), to prevent rupture in the event of overheating or overpressure. If temperatures approach the boiling point (water boils at 212° F), or if pressures reach close to the maximum design capacity (around 150 psi), the T&P valve is designed to open, relieving the dangerous pressure. This pressure is released via approved pipe material of at least 3/4 inch diameter, routed with proper slope for reliable gravity drain, to a safe location. Acceptably safe termination locations include floor drains, plumbing fixtures, sinks (with an adequate air gap at the flood rim) and outdoors (6 to 24 inches above the ground and pointing down). The exhaust pipe must have no traps, shutoff valves, or size reductions, and its termination must be unthreaded. Acceptable pipe material for this purpose is always copper or galvanized ferrous pipe, but many localities have independently approved the use of Chlorinated Polyvinyl Chloride (CPVC) piping. (Non-chlorinated) PVC is not acceptable.

Temperature-and-pressure relief valves are equipped with a lever that allows testing of their ability to fully open and flow without restriction. Water heater manufacturers recommend that homeowners regularly use this test function. Although this sounds like a good idea, these valves have a reputation for developing leaks after testing. Mineral deposits or particles of sediment can sometimes lodge in the valve, and constant drip-

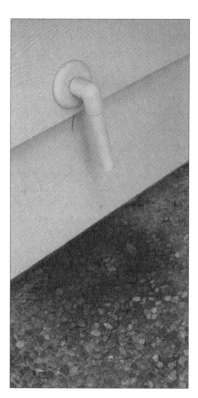

This temperature-and-pressure relief valve drain line serving the water heater is properly routed to the outside. It faces down, and appears safe. Is it made of CPVC or PVC? When this line is dripping, the valve is in need of replacement.

ping can be the result. Even though code-compliant T&P valve exhaust termination is to a "safe" location, constant dripping can be a nuisance, and may be viewed by some property owners as having been caused by the inspector. It may be best to simply report that the valve was not tested. In rare cases, where older heaters are encountered, separate valves for pressure relief and temperature relief will be found instead of the newer combination T&P valve.

In addition to the temperature-and-pressure relief valve, all water heaters have a built-in high temperature shutoff system. Electric heaters have a temperature limit shutoff device, with a reset button that is integral with the thermostat. Gas fired heaters use a high temperature gas shutoff system, which is built into the gas control valve and which cannot be reset. Once activated, replacement of the gas control valve is required. Temperature limit controls and T&P valves work independently, and have, in combination, been very successful in preventing overpressure ruptures.

As a water heater ages (7 to 12 years is their average service life), mineral deposits can form and accumulate near the bottom of the tank. This layer of sediment (mostly calcium carbonate), traps water, causing it to boil. Bubbles of steam then rise into the relatively cooler water, where they collapse with a loud gurgling noise. When this occurs, the remaining service life of the water heater is always in question, as the sediment accumulation has an insulating effect that causes the formation of hot spots in the tank near the burner or heat elements. As the tank metal is overheated, it weakens the steel and damages the porcelain interior. In electric water heaters, the life of the lower heating element can also be cut short by this process. Additionally, faucets and valves throughout the home can be fouled by the distribution of sediment particles via the hot water supply lines.

Regular flushing of the tank by use of the drain valve can increase heater life significantly, and some newer water heaters are designed with a curved dip tube (the pipe which feeds the incoming cold water to the bottom of the tank), in an effort to cause swirling of the tank-bottom water and sediment toward the drain valve. One may find that this drain valve, like the T&P valve, can be reluctant to stop dripping once used.

Product bulletins and recalls, which might be of interest to clients, should be, under appropriate circumstances, included in the inspection report. Examples of such bulletins come from water heater manufacturers American Water Heater Group (800-999-9515), A.O, Smith (800-527-1953), Bradford White (800-334-3393), Rheem (800-432-8373), and State Industries (800-365-0024). The bulletins refer to a polypropylene water heater dip tube distributed to the industry by a supplier in Ohio between 1993 and 1996. Under certain conditions this tube material can disintegrate, potentially causing 1) insufficient hot water, 2) clogged faucets, and 3) small white plastic particles found in washing machines or aerator screens. The particles are said to be non-toxic. About 16 million dip tubes may be affected, and some water heater manufacturers may replace the dip tube for free. This bulletin information was obtained from various newspaper and television reports, and a reprint of the "Consumer Reports" article released in July of 1999, which was redistributed widely by inspection industry newsletters.

Galvanic corrosion, also known as electrolysis, is an electrochemical reaction that causes dissimilar metals in contact with an electrolyte (like water) to corrode at a rate and order dictated by their placement on the galvanic scale. (This decomposition or corrosion of the less noble metal is accompanied by the production of an electrical charge, just as in a battery). In a water heater, a rod of magnesium or aluminum wrapped around a steel core is installed through the top of the tank to create a sacrificial anode, which corrodes completely before the steel of the tank can begin its corrosive breakdown. When no sacrificial metal remains on the rod, the tank itself begins to rust. Manufacturers recommend that sacrificial anodes be replaced every few years to extend the life of a water heater, but in reality, very few are ever replaced. Inspectors should look for the sacrificial anode accommodation at the top of each heater, and report its absence as an item in need of repair.

The cold water inlet must be served by a nearby full-bore shutoff valve, and fittings should be free of excess corrosion or evidence of leaks. Water connections at inlet and outlet lines should include the use of dielectric fittings, which electrically isolate and protect the components from galvanic corrosion. These can most often be identified by the appearance of plastic sleeves between the dissimilar metal pipes at their points of connection atop the heater case. Broken or missing parts, covers, or controls should be observed and reported, as well.

Inlet and outlet connections that are reversed will cause improper operation of the heater. Markings at the top of the heater case identify the correct fittings, but, generally, when viewed from the front, the cold water inlet, with its shutoff valve, is on the right, while the hot water outlet is on the left. If reversed, report this condition as in need of repair.

A watertight and corrosion resistant safety pan, of sufficient size and placement to properly catch leaks, and with a drain line sized and routed for reliable gravity flow, should be present in attic installations (or any

Proper gas-fired water heater installation includes a full-bore shutoff valve at the cold-water inlet line and dielectric fittings at inlet and outlet connectors for corrosion protection. A temperature-and-pressure relief valve drain line (of proper materials) must be routed for continuous positive gravity drain to prevent trapping water within the line, which could cause rupture in the event the valve was called upon to abruptly release. An approved double-wall "B"-class flue, properly located above the appliance flue collar, and with at least 1 inch of clearance to combustible materials, permits the scavenging of hot flue gasses while protecting nearby combustible materials from fire. A metal thimble at the flue's ceiling pass-through, also for fire protection, can be seen here. Minimum allowable vertical distance from flue collar to the flue termination point (for proper drafting) is 5 feet. An approved termination cap is required as well, to help prevent down drafting and to prevent water penetration into the internal flue and burner chamber. Water heaters located in a garage must be raised at least 18 inches to keep heat sources away from any combustible vapors that might accumulate at the garage floor.

other areas vulnerable to damage by leaks). Some corrosion or staining of the safety pan may only be caused by condensation that forms as cold inlet water fills a heater during heavy use. Water heaters installed in the attic require a permanently installed staircase or ladder, adequate openings for access and appliance removal or replacement, and sufficient attic flooring to allow safe inspection and service.

Water heaters installed in garage locations require special considerations for safety. First, any device capable of creating a glow, spark, or flame must be installed at least 18 inches above the garage's main floor. This applies not just to water heaters (both gas and electric), but to all heating appliances and electrical outlets as well. The reason for this is that fumes from gasoline, paint thinner, propane, and other flammable products often stored in a garage are heavier than air, and thus carry the potential to accumulate in combustible concentrations near the floor. Where water heating equipment (or central space heating equipment) is installed in a room or compartment adjacent to a garage (such as a laundry room) it may be installed at floor level *only if access to the room or compartment is from <u>outside</u> the garage and only if combustion air is taken from (and discharged to) the outdoors.* This means that a water heater in a room with direct access to the garage must be raised the compulsory 18 inches.

Inspectors will often find that a raised water heater which has been improperly replaced with a floor-level water heater will have a reverse sloping temperature-and-pressure relief drain line. When T&P relief drain lines are not sloped for reliable gravity drain, the potential exists for water to leak past and accumulate at the valve in what is effectively a water trap. If the valve should then be called upon to quickly relieve an overpressure condition, the inertia of the accumulated water in the drain line may well be sufficient to cause tank rupture, despite a properly functioning valve. Additionally, water trapped against the valve body may also cause corrosion, which can render the valve inoperable.

Another safety consideration is the vulnerability to physical damage caused by automobiles. A water heater located in a garage should be effectively protected from such hazards either by installation within a protected bay or niche, behind barriers, or out of the normal path of a vehicle.

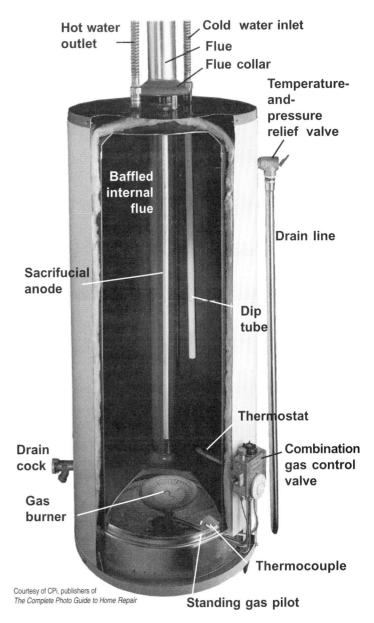

Gas-fired Water Heater

The permanently affixed label found on every heat-producing appliance must, by law, include information regarding the manufacturer's minimum allowable installation clearance from combustible construction. Those clearance requirements vary from model to model. Always find and read the manufacturer's label, comparing the requirement with the clearance provided. Inadequate clearance is a fire hazard, and must be reported as such.

Gas Fired Water Heaters

For the proper operation of water heaters using natural or propane gas, the availability of adequate combustion and draft air is required. Attics usually provide sufficient air by way of the soffit vents, turbine vents, ridge vents, or other standard attic ventilation provisions. Gas fired appliances installed in confined spaces should alert inspectors to look for the adequacy of such air availability. If installed in well-sealed utility closets, they must meet combustion and draft air needs by the use of grates or air ducts, installed so as to provide both combustion air to the burner compartment area, and draft air to the flue collar area. Such ductwork may be vented from approved living spaces, attics, or outdoor locations.

Gas fired water heaters must not be installed in a room used as a storage closet; nor are they permitted in a bedroom or bathroom unless they are within a sealed enclosure and installed in such a manner that combustion air is not taken from living spaces. Direct vent water heaters are not required to be installed within an enclosure as their combustion air is drawn in through the outer chamber of a double-wall vent pipe. Direct vent units must not be confused with power vent units, which do, in fact, use room air for combustion, while their flue gasses are forced out by a motor-driven blower, further increasing consumption of indoor air.

The outer panel cover that encloses the combustion chamber of a gas fired water heater is removed, and the inner cover is slid open or removed for inspection of the pilot, thermocouple, and burner area. The pilot flame should be mostly a soft blue, and large enough to completely surround the thermocouple. A safe distance from the burner compartment should be maintained when the temperature dial is turned up to light the burner, as the initial burner ignition can cause a heat pulse which may cause injury to eyes and face. Once lit, proper fuel-air mixture is indicated by a clearly defined soft blue flame with bright blue inner cone, resting directly on each burner orifice. If a yellow flame, or one that lifts steadily off the burner, or a lazy flame with undefined tips is encountered, adjustment is required.

Excessive rust or scaling in the combustion chamber or burner area must be reported, especially in newer units, where it may indicate the absence of a proper flue termination cap. The purpose of this cap is to prevent wind and rain from entering the flue. Any natural convection flue must extend at least 5 feet in vertical measurement from the flue collar (for proper drafting), and its diameter must be a minimum of 3 inches. A draft hood (or diverter) is required at the vent collar of the appliance, and its proper functionality must be assured. It is intended to divert any downdrafts from entering the internal center flue of the water heater, and it aids in scavenging of the exhaust gasses by permitting draft air to enter and help carry combustion byproducts up and out the flue. Smoke from a lighted match held next to the draft hood should be drawn fully up into the exhaust stream during burner operation. If it is not, the spillage must be reported as a condition in need of repair.

Additionally, all gas appliance flue vents must be of the double wall type, labeled with approval for use as a "B" class vent, and must terminate at least 2 feet above the roof and any vertical surface within 8 horizontal feet of the flue. When installed above any roof *with a pitch less than 6" rise in 12" of run*, vent termination can be as little as 1 foot above the roof.

Use of single-wall flues to vent combustion gasses is prohibited. Every appliance flue requires a non-combustible thimble, at least 4 inches larger in diameter than the pipe, at any location where it passes through ceilings or walls. No portion of connector or flue is permitted to slope upward less than ¼ inch per foot of horizontal run. Each vent pipe must be installed in accordance with its flow direction labeling and be assembled without screws or rivets. Inspectors will frequently discover B-class flue vents which are installed so as to violate the requirement that 1 inch clearance from combustibles be maintained, especially at the roof deck and ceiling passthroughs. All of these appliance venting requirements must be met with strict perfection to assure maximum safety. Any departure represents a recognized hazard, and must be so reported.

Gas branch line materials approved for gas service within a home include black iron, galvanized steel, corrugated stainless steel (and copper or brass *only* if the gas contains less than .3 grains of hydrogen sulfide per 100 cubic feet). Gas connectors, those used to connect appliances to the gas lines, should be of the stainless steel or epoxy coated type. Use of the older brass or copper connectors is hazardous, and should be reported as such. Connectors approved for use at water heater locations are to be a maximum length of 3 feet.

An approved gas shutoff valve must be installed within 6 feet of the water heater, just as is required with gas furnaces. The report should include disclaimer language specifying that the gas supply system inspection was limited to points of use, and only where supply connections are readily accessible.

Electric Water Heaters

Electric water heaters are equipped with one or two heating elements, each of which serves an independent thermostat. Double element heaters locate one element at the bottom of the tank, and one close to the top. Each element is energized by the demand of its thermostat, but only one is operable at any one time. A dedicated 30-amp branch circuit is typically provided, and current flow, as measured at the service panel with an amp probe or clamp-on multi-meter, will be the most reliable method of confirming correct operation. All visible wiring should be observed for proper use of wire nuts, damage to insulation, presence and condition of clamps and conduit, and invulnerability of conductors to physical damage and water penetration. Electric water heaters require a nearby electric service disconnect, within direct line of sight from the heater location, for the safety of service personnel. This can be the main service panel or breaker box, if appropriately located, or a separate shutoff installed near the appliance.

Obviously, the lack of hot water at sinks and tubs will be the first clue to a malfunction, but deeper analysis will give further clues to the improper operation of a dual element electric water heater. An appropriate volume of heated water, which has nonetheless failed to reach full temperature as set at the thermostat, may mean failure of the top heating element. Water which reaches the correct temperature, but is only delivered in small quantity before going cold, is usually indicative of a failing lower element.

Hydro-Therapy Equipment

(*This heading refers to jet-equipped indoor bathtubs that are filled for each use, as distinguished from spa tubs which remain filled, heated, and filtered continuously*).

As with standard bathtubs, observations are recorded regarding all issues of deterioration, damage, leaks, installation, materials, tile, grout, tub walls, surrounds, plumbing, and other relevant components. Additionally, hydro-therapy tubs (also called whirlpool tubs, or hydromassage tubs, and quite often referred to by the trademark brand name *Jacuzzi*), must be inspected for operational parameters beyond those of a standard bathtub. To do so requires that the tub be filled to a level just above the top jets, and operated. Damage can occur to circulating pumps if they are operated without water, and the inspector should not attempt operation of any hydro-therapy tub which cannot be filled.

The inspector should listen for unusual sounds from the pump motor, and may find that mildew, soap scum or other debris fouls the water. This is common in tubs that have been unused for long periods, and may not be a problem if all jets and aerators are functioning properly. Check to see that all jet discharge ports move or adjust as intended by their design. Also, operate aerator intake controls throughout their full range, observing that adjustment is effective. An access panel for pump-motor service is always required. Its absence is a reportable defect.

Timers or other electrically operated switches must be located a minimum of 5 feet from the tub deck. Many hydro-therapy tub installations incorporate a master wall switch as well as a tub-side switch. Those factory installed pushbutton switches located conveniently within the tub basin walls or atop the tub deck operate remote electrical slave switches pneumatically, and are perfectly safe.

Hydro-therapy tubs and their associated electrical components must be served by a circuit which is protected by a ground fault circuit interruption device. Dedicated GFCI devices serving hydro-therapy tubs might be found almost anywhere, perhaps hidden in a nearby closet, or directly within the electrical service panel. Verification of the presence of GFCI protection serving hydro-therapy equipment is done by manually triggering all GFCI devices, either with their test buttons or a GFCI testing analyzer, until the pump motor at the tub is rendered inoperable. In the event no GFCI device can be found serving a hydro-therapy tub, inspectors must warn the client of the hazard such a condition represents. GFCI devices which will not trip, continuously or inadvertently trip, fail to properly reset, or display evidence of arcing or burning will also be reported as in need of repair.

Review Questions - Plumbing Systems

(circle the letter next to the best answer for each question)

1. In regard to plumbing supply and drain systems:
   a. visible and accessible components are inspected
   b. hidden or underground components are not inspected
   c. plumbing vents are inspected
   d. identification of pipe materials is reported
   e. all of the above

2. Lead content has been reduced in plumbing supply line materials because:
   a. lead has been shown to be a health hazard
   b. the lead soldered joints deteriorate too quickly, causing undue potential for leaks
   c. use of lead solder creates a fire hazard due to the heat required to install it
   d. lead has become more expensive than alternative materials
   e. a. and b.

3. Characteristics of ferrous metal water supply lines include:
   a. a life expectancy of 75 years
   b. standard lengths assembled with soldered fittings
   c. a buildup of lead deposits within the pipes over time
   d. attraction to magnetic fields
   e. extreme vulnerability to waterhammer

4. In the presence of large amounts of corrosion at supply fittings, the inspector will report that:
   a. leaks were found
   b. evidence of suspected leaks was found
   c. no leaks were found
   d. the fittings were inspected
   e. ferrous metal supply lines normally corrode faster than other materials

5. A loud banging noise in water supply pipes, usually heard when faucets are turned off:
   a. indicates an accumulation of mineral deposits within the pipes
   b. is evidence of inadequate pipe diameter
   c. is normal, and is not reportable
   d. brings the danger of pipe explosion damage
   e. none of the above

6. A 1-inch (vertical) air gap between faucet spouts and the fixture flood rim at a tub or sink:
   a. can cause cross connection
   b. requires the installation of a mechanical anti-siphon device
   c. is required to prevent the siphoning of wastewater into supply lines
   d. represents a condition in need of repair
   e. a. and d.

7. When inspecting a tub with a shower enclosure, the inspector is *not* required to:
   a. look for evidence of water penetration at tile and grout areas
   b. look for evidence of water stains at adjacent rooms
   c. cut an access hole in wall board materials beneath any access panels provided
   d. observe for adequate water flow rate
   e. operate any shower diverter valve

REVIEW QUESTIONS 109

8. A glass shower enclosure:
   a. requires a dam at the entrance to the stall of at least 9 inches in height
   b. must be labeled by the manufacturer with safety glass identification
   c. must be at least 60 inches in height from the shower floor
   d. must be smaller than 990 square inches in floor area
   e. a. and b.

9. Commode inspection includes:
   a. checking for cracks in the porcelain bowl and tank
   b. looking for the presence of excess caulk at the floor-to-bowl area
   c. observing proper flush mechanism operation
   d. all of the above
   e. a. and c.

10. Plastic plumbing vents which pass through the roof:
    a. are not permitted
    b. must be covered with paint or other protection from ultra-violet damage
    c. are required to terminate at least 6 inches above the roof deck
    d. carry wastewater to the main water supply line
    e. b. and c.

11. No plumbing vent should:
    a. terminate in the attic space
    b. be larger than 1¼ inch in diameter
    c. terminate less than 6 feet from a property line
    d. terminate less than 12 horizontal inches from any vertical surface, such as a wall or chimney
    e. a. and d.

12. Plumbing drains must *not*:
    a. include a "P" trap at any fixture
    b. be vented
    c. be fitted with traps which have moving parts
    d. all of the above
    e. none of the above

13. The temperature-and-pressure relief valve in a water heater:
    a. regulates water temperature and pressure
    b. must discharge through a pipe of at least ¼ inch diameter
    c. must include a shutoff valve
    d. must discharge into a plumbing drain
    e. none of the above

14. The accumulation of sediment at the bottom of a water heater:
    a. can cause loud gurgling noises
    b. can cause hot spots at the top of the tank
    c. can cause a reduction in water heating efficiency
    d. is caused by the deterioration of the dip tube
    e. a. and c.

15. A sacrificial anode within a water heater
   a. decreases the life of the water heater tank
   b. is a made of the high temperature alloy manganese sulfide
   c. causes premature deterioration of the tank by galvanic corrosion
   d. causes premature deterioration of the tank by electrolysis
   e. none of the above

16. Any device or appliance capable of creating a spark or flame:
   a. must not be installed in a garage or attic
   b. must be at least 18 inches above the main garage floor
   c. must be protected by a GFCI device
   d. must bear the Good Housekeeping Seal of Approval
   e. must be installed with at least 1 inch clearance to combustible materials

17. Gas fired water heaters:
   a. do not require draft air or combustion air
   b. must not be installed in a room used as a storage closet
   c. may draw combustion air through the inner chamber of a double-wall power vent
   d. require a flue which slopes upward at least 1 inch per foot of run
   e. b. and c.

18. The flue serving a gas fired water heater:
   a. must be of the double-wall type
   b. must terminate at least 2 feet above a 6-in-12 roof and any vertical surface
      within 8 horizontal feet of the flue
   c. requires a non-combustible thimble at any wall or ceiling passthrough
   d. requires an approved vent cap
   e. all of the above

19. Electric water heaters:
   a. may have one or two heating elements
   b. must be served by a 20 amp circuit breaker or fuse
   c. require a minimum of 1 inch flue clearance to combustible materials
   d. are not equipped with a sacrificial anode rod
   e. must be equipped with a stainless steel or epoxy coated gas connector

20. Electrically operated switches which serve a hydro-therapy tub:
   a. must be located a minimum of 5 horizontal feet from the tub deck
   b. must be of the pneumatic type
   c. must be GFCI protected
   d. all of the above
   e. a. and c.

APPLIANCES

Learning Objectives

1. Learn how the many appliances found in the home are designed to work.
2. Understand the causes of home appliance failure.
3. Be able to identify those visible conditions that represent evidence of the need for repair in home appliances.
4. Be aware of the obligations borne by inspectors regarding the reporting of improper installation and operation of home appliances.
5. Recognize the hazards posed by malfunctioning or improperly installed appliances in the home.

Built-in Dishwashers

Almost all modern day kitchens are equipped with an automatic dishwasher. It is a convenience most homeowners won't do without. Expensive models are made with stylish design, electronic controls, digital displays, variable start delays, and cycle options tailored to any need. At the other end of the price scale are the economy grade models, lacking in style and sophistication, but nonetheless fully capable of good, basic cleaning functions. Regardless of price, all go about their business in about the same way.

Inspection begins with the condition of the door gasket and its attachment. Door panels should be well-secured in place. Dish racks, rollers, spray arms, and the overflow float switch should operate freely. The tub interior should be free of damage or rust, and the door latch, springs, and stops must work correctly. Check that the mounting tabs are well secured to the underside of the countertop, and that nearby cabinet drawers or pulls do not interfere with the opening door.

Electric service to a built-in dishwasher will often be located under the sink. If it is served by a plug-in cord, its length must be no shorter than 36 inches, no longer than and 48 inches. (Trash compactor cord limits are the same. Food waste disposer cords must be 18 inches to 36 inches in length). Cords lying on sink cabinet floors in a way so as to be vulnerable to physical damage or water contact should be noted. Any armored cable or conduit-enclosed wiring must be properly secured at each end.

There should be some provision for the prevention of discharge hose backflow, which can occur when sink drains clog and back up, allowing wastewater from the drain system to enter the dishwasher through its discharge hose. Newer installations usually include a dome shaped air break canister at the sink top to prevent wastewater from entering the appliance. At the very least, the discharge hose from the dishwasher should be routed with a loop extending high inside the sink cabinet interior, reducing the probability of backflow should the sink drain line back up. Inspectors calling out "absence of discharge hose backflow prevention measures" should know that some equipment manufacturers have recently begun to build such measures into the equipment as a standard feature.

Because of the likelihood that food particles will be discharged from the dishwasher as a matter of standard operation, the discharge hose should enter the sink drain ahead of the food waste disposer if one is installed. Disposers are manufactured with a dishwasher inlet fitting for this purpose. It is improper to install dishwasher waste lines to any other drain location when a disposer is present. When no disposer is present, the dishwasher waste hose must feed into the drain ahead of a trap.

Before starting the appliance, close the soap door and check it for proper latching, then position all the spray arms in a manner which would later evidence their failure to turn. Set panel controls for a regular wash cycle with heated drying, and start the dishwasher. Look for proper operation of knobs, levers, or other controls. Missing or broken parts will be reported.

Listen for unusual noise or vibration during fill, wash, and draining functions. It is a good idea to remove the decorative skirt at the front, if possible, to gain unobstructed view of the underside area, where leaks and evidence of leaks, like stains, puddles, rust, or mildew, will be most obvious. Once the drying cycle is reached, the door should be opened to ascertain the operation of the metal heating element at the bottom of the tub. Actually touching this coil while energized will result in serious burns, so care must be taken. Spray arms will now display a random pattern if operating freely, and a properly functioning soap door will be open.

In homes that have been vacant for an extended period, including new construction, the "rotten egg" smell of hydrogen sulfide may accompany the water supply. This is the result of a chemical reaction associated with the magnesium in the sacrificial anode(s) installed within the water heating equipment. When this odor is strong, it is recommended that inspectors do not operate the dishwasher unless it has been flushed. The buildup of hydrogen sulfide can cause explosion of the dishwasher when the electric heating element is cycled on. This is a rare occurrence, but one which can be averted by an alert and knowledgeable inspector.

Food Waste Disposers

Two different kinds of food waste disposer are in use. The most common is the continuous feed type, which is wired to a wall switch nearby, and permits continuous operation. The other, less common type is the batch feed disposer, which is activated by a stopper switch within its neck as the stopper is inserted and turned to the "on" position.

Overload protection is built into all modern day food waste disposers. A reset button can be found on most units, but some, with automatic reset, are designed without a manual reset control. An overload protection device that cannot reset is defective. Since the motors and circuits are manufactured as single sealed units, total replacement, rather than repair, is always required.

A food waste disposer should have its rubber splash guard in place. The guard prevents water and food particles from redecorating the kitchen walls every time the unit is operated. Using a flashlight, inspect the pivot-mounted grinding components, called hammers. Use a tool of some sort to poke down into the grinding chamber to determine that the hammers or flyweights move freely on their pivot pins. Rust or corrosion in excessive amounts will usually freeze up the hammers, and indicates the need for repair.

A visual inspection of the case exterior will reveal any leaks or evidence thereof, as well as improper wiring or drain line configurations. Plug-in cord length must fall between 18 inches and 36 inches for building code compliance. The unit must be mounted solidly to the sink, and there should be no unusual noise or vibration during operation.

Range Hoods

The primary purpose of the range hood is to trap airborne cooking grease. Those range hoods which exhaust to outdoor locations also carry smoke, moisture, and heat out of the living space. Hot airborne cooking grease congeals on the cooler surfaces of the metal mesh filter, which requires regular cleaning. This filter must be present, undamaged, and clean enough to perform its function.

Light and fan switches should be undamaged and functional. Excess noise or vibration, or inadequate fan speed or air flow must be called out. Accordion tubes of aluminum or plastic (similar to dryer vent connector material), will often be encountered, sometimes even supplied by the range hood manufacturer, but by current building code standards, only smooth, single-wall metal is allowable. This is a fire safety issue, and should not be ignored. Exhaust termination is not permitted in attic or crawl space areas, and outdoor exhaust terminations require a backdraft damper. Some regulatory bodies have concluded that it is in the best interest of the consumer to point out the mere absence of kitchen exhaust equipment, even though no building code currently requires such equipment. Each inspector must know the regulations by which he is bound, and should precisely follow the letter and spirit of the laws in his state.

Ranges/Ovens/Cooktops

Inspect for broken or missing knobs, elements, drip pans, and panels. Combustible materials, such as upper cabinets, must provide at least 24 inches of clearance above the burners. Each burner should be checked for damage and correct operation at all heat settings. Check to see that "burner on" and other signal lights associated with electric ranges are operating. Clock and timer functions often escape the inspector's scrutiny due to time constraints, and a statement to that effect should appear on the report.

Gas burners which fail to light consistently may need adjustment to the gas regulator or ignition source (whether standing gas pilot or electronic spark). Burner flames which are "lazy", raise off the burner head, display improper color or lack of definition, extinguish easily and inadvertently, or only light partially may indicate a gas pressure regulator or mixture control in need of adjustment. Be sure that the range top and burners are level and fit correctly in their recesses. Pilot lights, if any, should be on, and their heat should not create undue burn hazard conditions. Look for excessive grease in the burner jets, and see that gas tunnels are securely fastened and properly routed from pilots to burners.

Gas branch lines are always checked for use of proper materials. Gas connectors serving range tops must be no more than 3 feet in length, epoxy coated or stainless steel, served by an accessible gas shutoff valve within 6 feet of the appliance, and leak free.

Ovens should be set to 350° F and observed for temperature accuracy with an oven thermometer. An actual temperature which differs by more than 25° F from the 350° F setting should be reported. Look for broken or missing knobs, handles, glass panels, lights, and covers. Check the condition of the door gaskets, and be sure the door springs hold tightly in the closed position. Weak door springs which fail to support the door's weight are also reportable. If a latch is present, check its operation. Whether wall mounted or free standing, ovens must be securely installed. Grasp and pull the sides of the oven cabinet to determine the adequacy of mounting and anti-tip provisions.

Continuous-cleaning ovens are manufactured with an interior finish which can be damaged by the use of some oven cleaning chemicals. Ill-advised homeowners may, nonetheless, use chemical cleaners in their continuous-cleaning ovens, leaving a burnt, dark brown film on the interior surface. When this happens, the continuous cleaning effect is markedly diminished, and the chemical smell may be difficult to eliminate. Clients should be warned if the inspector has suspicions that this has occurred.

Gas burners or electric heating elements, and thermostat sensors (which are usually mounted high along a back or side wall of the oven interior), must be properly supported. Check that gas burners light without flare-up, and that flame color and definition are correct. Electric heating elements should heat to a dull red. A gas supply shutoff valve should be located within 6 feet of a gas oven, and a stainless steel or epoxy coated connector of no more than 6 feet in length (the maximum allowable for both ovens and clothes dryers), should be provided.

Built-in Microwave Cooking Equipment

Microwave ovens that are built in (or tabletop models installed in a cabinet designed for the purpose), should be tested for function by heating a cup of water. A small plastic cup for this purpose should be a part of the inspectors toolbox. Also, look for knobs, handles, and glass or plastic panels which are broken, missing, or cracked. Door seals, hinges, latches, and cook lights should be carefully inspected for proper functioning. Confirm the functionality of turntables, and check for excessive fan noise or vibration. Interior surfaces and components should show no evidence of scorching or arcing. Some inspectors utilize a microwave leak detector to confirm microwave containment, while others simply report any physical damage found at the case, door, latch, seals, and other containment components. If timer functions are not tested, a statement to that affect should be included in the report document.

Trash Compactors

It is important to observe the function of the ram plate, as a damaged screw drive, which can prevent ram actuation, may go unnoticed in the presence of normal motor sounds. A rolled-up newspaper, stood on end in the compactor will be crushed by a properly functioning ram mechanism. Trash compactors are generally a little noisy, but excessive noise or vibration is not acceptable. Look for secure mounting, drawer operation free of interference, and properly functioning deodorant dispenser operation. Check to see that pushbuttons and other controls are present, unbroken, and operational.

Bathroom Exhaust Fans and Heaters

All bathroom exhaust fans must exhaust to outdoor locations. The purpose of this is to prevent the unnecessary introduction of moisture into living, attic, or crawlspace areas, which can cause mildew or wood rot conditions. It is common practice to route exhaust vent tubes to soffit areas where attic ventilation grates are provided. This is acceptable, but venting through the roof (with an adequate rain cap), or outside walls (with some backdraft damper provision), is better.

Listen for unusual sounds and vibration, and check for proper fan speed and air flow. An accumulation of large amounts of dust at the fan housing can alert the inspector to a possible bypass condition, wherein attic or wall cavity air is circulated by the fan, often due to blockage of the intended exhaust route.

Electric resistance or heat lamp bathroom heaters should be operated and checked for functionality and safety. Be sure that mounting, safety grates, wiring, and controls are intact. Also, determine whether clearances to combustible materials and water sources meet the requirements set forth by the manufacturer's label, if one is present. Special bulbs intended specifically for heating should always be used. The presence of any other type of bulb should be brought to the attention of the client.

Gas fired bathroom heaters present many inherent dangers, and are no longer approved by building codes. Inspectors should refrain from operating them, and clients should be advised to do the same. Nonetheless, checkpoints for safety must be addressed, including the improper use of copper or brass gas lines and connectors, and the presence of the unmistakable odor of leaking gas. Safe installation will include consideration of clearance to combustibles, and the general condition of controls, housings, burners, and other components.

Whole-House Vacuum Systems

Whole-house or central vacuum systems are little different from portable shop type units used everywhere, except that the impeller motor, its canister, and catch bag are located in a remote location, usually a garage. They are invariably designed for dry use only, and cannot be used for cleanup of liquid spills. They have several advantages over portable vacuums, the most important of which include the discharging of air and the residual dust it carries to an outdoor or other suitable location. Noise created by the remotely located motor is less obtrusive to the operator, and the hoses which are inserted into the wall mounted inlet receptacles are much lighter and easier to maneuver than a self-contained, portable unit.

Visual inspection is limited to the observation of the general condition of the main vacuum unit and each inlet receptacle. The main unit should be securely mounted. Adequate airflow should be checked at all accessible inlets. Visible hoses, tubes, and couplings should be checked for damage or significant air leaks. Electrical switches, located at each inlet, should start the motor when hoses are inserted. Listen for unusual noise or vibration while the motor runs.

Residential grade central vacuums require a dedicated, 120-volt, grounded circuit of at least 15 amps. Most units are of the plug-in type, but be sure that all electrical splices and connections are within a proper junction box, well secured, and with cover plates in place.

Garage Door Operators

Automatic motorized garage door operators must be checked for secure mounting and proper operation. All must have a safety provision which automatically reverses direction of travel if there is an obstruction in the path of a closing door. Until recently, such a provision was by a simple pressure mechanism that reverses the motor's direction. Pressure switch equipped openers are tested by grasping the door during motorized closing and applying upward resistance to activate the reversing mechanism. Newer units utilize a pair of electric "eyes", mounted near ground level, to reverse direction in the event any obstruction is present. Passing an object through the eye's line of sight reverses door travel direction. Eye sensors must be installed within 6 inches of the floor.

Look for the required permanent hold-open device at the manual lock whenever automatic operators are installed. This prevents damage which may be caused by a motorized opener working against a locked door. Also check for the presence and proper operation of the door release catch and pull cord, intended to allow quick, manual separation of the door from the mechanized traveler in the event of power failure, malfunction, or emergency.

Never attempt to operate the automatic opener before carefully checking the condition of the door panels, locks, and hardware. Any inspector who causes damage by operating an unsound system may be asked to pay for its repair.

Residential overhead garage doors come in two standard sizes. Operators serving doors 8 feet in length require only 1/4 horsepower, while 16-foot models require at least 1/3 horsepower. Compliance should be observed wherever power ratings are listed on the motor housing. Note any unusual noise or vibration during operation, and check that all mounting hardware is securely attached. In the event that radio remote controls are unavailable for testing, a statement to that effect should be included in the report.

Doorbell and Chimes

Doorbells may be found at several doors, and different sounds are often programmed for each location. Buttons should be free of damage, well secured in place, and functional. Additionally, hard-wired bell transformers are usually found in the attic space, and can be inspected for improper wiring conditions, such as exposed splices, dangling conductors, and uncovered junction boxes. Electrical feed to the transformer is at 120 volts, and must not be overlooked in regard to electrical safety.

Dryer Vents

Dryer vents must terminate at an outdoor location to prevent the unnecessary accumulation of moisture (and in the case of gas fired units, combustion by-products), into living, attic, garage, or crawl spaces. A rigid metal vent pipe of at least 4 inches in diameter is required, with no screws protruding into the path of airflow to trap lint. Vent pipe joint configuration is directional for flow, with male ends feeding into female ends, and all joints must be sealed with duct tape or other sealant. Maximum allowable venting run is 25 feet (or less by 5 feet for each 90 degree bend). A backdraft damper is required, and exhaust must be unrestricted by screens or other obstructions. Termination must be a minimum of 3 feet from any property line. Flexible dryer venting *connectors* made of vinyl coated steel springs or aluminum accordion must be less than 6 feet in length, and cannot be used in concealed locations, such as behind walls or ceilings, or in attic spaces.

Review Questions - Appliances

(circle the letter next to the best answer for each question)

1. A plug-in cord serving a built-in dishwasher must be:
   a. between 36 and 48 inches in length
   b. between 18 and 36 inches in length
   c. of the armored cable type
   d. secured to the sink cabinet floor
   e. vulnerable to physical damage

2. The purpose of dishwasher discharge hose backflow prevention is to:
   a. protect the discharge pump from damage
   b. assure proper siphoning of the discharge water
   c. prevent wastewater from entering the dishwasher
   d. prevent food particles from entering ahead of the food waste disposer
   e. protect the ni-chrome heating element from over-cooling

3. All modern food waste disposers:
   a. are of the continuous feed or batch feed type
   b. utilize a manual overload re-set control
   c. are connected with 36 inch cords
   d. are reported as in need of repair in the presence of waterhammer
   e. a. and b.

4. Range hood exhaust vents must:
   a. be of aluminum, plastic, or smooth-wall metal
   b. terminate in attic or crawlspace
   c. be less than 8 feet in length
   d. be installed with an upward slope of at least ¼ inch rise per foot of run
   e. none of the above

5. Gas stovetop burners with electronic ignition which fail to light consistently:
   a. can be the result of using improper gas supply line or connector materials
   b. may need adjustment to the gas regulator or ignition source
   c. may require burner-head leveling
   d. indicate a condition of excess sulfur in the gas supply
   e. none of the above

6. Continuous-cleaning ovens:
   a. can be identified by the presence of a burnt, dark brown film on the interior surface
   b. can be damaged by the use of some oven cleaning chemicals
   c. normally develop a slight chemical smell
   d. are particularly vulnerable to door gasket failure
   e. must not be left unattended while the cleaning cycle is engaged

7. Proper operation of the ram plate in a trash compactor:
   a. is indicated by the presence of normal motor sounds
   b. may go unnoticed if motor operation is quiet
   c. will cause a rolled up newspaper, stood on end, to be crushed
   d. may be compromised by a malfunctioning deodorant dispenser
   e. a. and b.

8. Bathroom exhaust fan vent tubes:
    a. may be routed to soffit areas where attic ventilation grates are provided
    b. may be routed to outdoor, attic, or crawlspace areas
    c. must be of smoothwall metal construction
    d. must be vented through the roof
    e. none of the above

9. Gas fired bathroom heaters:
    a. are found mostly in premium homes
    b. are not normally operated for inspection
    c. are manufactured for zero clearance to combustible materials
    d. should only be used with special bulbs intended for this purpose
    e. a. and c.

10. Central vacuum systems found in the home:
    a. require a dedicated 120 volt circuit of at least 15 amps
    b. are never designed for liquid cleanup
    c. should be checked for adequate airflow at all accessible inlets
    d. all of the above
    e. a. and c.

11. Automatic motorized garage door operators are required to:
    a. reverse direction automatically if there is an obstruction in the path of a closing door
    b. have the door release catch at the traveler permanently rendered inoperable
    c. be of at least 1/3 horsepower when used with 16 foot doors
    d. all of the above
    e. a. and c.

12. Clothes dryer vents must:
    a. be less than 25 feet in length
    b. be of rigid metal pipe, at least 4 inches in diameter
    c. be equipped with a backdraft damper
    d. not terminate less than 3 feet from a property line
    e. all of the above

2
Optional Inspections

SWIMMING POOLS AND EQUIPMENT
(INCLUDING SPAS & HOT TUBS)

Learning Objectives

1. Learn how the various types of residential pools and spas are designed to work.
2. Recognize visible conditions which represent evidence of the need for repair in residential pools and spas.
3. Be aware of the obligations borne by inspectors regarding the reporting of adverse conditions found in residential pools, spas, and associated equipment.
4. Become familiar with the many hazards residential pools and spas present, and the measures which must be taken to maximize pool area safety.

Pools, spas, hot tubs, and their associated equipment are complex systems which must be carefully inspected to determine whether unsafe, unsound, or unsanitary conditions exist. This section is intended to give the home inspector a basic understanding of the responsibilities imposed on those who choose to perform this very important inspection.

Water Quality

An empty pool, or one filled with stagnant water, cannot be completely or properly inspected. Such pools will require maintenance, repairs, cleanup or filling before pumps and other equipment can be operated. Since this is beyond the scope of a visual inspection, clients should always be referred to a qualified pool care professional when such conditions exist.

Although of considerable importance, evaluation of water chemistry is outside the scope of the home inspector's responsibility. Water chemistry is ever-changing, and must be tested regularly for proper evaluation. Obvious deficiencies, however, such as turbid or otherwise fouled water, the growth of algae, or the accumulation of calcium carbonate deposits, should be reported.

Poor water quality within an operational pool will hamper the inspection, so whenever possible, it is best to have the owner "shock" the pool a day or two before inspection. This permits better observation of interior surfaces and underwater steps, ladders, lights, drains, return inlets, and hydro-jets.

Pool Safety

Safety is of paramount importance in a pool area, and any circumstance or condition that, in the opinion of the inspector, represents a hazard to its users must be reported. It is important, for instance, to report the lack of nearby rescue devices (like flotation rings or a sheperd's crook of suitable length). Depth of the water should be clearly and permanently indicated at appropriate intervals around the pool. These depth markings help unfamiliar users judge the safety of their selected entry points. Inspectors should also note the presence of any hazardous items stored or located near a pool. Codes, for example, require that glass doors or windows within 60 horizontal inches of a pool-edge walking surface be fitted with safety glass (unless the glazing is greater than 60 inches above the walking surface).

Pool Construction

The 1995 CABO One and Two Family Dwelling Code defines a swimming pool as any structure "intended for swimming or recreational bathing that contains water over 24 inches (610 cm) deep", including "in-ground, aboveground, and on-ground swimming pools, hot tubs, and spas". For the purposes of a visual inspection, swimming pools and installed outdoor spas and hot tubs will be considered equivalent, except where otherwise noted within this text.

Permanently installed swimming pools are divided into two classes: in-ground (totally or partially); and above-ground. Materials commonly used to create the watertight shell of in-ground pools include concrete (poured or gunite), fiberglass, and vinyl. Above-ground pools will almost always have a vinyl liner or a fiberglass shell. In some cases, on-ground hot tubs will have a watertight shell of wood slats (typically of redwood, cedar, cypress, teakwood, or oak), in a barrel-like construction. The type of construction and the materials used must always be identified for the client.

Interior Surfaces

Before visual inspection of the pool interior can be properly made, all water moving equipment should be turned off, to calm the water for better viewing. The inspector should report the presence of any irregularities, such as cracks, thinning or crumbling plaster, liner wrinkles or tears, stains or other discoloration, and chips or gouges on finished surfaces. Any evidence found of previous repairs should be reported, as well.

The condition of ceramic tiles which line the interior perimeter of plaster-coated pools should be observed. Although not required in a swimming pool, these tiles *are* required in plaster-coated spas and hot tubs to facilitate the cleaning of body oils and mineral deposits which collect there. The absence of these tiles, where required, is a reportable defect. All tile surfaces should be checked for the damage caused by the use of abrasive cleaners.

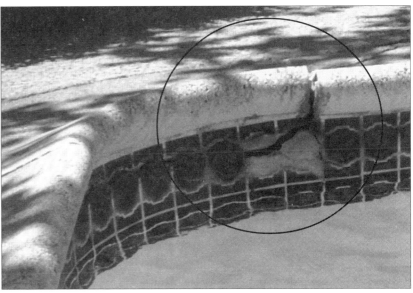

Damaged tiles and heaved coping stones at this pool's edge are evidence of structural settlement.

Plaster surfaces should be generally smooth. The presence of a rough, sandpaper-like texture is an indication that acidic water conditions (either current or previous), have etched the surface, or that the plaster was poorly applied. Very rough plaster surfaces that are likely to cause abrasion to swimmers should be reported as hazardous.

The finish surface of fiberglass pools should be inspected for the damage caused by improperly cleaning with chemicals or abrasives. Obvious scratches or a dull luster are the result. Also, the inspector should be alert to fiberglass surfaces that have been painted. Fiberglass surfaces normally do not require painting. When paint is found, inspectors should be alerted to the possibility that surface damage has been concealed.

Lights, Steps and Ladders

The function and condition of underwater lighting should be carefully observed. Look for cracked covers, flooding, and missing or damaged parts, such as retaining rings or gaskets. The lack of underwater lighting to illuminate the pool bottom can be hazardous, but underwater lighting in smaller pools, spas, and hot tubs with water depth less than 4 feet, is not required. The main purpose of such lighting is to make it easier to spot troubled swimmers at night.

Underwater lights should be specifically designed for the purpose, UL listed, and installed a minimum of 18 inches below the water line. Any wet niche fixture should be secured to the shell with a locking device that that requires the use of a tool for removal. Visual verification of such things as UL listing labels and cover locking devices is rarely possible due to the installed location of the fixtures, but obvious deficiencies should be reported.

The presence and condition of steps and ladders for pool entrance and egress should be noted. Local codes vary, but there should always be at least one ladder or set of steps in every pool. If a pool is not of uniform depth, the deep end should have an in-pool ladder. All permanently installed ladders must be in good condition and securely mounted. Suitable railings for ladders should be present for safe entry and egress.

Level

Great care must be taken during the installation of every pool to be certain it is level. Measuring the vertical distance between waterline and coping at 3 or more locations will quickly reveal any out-of-level condition. Measurements found to be different by more than ¼ inch should be reported. Any out-of-level condition greater than 1 inch should alert the inspector to the likelihood of significant post-installation shifting. Hydrostatic pressure from ground water can have a significant affect on the stability of in-ground pools in areas with high water tables or expansive clay soils. Ideally, a hydrostatic relief valve or plug should be installed in the sump of the bottom drain, allowing water pressure to be released instead of forcing the pool out of its installed position. These devices are not readily visible, and verification of their presence is difficult.

Diving Boards and Slides

Diving boards and slides can enhance the enjoyment of any pool, but they also represent a considerable potential for injury. Many pool-related injuries result from the improper installation or use of this equipment. Any condition found which creates an unnecessary hazard should be reported as in need of repair.

Where diving boards are in place, they should have a continuous non-slip surface over their entire length, and be in generally good overall condition. Inspect carefully for any sign of cracking or weakening at stress points. Rubber shock absorbers or springs at the fulcrum should be properly mounted and in good condition. See that hardware holding the diving board to its pedestal is secure and free of corrosion. The pedestal must be securely anchored to the deck, and structurally sound.

Slides should be securely anchored to the deck and sliding surfaces should be smooth. Fiberglass slides are checked for splitting, delamination, damage caused by improper cleaning, and adverse conditions concealed by paint. Plastic slides are vulnerable to ultra-violet deterioration, evidence of which is color-fading, cracking, or crumbling of the plastic material. Water tubes, installed to wet the surface of a slide for reduced friction, should be tested for adequate flow and complete water recovery into the pool (without dripping onto the deck). Check that steps, ladders, railings, and hardware serving slides or diving boards are secure, suitable for the intended purpose, corrosion free, and in good condition.

Inspectors should report as hazardous any slide that delivers users into water where the depth is less than the vertical height of the slide. (A slide which brings the user into the water at a very shallow angle may be given some latitude here). Four feet is the minimum safe water depth for slides in all cases. The end of a slide must extend sufficiently out over the water to assure clearance from deck or coping. Diving boards and platforms of 3 feet or less in height require a minimum water depth of 9 feet for a horizontal distance of at least 18 feet, according to safety experts. Slides and diving boards should be located well apart to prevent injury to users by collision.

Manufacturers of slides and diving boards list water depth and clear area requirements for the safe use of their products. The manufacturer's minimum safety requirements, when available, should always be met, but where local codes specify more stringent rules, their regulations must be followed. It is incumbent upon each inspector to become familiar with code requirements in his service areas.

Walking Surfaces

The area immediately around a pool should have a deck wide enough to allow free movement and safe walking, with adequate space for slides and diving boards. Deck material should not be slippery when wet, and must slope away from the pool (with a minimum of 1 inch drop over 4 horizontal feet), to prevent rain and splashed water from washing dirt and debris into the pool. The walkway slope should not, however, be so great as to create a walking hazard. Tripping hazards created by such things as shifting wood or concrete sections, or improper construction, should be reported. Decks must also be self-draining, with no low areas which might permit ponding or the growth of algae.

A ring of stones, castings, or other material (called coping), is found surrounding most in-ground pools. The coping is inspected to assure that no sections are loose, damaged, or missing. The coping will be slightly higher than the deck, or will form into an upturn at the poolside edge to provide a water dam. The upturn is an added measure of protection from water running into the pool from the deck. Seams between decking and coping must be well sealed with mortar, caulk, or other filler to prevent water from entering the joints.

Structural components of above-ground pools are inspected for damage and deterioration. Bracing and wall panels should be in good condition, and show no signs of deformation. Hardware must be secure and free of corrosion. Wood panels should be no less than ½ inch pressure treated marine grade plywood. All wood which comes in contact with the ground should be pressure treated or of a rot-resistant and insect-resistant species (such as redwood or cedar).

Above-ground pools require at least one ladder that leads up from the ground and down into the pool. Many above-ground pools have a raised deck at the pool's edge which partially or completely surrounds the pool. A deck of 30 inches or more in height, and the stairs leading to it, should be equipped with a suitable outside guardrail or handrail to prevent falls to the ground. All decks, ladders, steps, and stairs are inspected for condition and secure mounting. Some raised decks attach directly to the pool's edge. Those that are freestanding must be located and well secured in a way that prevents pinch injury or damage to the pool structure. Decks must drain away from the pool, and afford adequate traction when wet.

Mechanical Equipment

All visible plumbing should be checked for damage and leaks, and all gate valves must operate freely. Since many equipment configurations are designed in the field at the time of installation, it is impossible to describe every combination of pumps, valves, and piping which might be encountered. For this reason, all gate valves should be clearly labeled to identify their functions and operating positions. Plumbing and equipment that is not easily accessible for convenient servicing is also reportable.

Without labeling, the pipe configuration at this pool pump and filter system would be indecipherable.

It is beyond the scope of a visual inspection to test for leaks in underground piping, but visible evidence of leaks, such as inexplicably soggy ground or percolation, must be called out as suspected defects. Underground leaks in air lines from blowers associated with spas and hot tubs are often identified by air bubbles coming up through cracks and seams in decking or coping.

The waste drain discharge should be located by the inspector whenever possible. No water should be flowing here while the pump is running unless the waste drain valve is open. An improperly functioning waste valve that allows unwanted draining is a common defect, and must be reported as in need of repair. Waste drains require an air gap or backflow preventer at any drainage pipe into which they discharge, and must never be connected to wastewater plumbing lines.

If a pool is permanently connected to the dwelling's main water supply, a backflow preventer is required there as well, to prevent pool water from being drawn into the potable water supply. This anti-siphon device should be installed at least 12 inches higher than the pool deck, although some localities require a greater height.

All pumps should be operated to assure proper function and adequate flow. Excessive vibration, commonly caused by impeller damage or the presence of debris, indicates the need for repair. Unusual noises (such as grinding or squealing caused by bearing wear or faulty ceramic seals), are also reportable. A sound like marbles rolling around inside the pump is caused by cavitation (air bubbles within the pump housing), which can damage the impeller over time.

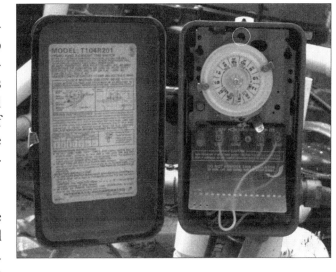

No pump should be resting directly on soil or supported solely by its piping. Water drawn into the pump must first pass through a strainer to filter out large debris. Strainers can be at poolside, as surface skimmers or bottom grates, or they may be ahead of (or integral with), the pump housing. All pumps must be capable of self-priming. A pump which fails to completely prime may have a leak on the intake side of the piping (assuming all draw points are properly submerged).

Clock and timer controls are inspected for secure mounting, the presence of internal electrical covers, and signs of soot or charred wiring within the timer box. Many timers have a "clock movement" verification hole where the movement of gears can be seen, otherwise, checking and rechecking clock positions over a period of time will confirm clock movement. Changeover functions can be verified by manually rotating the clock dial (as per the manufacturer's instruction label), until a trip tab passes the set point. Alternating passes of the trip tabs should turn the switching mechanism on and off. Clock and timer controls are protected by an external cover, which should be present and equipped with a properly functioning latch.

This is a typical clock timer for pool-water pumps. Note the opening through which the clock's gear movement can be verified.

Blowers (for the introduction of therapeutic air bubbles into a pool, spa or hot tub) must be mounted well above the waterline to prevent flooding. (Blowers mounted inside the cabinet, below the waterline, of listed, manufactured, self-contained portable spas or hot tubs are specially designed for this configuration, utilizing a backflow prevention valve, and are thus perfectly acceptable.) All blowers should be observed for proper function and adequate air delivery. Although inherently noisy, irregular operating sounds or excessive vibration should be brought to the client's attention.

Blowers and booster pumps may have electrical timers controlling their functions. Timers are subject to inspection for proper functionality and overall physical condition. Most blowers, though, are controlled by remote pneumatic switches, which utilize air pressure to remotely activate an electrical slave switch. Because remote pneumatic controls have no electrical components, they can be safely and conveniently located within easy reach of pool occupants. Pneumatic plungers and tubing should be operated to assure reliable functioning.

Drains, Skimmers and Returns

Inspection includes observation for the presence and condition of bottom drains and grates. Bottom drain location should be at the deepest point in a pool to permit efficient filter operation and, when required, draining. Surface skimmers are inspected to assure that strainer baskets are in place and in good condition. Weir gates or float valves found within the skimmers are also checked. Skimmer covers should be approved for the purpose, in place, undamaged, and installed in such a way so as not to create a tripping hazard. Always remove the strainer basket and inspect the draw pipe below. Look for damage at the end of this pipe, which is often fitted with a connection flange for the attachment of vacuum equipment.

Ideally, several return inlets from filter or booster pumps will be strategically located around the pool to provide movement of the water's surface. Proper swirling of the water helps keep floating debris and body oils from accumulating in still water areas, and will enhance the function of surface skimmers. With pumps running, inspectors should observe the water's surface to evaluate the adequacy of this action. Some return inlets have direction-adjustable nozzles for this purpose.

Spas and hot tubs have specially designed return inlets that provide a mixture of air and water in order to create a more satisfying hydro-massage. Two types of air inlets are in common use. The standard venturi-jet draws air through a tube from above the waterline, and will often have a threaded adjusting knob to adjust the volume of air to be mixed with the water. Hydro-jets make use of a blower to give added air volume to the water jets, and often a separate array of air-only nozzles. Whichever type is found, all flow control valves should be tested for proper function. Components which are cracked, damaged, or missing, or fail to deliver sufficient air flow, are reported as in need of repair.

When circulation pumps are running and piping is completely primed, flow from return inlets should contain no air bubbles. Air bubbles would be indicative of a leak along the suction side of the piping (unless, of course, the returns are intended to deliver air from a blower). Evidence of any leaks, even though no leak may be found, is a reportable condition.

Waterworks, such as fountains or waterfalls, may either be powered by dedicated pumps or be connected to return piping from the filter pump. All water from this equipment must return to the pool without splashing on decks or draining away. Backs and sides of waterfall construction should be inspected for leaks and damage. Nozzles and fountains are observed for damage and proper delivery. The appearance of moss, algae, or encrusted mineral deposits found anywhere on the structure may be an indication of leaks, and should be accurately described in the report document.

Pool water heaters, gas or electric, must be operated to assure proper function. Before attempting to operate any heater, the inspector must verify that circulation pumps are running and that valves are positioned to permit water flow through the heat exchanger. Failure to do so may result in heater damage. With heater controls on, the thermostat setting is slowly turned higher until engagement (usually with an audible click).

Any gas pilot flame should be steady, blue in color, with a slight yellow or orange tip, and large enough to fully engulf its thermocouple or millivolt pilot generator. The burner flame should also be blue with slight yellow or orange tips, and should display a steady burn that does not lift off the burner rails. A lazy flame, or one which is mostly yellow or orange, indicates improper gas pressure or mixture. The firebox area should be free of corrosion and debris, and any heat or wind shields present should be properly secured.

The installation of the heater should provide adequate room for servicing and clearance from combustible materials, as specified in the manufacturer's label or local codes. No heater should be installed at grade level or in direct soil contact. A level, one-piece, non-combustible pad that raises the unit at least 2-4 inches above grade is ideal. Gas heaters installed outdoors must be approved (and so labeled), for outdoor use. Gas heaters installed indoors must be provided with adequate combustion and draft air.

Gas supply lines and connectors must be of approved materials. Underground steel gas piping must be covered in a sleeve or coating which continues above the soil at the point where the pipe extends up through the finish grade. Only epoxy-coated or stainless steel gas flex connectors are allowable. Copper tubing and bare brass flex connectors are not permitted. A gas cutoff valve is required within 6 feet of the main gas control valve. As always, check for gas leaks.

Heating elements in electric heaters are tested with an amp probe. Amperage drawn is compared to the full load amperage (FLA), rating listed on the manufacturer's label. (This test can be dangerous to the inspector if performed without the proper caution and knowledge of electricity, so extraordinary care should be taken). Any amperage draw measurement significantly higher or lower than the FLA rating listed by the manufacturer is a reportable defect. Wiring or other components that appear to be charred or burned must also be called out.

Both electric and gas heaters should be checked to assure that none of the safety devices, such as high limit sensors or flow switches, have been bypassed. A thermostat stop or a high limit device should always be present. Their purpose is to disengage the heater when the water in a spa or hot tub reaches a maximum allowable temperature of 104° F. Maximum allowable temperature for a swimming pool is 90° F. Additionally, check that the direction of water flowing through the heat exchanger complies with the manufacturer's labeling.

The three types of filters in common use are the high-rate sand filter, the cartridge filter, and the diatomaceous earth filter. Inspectors are required to report the type in use to the client. The high-rate sand filter and the diatomaceous earth filter require routine back-washing, which is done with a series of manually operated valves. It is not advisable for the inspector to actually test the filter backwash function, as this can result in the loss of filter medium under some conditions. Inspection must include, however, verification of the *presence* of a proper bypass or backwash valve configuration, as well as a test for the functional operation of the valves (which, when performed by the inspector, should be done with the filter pump off). Cartridge filters are maintained by removal and cleaning or replacement, so no backwashing provision is required. Opening a filter canister or otherwise evaluating any filter material is beyond the scope of a visual inspection.

Filters are inspected for signs of leaks, damage, corrosion, or other deterioration. Pressure gauges, which measure and indicate pressure drop across the filter medium, must be present and functional. Either a manual or automatic bleeder at the top of the filter body, designed to remove air from the filter shell, must be present and functional. A filter mounting base of adequate size and strength is required. Just as with heaters, filters must not come in direct soil contact, unless they are designed for such installation with a suitable integral base. Filters found leaning or supported by their piping require repairs.

In residential swimming pools, it is desirable to have a pump/filter system which can, at a minimum, filter the equivalent of the pool's entire volume in less than 12 hours. Pools which get heavy use require greater capacity. Calculations for pool volume and pump adequacy are made by pool designers, and are normally outside the expertise of the home inspector, but clear and obvious deficiencies should be pointed out.

Automatic cleaning equipment is powered by water pressure (or vacuum) generated by the circulating pump. Designed to be connected to a surface skimmer intake pipe (in the case of vacuum equipment), or a return pipe (in the case of agitators), they move freely about the pool, performing their duties unattended. Hoses must be in good condition, of adequate length, with unobstructed room for travel. Check for worn or missing pieces, and look for tears or holes in collection netting. Finally, hoses must be inspected for leaks, which can reduce cleaning efficiency.

Pool Area Electrical Systems

It is universally recognized that the presence of water near otherwise safe electrical devices can create a potential for electric shock. It is, therefore, essential to inspect all electrical wiring and devices in a pool area, whether or not they are directly related to pool equipment. Any electrical system, component, or condition that represents unnecessary danger must be reported as hazardous and in need of repair. Inspection items for which safety cannot be verified due to inaccessibility, damage, malfunction or other reason require an explanation within the report, warning the client of potentially hazardous conditions.

The National Electric code (NEC), draws some distinctions between swimming pools, spas and hot tubs, and that class of portable spas and hot tubs described as Listed, manufactured, and self-contained. Generally, electrical devices installed within the cabinets of portable spas and tubs are exempted from some of the requirements which apply to swimming pools and integral or built-in spas and hot tubs. Where such exemptions or significant differences exist, notation is made within this text. Where no such notation is made, general guidelines for swimming pools should be followed.

Pool equipment utilizing a cord to connect to a power source must be plugged into a single-outlet receptacle that uses a twistlock device whenever the outlet is located less than 10 horizontal feet from a pool wall. Such outlets are not permitted less than 5 horizontal feet from a pool wall. Equipment plugged into receptacles located greater than 10 feet from the pool wall do not require a single outlet receptacle or twistlock device.

The enclosure for any receptacle used to power any corded pool equipment must be suitable for wet locations, and be of the type that is weather-protected, with or without the cord in place. Maximum cord length permitted for corded equipment is 3 feet. Maximum amperage rating for corded equipment is 20 amps. Listed, manufactured, self-contained portable spas and hot tubs may utilize a cord no greater than 15 feet in length. All cords should be properly sized for the equipment they serve, but in no case can they be less than #12 AWG copper, limiting corded pool equipment to a maximum of 20 amps.

No service receptacle may be installed less than 10 horizontal feet from pool walls (no less than 5 horizontal feet from the walls of spas and hot tubs). At least one GFCI protected convenience receptacle is *required*, no less than 10 feet and no greater than 20 feet from swimming pool walls (no less than 5 feet nor greater than 10 feet from the walls of a spa or hot tub). The required convenience receptacle must be installed no higher than 6'6" above grade or deck.

No lighting or paddle fans may be installed over the water or in an area extending less than 5 horizontal feet from a pool wall, unless it is 12 vertical feet, or higher, above the water. NEC does permit existing, securely mounted fixtures to be less than 5 horizontal feet from a pool wall if the fixture is no less than 5 feet above the maximum water level, and is GFCI protected.

All electrical switches must be greater than 5 horizontal feet from pool walls, excepting, of course, pneumatic switching devices that activate remote switches. All electrical junction boxes must be at least 8 inches above the highest possible water level, no less than 4 inches above the deck, and no closer than 4 horizontal feet from the pool wall. Such junction boxes must be corrosion-resistant, suitable for the purpose, and (if metallic), grounded. Junction boxes that contain wiring or devices using 15 volts or less may be flush-mounted with the deck, but must still be a minimum of 4 horizontal feet from pool walls. These low-voltage flush mounted junction boxes must be potted to prevent water penetration.

Power lines over the water and any area extending 10 horizontal feet from pool walls, or to the edge of the base of any diving board or platform must be at least 22 feet above the water level or the base of the diving board or platform. Overhead power lines within 10 horizontal feet of any portion of a diving board or platform must be a minimum of 14 feet above the highest standing area of the diving board or platform. Additionally, coaxial cables and antennae must be a minimum of 10 feet above the water or any portion of a diving board or platform.

Lighting fixtures installed between 5 and 10 horizontal feet from a pool wall require GFCI protection if installed less than 5 vertical feet above the maximum water level. All 120-volt pool equipment, 240-volt single-phase pump motors, outdoor receptacles (regardless of distance from the pool), and underwater lighting circuits, also require GFCI protection. Even if the underwater lighting uses low voltage, the primary feed to the transformer must be GFCI protected. Inspectors should verify the presence and test the operation of all GFCI devices.

All 240-volt pool equipment must be grounded, and each requires a separate, dedicated circuit. All pool heaters, as well as pumps or blowers with drive motors in excess of 1/8 horsepower, require a service disconnect within 50 feet of, on the same wall as, and within a direct line of sight from the equipment. Either a standard or twistlock receptacle (for corded equipment), meets this disconnect requirement. Pool equipment wiring must be run within approved electrical conduit, with proper fittings in use. Where extension cords are permitted, no conduit is required. All disconnects must be located a minimum of 5 feet from pool walls.

Electrical bonding and grounding of all metal and otherwise conductive components associated with (or located near), a pool is necessary to reduce the hazard of electric shock. A copper wire of at least #8 AWG must connect the structural rebar within the pool structure and deck, wet niche fixtures of underwater lighting, slides, diving boards, ladders, pumps and their associated equipment, and any other exposed metal apparatus within 5 feet of pool walls. Securely attached metallic electrical tubing and existing Romex cable are exempted from this unified electrical bonding requirement. All receptacles, lighting fixtures, junction boxes, transformer enclosures, and pool equipment should be properly grounded as per the manufacturer's specifications *and* local code requirements.

Barriers

Fences, walls, or other barriers are required to limit access to the pool area, and ultimately to help prevent drowning accidents. The only exception permitted by the 1995 CABO One and Two Family Dwelling Code is for Listed, manufactured, self-contained portable spas and hot tubs with a safety cover which complies with ASTM-ES-13 standards. Non-portable spas and hot tubs have no barrier requirement exemption.

Pool barriers are purposely constructed in a way to restrict climbing. They should also be located such that other permanent structures or equipment cannot be used as a climbing aid. The proximity of trees, equipment, woodpiles, or other structures that might compromise this intent should be pointed out, and their removal or alteration suggested.

The top of a barrier must be a minimum of 48 inches above the ground (as measured from the side facing away from the pool). Any gap between the barrier and the ground should be less than 2 inches. No protrusions or indentations that create a foothold are permitted in the outside wall of any solid barrier. With any barrier that includes both horizontal and vertical members, all horizontal members less than 45 inches apart are to be installed at the pool side. Where horizontal members are spaced less than 45 inches apart, the vertical members must have a maximum spacing of 1¾-inch. Where horizontal members are at least 45 inches distant, vertical members must be spaced such that passage of a sphere greater than 4 inches in diameter is restricted.

Mesh openings in chain link fencing can be no larger than 1¼-inch square. Larger openings are permitted if slats that effectively reduce the openings to 1¾-inch are securely attached. Diagonal member barriers, such as lattice fencing, must be constructed with openings of less than 1¾-inch.

All access gates should be equipped with locking devices. Gates must be self-closing, self-latching, and be hinged to open *away* from the pool. (Gates not intended for pedestrian traffic need not be self-closing). Where a latch release mechanism is less than 54 inches above the ground, it must be installed on the poolside, at least 3 inches below the gate's top. Further, any gate and surrounding barrier must have no opening greater than ½ inch within 18 inches of the latch mechanism.

Where the wall of a building serves as part of a pool area barrier, *one* of the following three conditions must be met: 1. Doors that access the pool area should be self-closing and self-latching, with latch releases located no less than 54 inches from the floor. 2. Doors that access the pool area should be equipped with an alarm that sounds when the door is opened, and is audible throughout the dwelling. Such an alarm must sound for at least 30 seconds, and automatically reset for the next occurrence. A

momentary shunt switch that deactivates the alarm for no more than 15 seconds may be installed if located at least 54 inches above floor level.
3. The pool may be equipped with a powered safety cover in compliance with ASTM-ES-13-89 standards.

The pool structure itself may serve as a barrier in above-ground pools if all the requirements regarding climbability, as described herein, are met. Wherever an above-ground pool relies on the pool structure to meet these requirements, access ladders or steps must be lockable or removable. Alternatively, ladders or steps must be surrounded by a barrier that meets all in-ground pool barrier requirements regarding height, latches, locks, climbability, etc. If such a pool structure does not meet the 48-inch minimum height requirement, a barrier must be installed on top of the pool edge to bring it into compliance.

Some local ordinances allow for the use of safety netting systems as an alternative to conventional barriers. Where safety netting is present and approved, it should be inspected for damage, deterioration, and proper installation (in accordance with the manufacturer's specifications). Powered cover systems must be tested to assure full opening and closure. Netting with openings which allow a 4 inch sphere to pass, or which is so loosely installed as to permit submersion of a child, is hazardous, and must be called out as in need of repair.

This pool's thermal cover in no way acts as safety netting. The two must not be confused.

Review Questions - Swimming Pools And Equipment

(circle the letter next to the best answer for each question)

1. According to the 1995 CABO One and Two Family Dwelling Code, a swimming pool is any structure intended for swimming or recreational bathing that contains water over _____ inches deep:
   a. 12
   b. 18
   c. 24
   d. 36
   e. 42

2. To prevent disassembly of underwater lighting fixtures by pool users:
   a. warning signs must be posted around the pool
   b. lights should be installed as close to the pool bottom as possible
   c. a locking device that requires the use of tools for removal is required
   d. a wire grate must be installed over all underwater lighting fixtures
   e. all of the above

3. During visual inspection of a pool's interior surface, the inspector need *not* be concerned about any visible:
   a. cracks in concrete or fiberglass
   b. thinning or crumbling plaster
   c. tears or holes in liners
   d. stains or discoloration
   e. none of the above

4. The required minimum depth of underwater lighting fixtures is:
   a. half the depth of the water where the fixture is installed
   b. 18 inches below the water line
   c. 24 inches above the water line
   d. there is no minimum depth requirement
   e. dependent upon the voltage rating of the device

5. When an out-of-level condition equaling 1 inch is observed in an in-ground pool, the inspector should:
   a. suspect that the pool has shifted from its installed position
   b. inform the client that the degree of departure from level is within normal limits
   c. test for the functionality of the hydrostatic valve or plug
   d. recommend draining and leveling of the pool
   e. none of the above

6. When considering the safe minimum depth of a pool in the area of a diving board or platform:
   a. the equipment manufacturer's safety specifications should always be met
   b. local code requirements should always be met
   c. the greater depth specified by either the manufacturer's safety specifications or local code requirements should be met
   d. the inspector should suggest the removal of all diving boards and platforms
   e. an opinion of safe minimum depth requirements is beyond the scope of a visual inspection

REVIEW QUESTIONS 137

7. Pool slides should be installed in such a way as to assure:
    a. secure attachment to the deck
    b. that water running off the slide does not return to the pool
    c. that point of entry into the pool is at a depth appropriate for the vertical height of the slide
    d. all of the above
    e. a. and c.

8. Openings in any pool safety netting must not allow a sphere greater than _____ inches in diameter to pass through:
    a. 7
    b. 6
    c. 5
    d. 4
    e. 3

9. The deck around an in-ground pool should be:
    a. wide enough to allow safe walking
    b. sloped toward the pool to allow splashed water to flow back into the pool
    c. surfaced so as not to be slippery when wet
    d. all of the above
    e. a. and c.

10. Visible leaks in pool equipment piping are not of concern if:
    a. pool equipment and components are not vulnerable to water damage
    b. any leaking water is allowed to drain back into the pool
    c. water loss due to leaks is calculated to be less than 1% of pool volume over a 24 hour period
    d. leaks drain away into an approved drain
    e. none of the above

11. Pump motors should be:
    a. installed in a location visible from the pool's closest edge
    b. installed above grade level
    c. well supported by the connecting pipes
    d. provided with 2 inches of clearance from combustible materials
    e. all of the above

12. Water flow from the return outlets in a pool might contain air bubbles if:
    a. they are part of a venturi-jet system
    b. a leak exists on the suction side of the pipe system
    c. the pump and piping system are not fully primed
    d. all of the above
    e. none of the above

13. Clock timers associated with pump equipment should:
    a. be securely mounted
    b. be checked to assure that timer and changeover mechanisms function properly
    c. have a protective cover over the electrical terminals
    d. have a functional cover and latch
    e. all of the above

14. Automatic cleaning equipment is usually powered by:
    a. an electrical outlet that is required near the pool for the purpose
    b. compressed air generated by the blower
    c. suction or pressure created by the circulating pump
    d. water movement at the water's surface
    e. none of the above

15. Which of the following is not an acceptable gas connector for pool heaters?:
    a. a stainless steel flex connector
    b. a bare brass flex connector
    c. an epoxy coated flex connector
    d. rigid black iron pipe
    e. b. and d.

16. Spa heaters should have a device limiting water temperature to a maximum of:
    a. 98.6° F
    b. 100° F
    c. 102° F
    d. 104° F
    e. 106° F

17. Electrical junction boxes should be no closer to a pool wall than 4 horizontal feet and at what minimum height above the pool deck?:
    a. 24 inches
    b. 12 inches
    c. 10 inches
    d. 6 inches
    e. 4 inches

18. Which of the following does not require GFCI protection?:
    a. lighting fixtures located less than 5 feet above grade and less than 10 feet from a pool wall
    b. pool equipment which operates on 120 volts
    c. receptacles greater than 5, but less than 10 horizontal feet from a pool wall
    d. underwater electric lighting
    e. lighting fixtures greater than 5 horizontal feet from a pool wall which are also greater than 5 feet above maximum water level and rigidly mounted to a structure

19. Pumps and blowers are required to have a dedicated electrical disconnect if the horsepower rating exceeds:
    a. 1/10 horsepower
    b. 1/8 horsepower
    c. 1/6 horsepower
    d. 1/3 horsepower
    e. none of the above

20. Overhead power lines within 10 horizontal feet of a pool's edge:
    a. are not permitted
    b. must be properly insulated
    c. are safe if no diving board or platform are present
    d. must be a minimum of 22 feet above the pool deck
    e. none of the above

21. All of the following must be included in a unified electrical bonding with #8 AWG copper wire except:
   a. electrical metallic tubing secured to a building less than 5 feet from a pool's edge
   b. wet niche fixtures of underwater lights
   c. metal slides, ladders, and diving boards
   d. metallic fencing less than 5 feet from a pool's edge
   e. steel re-bar in a pool's structure

22. The maximum allowable length of a plug-in cord serving a Listed, manufactured, self-contained portable spa is:
   a. 3 feet
   b. 6 feet
   c. 10 feet
   d. 12 feet
   e. 15 feet

23. The main purpose of a barrier around a pool is to:
   a. help prevent accidental drowning
   b. control the accumulation of debris that might foul the filtration system
   c. provide privacy for the users
   d. protect the pool water from contamination caused by pets and other small animals.
   e. none of the above

24. The minimum allowable height of a barrier installed to restrict pool area entry is:
   a. 60 inches
   b. 54 inches
   c. 48 inches
   d. 42 inches
   e. 36 inches

25. A door which permits entry into a pool area from inside a dwelling needs no special equipment if:
   a. the pool is equipped with an approved powered safety cover
   b. no children under the age of 12 live in the dwelling
   c. pool danger warning signs are conspicuously posted on the inside of the door
   d. the pool has been drained
   e. the door has a residential deadbolt locking device

26. Gates are required to meet the same safety criteria as a fence, and should also:
   a. be self-closing
   b. open away from the pool area
   c. be equipped with a locking device
   d. have a latch located on the pool side if the latch is less than 54 inches above the ground
   e. all of the above

Winged Ant

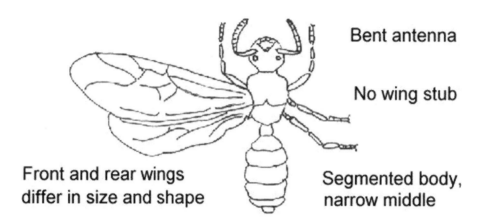

Bent antenna

No wing stub

Front and rear wings differ in size and shape

Segmented body, narrow middle

Winged Termite

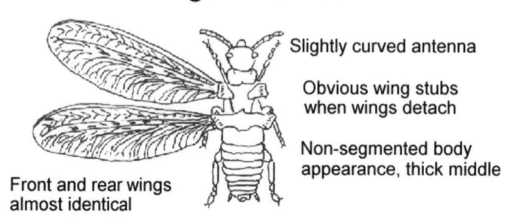

Slightly curved antenna

Obvious wing stubs when wings detach

Non-segmented body appearance, thick middle

Front and rear wings almost identical

Wood Destroying Insects

Learning Objectives

1. Learn to recognize the most prevalent and destructive wood destroying insects.
2. Understand the destructive nature of the various wood-destroying insects.
3. Be able to identify those visible signs which represent evidence of infestation and insect damage.
4. Recognize the obligations borne by inspectors regarding the identification and reporting of adverse conditions caused by insects.
5. Be aware of the conditions which are most conducive to insect infestation.

Depending on regulations in each state, inspection for the presence of (or damage done specifically by) wood destroying insects may require special pest control licensing. Mastering the science of insect identification and control requires extensive study in the field of entomology. Pest control licensees are often called upon, in addition to home inspectors, to help buyers of residential real estate assess the condition of the subject property. Many lenders and mortgage insurers require such inspections before loan approval is granted to the buyer.

Without proper knowledge and certification, home inspectors should not attempt to perform insect-related inspections, but should recommend that a licensed pest control operator be employed to conduct an inspection and render a professional opinion regarding the presence or absence of insect activity and damage.

Contrarily, failure by the home inspector to comment on the known presence of wood destroying insects, or any visible damage done by them, would seem to violate the inspector's obligations. To remain within the spirit and letter of the laws that govern home inspectors, while remaining outside of the pest control field, requires that comments within the inspection report document be carefully stated.

Inspectors without a pest control license must refrain from specifically identifying any wood destroying insects, such as termites, powderpost beetles, and carpenter ants. Insect damage can be described simply as "damaged, rotted or deteriorated" wood members, and when known, the presence of "wood destroying insects" can be reported. The client should then be advised to consult with a pest control licensee for expert evaluation regarding the conditions found.

With that in mind, this section is limited to the basic background knowledge every home inspector should have. This section is not intended to fulfill the educational requirements for pest control professionals, and its treatment of the subject is deliberately superficial. Those home inspectors who wish to perform bona fide pest inspections must contact their state regulatory agencies for details regarding qualifications, courses, testing, and licensing.

Insects which typically cause wood damage are not often seen by the inspector. The damage done by them is the most obvious clue to their presence. Although termites, wood boring beetles, carpenter ants, and wood attacking wasp and bee adults may occasionally be visible, the immature insects (eggs, larva (or grubs), pupa (or nymph), are usually found only by cutting into infested wood.

Conditions conducive to insect attack *should* be reported to the client. These include grading which permits standing water to accumulate near the foundation, finish grading or mulch which conceals too much of the foundation walls (leaving a short or hidden path from ground to sill or brick ledge), diseased trees in close proximity to the structure, vegetation in direct contact with the structure, scrap lumber or firewood stacked against the building, and cracks in foundation walls or floors which might permit insect entry. Worker termites can enter through a crack as small as the width of an average human thumbnail.

Wood destroying insects may attack standing trees or fresh logs, as well as sawn or seasoned lumber. Suitable temperature and moisture levels are required for insect activity, and fungus or dry rot increase vulnerability to infestation. Insect-damaged wood generally will be found to have tunnels or cavities bored into them, often filled with frass (wood powder) or fecal pellets. Frass may be found to have been pushed through small holes, leaving evidence of new insect activity.

Wood destroying insects can be found in all parts of the US. Subterranean termites are the most abundant, but drywood termites are found in high numbers in the warm and humid southern regions. Regardless of population or climate, subterranean termites are the most destructive wood boring insects found anywhere in the US.

Termites

Primary reproductive termites, also known as swarmers, have non-segmented bodies with one pair of antennae, and pigmentation ranging from very light to black. They are the only type of adult individual in the caste with wings (two pair, all of equal size and shape). Like all termites, the primary reproductives have three pair of legs. Secondary reproductive subterranean termites are similar, but have little or no pigmentation, and are wingless. The soldier is also wingless, and its pigmentation is limited to the head and mouth parts (which are usually much larger than those of the others). Workers are the most populous of the caste. They are smaller than the others, colorless, and wingless.

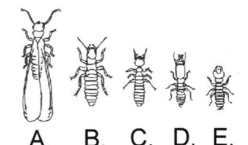

A. Primary reproductive
B. & C. Supplementary reproductive
D. Soldier
E. Worker

Evidence of the presence of *subterranean termites* includes the rare appearance of the swarmers, or more likely, the discarded wings accumulating at sources of light, especially windows. Activity may be found inside shelter tubes or infested wood. Shelter tubes are often visible at foundation locations, which allow termites to safely travel into the structure in their search for wood. Dark or blistered wood elements which are weak, hollow-sounding, or powdered are good clues. Once broken apart, the cavities may hold a light colored sponge-like substance (called "carton") and soil.

Drywood termites discard pellets of excrement outside their galleries. The pellets are hard, elongated, six-sided, and about 1 mm in size. They can accumulate on the surfaces below the tiny holes, called kick-holes, through which they are ejected from the galleries. Swarmers or their discarded wings may be found, but the kick-holes may be filled with secretions, and therefore hard to see. Smooth-walled chambers inside infested wood are connected by tunnels, and chambers are generally free of deposits other than pellets.

Dampwood termites, as their name implies, require high moisture levels in the wood they colonize. Because of this, only wood that is decayed or water damaged is susceptible to infestation. Where they are of concern, swarmers or their wings might be found, but inspection of the inside of suspected woods yields the best evidence of their presence. Gallery interiors have a velvety appearance and contain pellets of excrement.

Arboreal termites are tree-nesting insects, and generally do not invade occupied residential structures, although barns and sheds may be infested. Large shelter tubes on trees, posts, or (rarely) walls are visible, leading from the ground to smooth, round nests made of wood debris and secretions.

Wood-Boring Beetles

Most adult wood-boring beetles are between 1mm and 25mm in size. All have one pair of hardened outer front wings protecting a pair of folded, larger membranous wings. They are not often seen unless infestation is severe. The larvae, or grubs, which do the bulk of the wood damage, are wingless, legless, and worm-like. They generally are lightly pigmented, with dark mouth parts. The larval existence is exclusively inside of wood, and is rarely seen. Only after their development into adult beetles (and after the damage is done), do they bore exit holes.

Small (3mm to 7mm) circular entry holes leading to egg tunnels may be found, but the exit holes made by emerging adults are usually filled with frass. Wood powder and small oval pellets of excrement will be found beneath the exit holes made by the first or second generation of some beetles. This is to say that discovery of infestation earlier than the emergence of the second generation of adult beetles can be very difficult. Apparent blistering of wood surfaces can be evident in severe cases, leaving only an outer shell filled with frass which bulges the wood surface. Some beetle larvae are so voracious as to be detectable simply by listening to the sounds of boring and chewing in the wood they attack.

Carpenter Ants

Wood destroying ants can be as large as 3/4 inch in length and have three distinct body segments (head, thorax, and abdomen). The segments are configured with thin attachment joints, leaving them much thinner in appearance than termites. The largest of all is the queen, which may or may not be found with wings. The slightly smaller adult males have wings, but the workers, which are smaller still, are always wingless. Unlike the termite wings, the front wings of ants, which usually have a notch in the front edge, are considerably larger than their rear wings. Pigmentation ranges from black to reddish brown.

The larvae are small, worm-like, and devoid of pigmentation. They have no legs, and are completely dependent on the care of the adults. As they mature into the pupal stage, they are encased in light colored egg-like cocoons. Unlike termites and beetles, ants do not actually eat the wood, but burrow into it only for nesting. Very dry wood is less susceptible to colonization.

Adult carpenter ants can be seen inside a home mostly at night as they search for water. Outdoor activity is largely seasonal, but indoor activity can be year-round. Spring and summer brings swarming, and with it an accumulation of individuals, usually concentrated near the windows. The telltale frass they expel from cracks in the infested wood can contain tiny bits of ant or other insect parts. The holes or slits from which the frass is expelled may be visible, and the smoothwall galleries they carve inside the wood might be mistaken for termite damage, except that frass is expelled only from ant galleries.

Wood Wasps and Carpenter Bees

Infestation by wood wasps and carpenter bees is less prevalent than that of termites, beetles, and ants. The damage caused by wasps and bees is generally less severe, as well. In those rare cases of severe infestation, the presence of wasps and bees becomes more a nuisance than a structural concern. Exit holes in building materials are large and obvious, and the adults can be noisy and menacing. It is unlikely that a home inspector would be called upon to confirm the existence of such pests. When encountered, these insects are easily distinguishable from termites, beetles, and ants.

Review Questions - Wood Destroying Insects

(circle the letter next to the best answer for each question)

1. Home inspectors without a pest control license should:
    a. identify any wood destroying insects encountered
    b. inform only the client's lender of conditions found regarding wood destroying insects
    c. recommend that a pest control licensee be employed
    d. only perform insect-related inspections by agreement with the client
    e. none of the above

2. Home inspectors who wish to perform termite inspections should:
    a. contact their state regulatory agencies for details regarding licensing
    b. explain that insects which cause damage are not often visible to the naked eye
    c. explain that termites are only seasonally present
    d. study the field of astronomy
    e. b. and c.

3. Conditions conducive to insect attack include:
    a. improper grading around the foundation
    b. scrap lumber stacked against the building
    c. cracks in foundation walls or floors
    d. all of the above
    e. a. and b.

4. The most destructive wood boring insects found in the US are:
    a. termites
    b. powderpost beetles
    c. carpenter ants
    d. wood wasps
    e. carpenter bees

5. Those termites with wings:
    a. are called primary reproductive termites
    b. are called swarmers
    c. have large wings in front, with smaller wings in back
    d. a. and c.
    e. a. and b.

6. Termite workers:
    a. are colorless
    b. are the most populous of the caste
    c. have no wings
    d. are smaller than swarmers and soldiers
    e. all of the above

7. Subterranean termite shelter tubes:
    a. allow termites to safely travel into the structure
    b. do not contain active termites
    c. are not visible at foundation locations
    d. are of a light colored sponge-like substance
    e. a. and d.

Review Questions

8. Pellets of excrement discarded by drywood termites:
   a. accumulate on surfaces below kick-holes
   b. are hard, elongated, and about 1mm in size
   c. are made of a light-colored sponge-like substance called carton
   d. all of the above
   e. a. and b.

9. Dampwood termites:
   a. create galleries that are smooth-walled
   b. cause accelerated water damage to wood
   c. infest mostly decayed wood
   d. create galleries that are devoid of pellets
   e. nest in trees

10. Adult wood boring beetles:
    a. are responsible for the bulk of the damage to the wood they infest
    b. have one pair of large, hardened wings protecting a pair of smaller wings
    c. bore exit holes after they develop into larvae
    d. are between 1 cm and 25 cm in size
    e. none of the above

11. Wood boring beetle larvae:
    a. have 2 pair of wings
    b. develop into grubs
    c. are lightly pigmented with dark mouth parts
    d. have 3 pair of legs
    e. feed on small worms

12. Evidence of the presence of wood boring beetle larvae may include:
    a. the existence of small exit holes, made by the emerging larvae
    b. powder and pellets beneath exit holes
    c. apparent blistering of wood surfaces
    d. all of the above
    e. b. and c.

13. Carpenter ants:
    a. appear thicker than termites
    b. have four distinct body segments
    c. may be as large as 3/4 inch in length
    d. have no pigmentation
    c. none of the above

14. The larvae of carpenter ants:
    a. have 3 pair of legs
    b. provide complete care for the adults
    c. construct light colored egg-like cocoons
    d. burrow into the wood primarily for food
    e. are small and worm-like

15. Wood wasp and carpenter bee infestation:
    a. can be noisy and menacing
    b. is more prevalent than that of beetle or ant infestation
    c. is identified by tiny, inconspicuous exit holes
    d. is not usually obvious to the homeowner
    e. a. and c.

148 PROFESSIONAL HOME INSPECTION RESULTS

Private Well Water Pumps

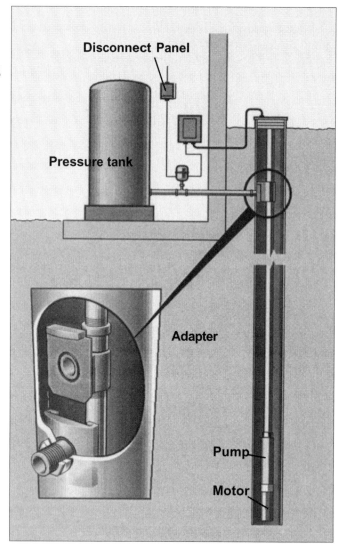

A submersible pump is a single unit that is submerged in the bottom of the well and uses a series of stacked impellers to drive water to the surface.

Courtesy of CPi, publishers of *The Complete Photo Guide to Home Repair*

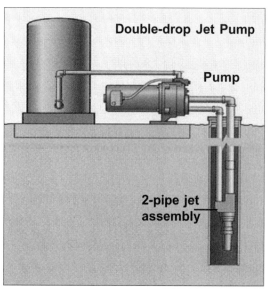

Jet pumps are located on the surface.

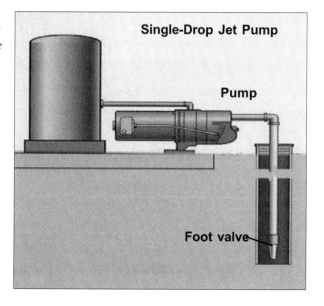

Private Water Wells & Septic Systems

Learning Objectives

1. Be able to identify the most common types of private water well and septic system equipment.
2. Understand the intended function of various water well and septic system components.
3. Recognize those visible signs that represent evidence of malfunction and the need for repair in private water wells and septic systems.
4. Be aware of the obligations borne by inspectors regarding the identification and reporting of adverse conditions found in private wells and septic systems.
5. Become familiar with hazards associated with improper installation, maintenance, and operation of water wells and septic systems.

Water Wells

Wherever it is not possible to access a public water supply for domestic use, a water well and pumping system is installed. Such a system usually includes a pump, a storage tank, and a pressure switch (which regulates tank pressure). Relatively steady pressure is maintained by an air chamber inside the tank. Over time, water absorbs the air and creates a condition called waterlogging. When this occurs, the pump will "short-cycle" to maintain pressure within the desired limits. Pump operation or pressure switch cycling would then be obvious each time there is even a small water demand. The waterlogging condition is not difficult to repair, requiring only a tank draining operation which allows air to once again occupy an appropriate portion of the tank's volume. Sometimes, permanently installed air pumps are found serving the tank. Another method employed to address waterlogging is the separation of water and air within the tank by rubber bladder or diaphragm. Irrespective of the equipment found, all tanks are vulnerable to waterlogging.

Depending on the specific site, the aquifer (an underground water-bearing formation of rock, gravel or sand), may be defined as shallow (less than 25 feet deep), or deep (greater than 25 feet and often beyond 500 feet). Pollutants can foul any well, regardless of its depth, but it is unreasonable to expect any home inspector to have reliable knowledge of the exact location of all potential sources of well water contaminants. Well owners should be advised to assure the safety of their water by regularly testing for coliform, bacteria, hardness, chemicals, and debris.

Pumps can be of the submersible type, the jet type, or the obsolete piston type. Pump type must be identified for the client. The submersible pump is most appropriate for deep wells. Its pump, motor, and electric service are designed to be inserted directly into the well. Submersible pumps are quiet, and little can be observed of their operation without removing them from the well. Adequate flow into the tank should be observed by monitoring the pressure gauge and listening to the pressure switch, evaluating practical functionality.

The jet pump is located at ground level, and may be of either the shallow or deep well type, identified by the number of pipes (or "drops") entering the well. Single drop jet pumps serve shallow wells. Double drop jet pumps recirculate a portion of the water reaching the surface, driving it back down into the well to pressurize the primary water pickup within deeper wells.

Piston pump *motors* are invariably at ground level, but the piston assemblies are often found in the well. Piston type well pump systems are not as efficient or reliable as the more modern submersible or jet pumps. Belts wear out quickly, and vibration caused by the reciprocating parts causes stress on moving components, casings, and gaskets.

Pressures within the storage tank are normally maintained between 20 and 40 pounds per square inch (psi). Some tanks are designed to safely handle 60 psi, and pressure switches (and gauges) within such tanks will be set and calibrated accordingly. Pressure readings above this maximum are evidence of malfunction. Pressure gauge readings that do not hold steady while no demand for water is made indicate that the system is not able to hold pressure, and a leak condition should be suspected. Look for a pressure relief valve somewhere along the piping system near the tank. If either the relief valve or the pressure gauge are missing, it should be reported as in need of repair.

Clients should be made aware that the scope of evaluation for private wells during any non-invasive visual inspection is really quite limited, and hidden or underground auxiliary tanks or equipment may go unfound. Proper inspection procedures include the simultaneous operation of at least 2 fixtures to test for adequate flow and normal operation of the pressure switch. Careful observation of the condition of all visible and readily accessible parts, equipment, and components (including wiring and suitable overcurrent protection), is also required. Be sure to inspect for proper grading and drainage at the well head area. This is important to reduce the risk of garden chemicals or other surface contaminants finding their way into the well.

Septic Systems

Since virtually all components are underground, there are few clues to the use of a septic system in a home. From a performance standpoint, a septic system is indistinguishable from a municipal sewer system. No assumption should be made that the existence of a street-side public sewer system assures that connection from the subject property was ever made. Unless septic system components are found, accessing municipal records is the most reliable way to determine which system is in place at the property in question. Every inspected domicile will be served by a sewer connection, a septic system, or a simple cesspool. A cesspool is nothing more than a brick-lined hole in the ground, into which the main house drain empties. Cesspools are no longer permitted in new construction, but may be functioning as intended, and so need no repair. When they are not functioning as intended, though, most municipalities require that they be replaced with a proper septic system or connection to a city sewer line.

A septic system is designed to retain solid wastes in a tank until decomposition occurs. The effluent, or liquid waste (comprised of wastewater normally introduced into the system and byproducts of the bacteriological breakdown of solid wastes), flows by gravity out into a drainage field or bed (also known as a leaching field), where it is absorbed into the ground at a safe and calculated rate of flow. A seepage pit may be used instead of a leaching field where soil conditions or leaching field size are inadequate.

A properly sized and maintained septic system may serve for 30 years or more, but care must be taken to maintain proper operation. Surface drainage at the leaching field site must be properly maintained to maximize system efficiency. Tank cleaning is required every few years to remove accumulated solid wastes and to prevent backups. Food wastes from a sink disposer and household chemicals like chlorine bleach, drain cleaners, motor oil, and paint thinner can cause a buildup of solids in the tank, as they destroy the bacteria required by the system for decomposition of solid wastes. Without proper decomposition, these solids will clog the drainage field. Though tanks can be cleaned of solid buildup, and bacteria can be re-introduced, the installation of new drainage fields will be required when they are clogged and thus fail to adequately drain into the soil below.

Inspection reporting includes results of observations relating to any visible and accessible components. Check the operation and functional drain flow at all plumbing fixtures, and look for evidence of effluent seepage at soil surfaces near tanks, leaching fields, pits, or beds. Saturated or muddy surfaces at the leaching field may indicate failure of the septic system, especially when accompanied by that distinctive odor so easily recognized. Vegetation, benefiting from the natural fertilizers found in the effluent, will always be unusually thick and green over a leaching field struggling to drain.

Safety regulations are numerous regarding minimum distance requirements for septic system components. In addition to the distances outlined in the chart below, proximity to sharp slopes, soil breaks or faults, easements, swimming pools, sprinkler systems, or other environmentally sensitive locations should be reported to the client whenever they are known.

Minimum Safe Distances for Septic System Components

	Septic tank	Soil Absorption Sys	Water Tight Sewer Pipe
Water wells**	50' *	100' **	20'
Underground cisterns	50' *	100' **	20'
Pump suction pipes	50' *	100' **	20'
Public water supply lines	5'	10'	5'
Streams, ponds, lakes	50' *	75'	20'
Foundation walls (struct)	5'	15'	0
Property lines	10'	10'	0

*if influent and effluent lines are constructed with solvent weld or watertight sewer pipe, holding or septic tanks designed for submergence (concrete, reinforced, or equal) may be within 20' of ponds, cisterns or water wells.
**minimum distance from *public* water wells to soil absorption system 150'.

The inspector should look for the presence of some access portal into the tank and report its location if found. Portals may be buried a few inches under the surface of the ground, and thus will not always be visible. Damage can occur to fiberglass or plastic tanks if a rod is used to probe for the portal; a practice best avoided. Under no circumstances should a home inspector attempt entry into the tank without very specialized skills and experience, as septic system gasses can be harmful or fatal in high concentrations. The location of any drain field, if known, should be reported, as well. Finally, inspect for general condition and operation of any supplemental equipment, such as aerators and dosing pumps.

Review Questions - Private Water Wells & Septic Systems

(circle the letter next to the best answer for each question)

1. Elements found in a private water well system usually do *not* include:
    a. a pump
    b. a desalinization bladder or diaphragm
    c. a storage tank
    d. an air chamber
    e. b. and d.

2. A waterlogging condition in a private water well system:
    a. causes the pump to short-cycle
    b. occurs when air absorbs the water in a storage tank
    c. is unlikely in tanks containing a rubber bladder or diaphragm
    d. is costly and difficult to repair
    e. causes relatively steady pressure at supply fixtures

3. An aquifer:
    a. is usually less than 25 feet deep
    b. is usually beyond 500 feet deep
    c. is a water bearing formation of rock, gravel, or sand
    d. pollutes any well, regardless of depth
    e. none of the above

4. Private water wells should be regularly tested for coliform, bacteria, water hardness, chemicals, and debris:
    a. to assure compliance with Department of HUD regulations
    b. to assure compliance with OSHA regulations
    c. to assure compliance with EPA regulations
    d. to assure compliance with FHA regulations
    e. to assure the safety of the water

5. In regard to private water well pumps, the following is true:
    a. jet type pumps are obsolete
    b. submersible pumps can be readily inspected without removing them from the well
    c. submersible pumps are most appropriate for deep wells
    d. jet pumps can be of the single drop or double drop type
    e. c. and d.

6. Private water well pressure gauge readings which do not hold steady while no water demand is made indicate that:
    a. pump operation is normal
    b. the required pressure relief valve is not present
    c. the system uses a double drop jet pump
    d. the well is almost dry
    e. the system is not holding pressure, and may have leaks

7. Proper inspection for adequate flow and pressure switch operation in a private water well includes the simultaneous operation of at least:
    a. 4 fixtures
    b. 3 fixtures
    c. 2 fixtures
    d. 1 commode and 1 tub/shower faucet
    e. none of the above

8. The existence of a street-side public sewer system:
    a. assures that the connection to the subject property has been made
    b. is evidence of the existence of a private septic system on the property
    c. requires that the inspector access municipal records for identification of system type
    d. is not a guarantee that the subject property has no septic system
    e. is evidence that the subject property is served by the public water supply

9. Whenever septic system components are not found on the property:
    a. wastewater drains are presumed to have been connected to a public sewer system
    b. municipal records become the most reliable source of information regarding drain system type
    c. the drain system should be reported as in need of repair
    d. the client should be advised of the presence of obsolete wastewater equipment components
    e. c. and d.

10. A properly sized and maintained septic system may last:
    a. 10 or more years
    b. 30 or more years
    c. 60 or more years
    d. 75 or more years
    e. 90 or more years

11. Cleaning of a septic tank is required every few years to:
    a. remove accumulated solid wastes and to prevent backups
    b. purge the system of household chemicals
    c. destroy bacteria
    d. reduce odors
    e. a. and c.

12. The minimum distance permitted between a septic tank and a property line is:
    a. 50 feet
    b. 15 feet
    c. 10 feet
    d. 5 feet
    e. none of the above

13. The minimum distance permitted between a soil absorption field and foundation walls is:
    a. 5 feet
    b. 10 feet
    c. 15 feet
    d. 20 feet
    e. 50 feet

3
Miscellaneous Optional Inspections

Learning Objectives

1. Learn which of the various types of common inspection items are identified as optionally inspected.
2. Understand the intended function of those optionally inspected items found less often in homes.
3. Recognize those visible signs which represent evidence of malfunction and the need for repair in optionally inspected items.
4. Be aware of the obligations borne by inspectors regarding the identification and reporting of adverse conditions found in various optionally inspected items.
5. Become familiar with the hazards and potentially adverse consequences associated with the improper installation, maintenance, and operation of those inspection items found less often in the home.

Lawn Sprinklers

Residential lawn sprinklers are irrigation systems designed to provide consistent and controllable water conditions for plants, shrubs, lawns, trees, and gardens, with some degree of automation. Generally, an electronic panel controlling the time, duration, and sequence of several watering zones is located in an outdoor or garage location. A network of underground pipes is run to those locations where irrigation is desired. The panel controls low voltage solenoid-operated valves, which permit the flow of water under normal supply system pressure to spray- or dripheads located along each irrigation run. Zoning is required to maintain sufficient pressure for good water volume, reach, and pattern at each head.

A backflow preventer, a type of vacuum break serving an anti-siphon function, is required to minimize the risk of garden water siphoning into, and thus contaminating, the supply water system. Its location can vary, but it will usually be found at the building water supply entrance. The backflow preventer must be mounted at least 12 inches higher than any of the spray heads in the system to be optimally effective, and its absence or improper elevation is reportable as an item in need of repair. Actual effectiveness of the backflow preventer is not tested by home inspectors. A system shutoff valve is required at the supply line, and it should be inspected for damage, leaks, excessive corrosion, and general condition.

Only manual operation of each zone or station will be tested, as operation of clock or timer functions is impractical, due to time constraints. Water flow and pressure are observed for adequacy. Each station must be identified for its general service location, and any evidence of underground leaks should be noted. Report spray patterns which unnecessarily wet public walkways, streets, or structures, especially at windows or wood siding. Identify significant areas of non-coverage. Overgrown vegetation must not interfere with spray patterns or full deployment of pop-up heads.

Look for secure mounting of the control panel, and the general condition of all visible components. Report the presence of any rain sensors found. Rain sensors serve to cancel programmed operation of the system when rainfall is adequate.

Outbuildings

When outbuildings, like garden sheds, barns, and gazebos, are inspected, structural performance and evidence of water penetration are observed, just as in the subject property main structure. Where applicable, inspection will include foundation, grading and drainage, roof coverings, roof structure and attic, interior and exterior walls, ceilings and floors, doors, windows, fireplaces, chimneys, porches, and decks.

Mechanical systems within outbuildings will also be inspected for performance in the same way as those within the main structure. These will include electrical panels and branch circuits, heating and air conditioning, ducts and vents, plumbing supply lines, drains and vents, tubs, commodes, showers, water heaters, and built-in appliances.

Note that fully habitable structures (such as garage apartments or service quarters) are part of the primary inspection, and cannot be considered optionally inspected. They must be fully inspected for all systems, and should be referenced within the report document as the inspector finds would best suit the client.

Outdoor Cooking Equipment

Inspection of outdoor cooking equipment begins with identification of the heat source, whether natural gas, propane gas, or electricity. Permanently installed heat producing appliances should be located sufficiently clear of combustible materials for safety. A distance of at least 24 inches is recommended. Stable and level mounting is checked. Inspect for cracks, rust, or burn-through in metal bodies, and observe the condition of any firebrick and mortar.

The unit must be operated, and notation is made if any spark igniters fail to work easily and consistently. Observe and report deficiencies found at all handles, control knobs, burners, grilles, rotisserie components, and heat diffusers (such as lava rocks or metal shields).

Natural gas units must have appropriate gas branch line materials, which may include polyethylene (an approved material for underground gas branch line use). Connectors must always be of the stainless steel or epoxy coated variety. Some portable gas fired grilles will be connected to the gas supply branch line by way of a long flexible rubber hose, which must be labeled for use with gas appliances, and is restricted to a maximum length of 15 feet. A shutoff valve is required within 3 feet of the appliance. All accessible gas valves and connection fittings should be checked for gas leaks.

Gas Lines

Full scientific evaluation of gas service supply system performance requires special tools, training, and licensing. Unless the inspector is properly qualified to perform this inspection, it is recommended that a statement be included in the report disclaiming responsibility for gas line inspection.

Gas lines are, however, inspected at points of use, where readily accessible. Observations are made during the inspection of those appliances which utilize gas. It is also good practice to check the outdoor gas meter for detectable leaks, especially where take-off valves are installed for service to fireplaces, coach lights, pool heaters, or outdoor cooking equipment. Point-of-use gas leak detection can be accomplished by sense of smell, use of an electronic combustible gas detector, or by soap-solution bath.

Acceptable gas branch line materials include the following:

1) Black iron, with welded, threaded, or flanged joints. Schedule 40 pipe with malleable black or galvanized fittings only. If outside or below grade, piping must be protected by approved corrosion control methods. When dissimilar metals are joined underground, dielectric fittings or couplings must be used.

2) Galvanized steel pipe, with threaded or flanged joints. Schedule 40 pipe with malleable black fittings only. If outside or below grade, piping must be protected by approved corrosion control methods. When dissimilar metals are joined underground, dielectric fittings or couplings must be used.

3) Corrugated stainless steel tubing, with proprietary mechanical fittings. Must be listed and labeled for gas use, and installed as per manufacturer's instructions. Above grade use only.

4) Soft copper, type K or L tubing, with flared or brazed joints. Not permitted if the gas contains more than an average of .3 grain of hydrogen sulfide per 100 standard cubic feet of gas.

5) Rigid copper or brass pipe, with threaded or flared joints. Not permitted if the gas contains more than an average of .3 grain of hydrogen sulfide per 100 standard cubic feet of gas.

6) Plastic pipe, with solvent cement, adhesive, heat fusion, compression coupling, or flanged joints. Only permitted underground, outside of building. Not permitted within or beneath a building.

(Note: Gas *appliance connectors* are required to be of the epoxy coated or stainless steel type).

Security Systems

Security alarm systems have become commonplace, and inspectors will frequently be asked to inspect them. Operation of any but the simplest systems can be daunting to the uninitiated, due to the variety and complexity of programming options provided with modern control panels. Additionally, system codes or keys may not be available to the inspector, and testing of those systems designed to dial central monitoring stations or police can bring a surprise visit. For these reasons it is often advisable to inspect security systems without actually testing functional operation. If this is done, a statement to that effect is required in the report.

Begin with determining the type of security system, reporting whether monitoring devices are hard-wired, radio controlled, or a combination of the two. Describe the location of control panels, keypads, and monitoring sensors. An infinite variety of magnetic switches might be found hidden in door jambs or window frames for perimeter protection. Infra-red, ultra-sonic, or microwave motion sensors are common interior "trap" devices, and their functionality can sometimes be ascertained by tiny monitoring lights provided within their housings. Most modern systems have a "test" function which sounds an audible alert (or annunciator) when a detection device is triggered. In the "test" mode, inspectors can easily determine which doors, windows, and interior spaces have detection devices. Reporting should include the location of integral smoke, heat, or ionization fire protection equipment.

Telephone interconnects are usually easy to identify at the control panel, and the presence or absence of battery back-up should be noted. It may be difficult to locate any local, external siren or other sounding device in the absence of an actual equipment test, but its presence should be noted if found. Sounding devices may be found in attic spaces, outdoors, or hidden within an HVAC return air plenum. This last location is not ideal, as wiring and other components that are not "plenum rated" may emit toxic fumes in the event flames are drawn by convection (or the furnace blower) into the plenum during a fire.

Sophisticated video monitoring equipment may be found, indoors or out. Unless operation of such equipment is clearly and unequivocally within the realm of the inspector's expertise, only specially trained and qualified technicians should attempt to provide detailed inspection evaluation.

Fire Protection Equipment

All homes should have smoke alarms or other fire protection equipment. Whether hard-wired or battery operated, one smoke or fire detector must be located in each bedroom, and one in each hallway that leads to a bedroom. At least one smoke detector should be installed per floor, regardless of bedroom locations. Whenever alarms are not found at each required location, clients must be advised to install the additional units.

Some states require inspectors to operate the test buttons of each smoke or fire alarm unit present to assure proper functioning. Bear in mind that smoke alarms found in multi-family dwellings may be interconnected to other units within the building, so any testing procedures used should be with the approval of the property owner or manager. Also, be aware that homes with interconnected security and fire alarms may be configured to automatically dial police, a fire department, or a monitoring station. When such is the case, measures should be taken to avoid falsely alerting authorities. Where it is not required or prudent, inspectors may choose not to test the functionality of any alarms present, but must always include a statement to that effect in the report, explaining why functional operation was not tested.

Review Questions - Miscellaneous Optional Inspections
(circle the letter next to the best answer for each question)

1. Lawn sprinkler backflow preventers:
   a. must be located lower than the lowest spray head in the system
   b. are usually tested for effectiveness by the inspector with a vacuum gauge
   c. are normally located at the building water supply entrance
   d. cancel programmed operation in the event of rain
   e. help minimize the risk of garden water migrating into the drain system

2. When inspected, garden sheds, barns, and gazebos:
   a. do not require the same level of inspection as the main structure
   b. are usually excluded from inspection for proper grading and drainage
   c. should be inspected only for structural systems
   d. must be at least 12 feet from the main structure for code compliance
   e. none of the above

3. When inspecting outdoor cooking equipment, the inspector:
   a. must identify and report the heat source
   b. should not attempt to light or otherwise operate the unit
   c. must report the use of underground polyethylene branch line materials as in need of repair
   d. must report the use of stainless steel gas connectors as in need of repair
   e. a. and b.

4. Acceptable gas branch line materials within a residential structure include:
   a. black iron
   b. plastic pipe
   c. galvanized steel pipe
   d. all of the above
   e. a. and c.

5. Acceptable methods for detection of gas leaks at fittings near points of use do *not* include:
   a. a soap-solution bath, which will display bubbles at leak points
   b. use of an electronic combustible gas detector
   c. sense of smell
   d. ignition of potentially errant gas by lighted match or other flame source
   e. c. and d.

6. When inspecting a security alarm, the inspector must:
   a. determine and report whether monitoring devices are hard-wired, radio controlled or a combination of the two
   b. describe the location of control panels, keypads, and monitoring sensors
   c. include the inspection of integral fire protection equipment
   d. test the functional operation of all alarm circuits
   e. a. , b. and c.

7. Smoke or fire alarms are not required to be located:
   a. in each bedroom
   b. in each hall that leads to a bedroom
   c. in kitchen locations
   d. in attic spaces containing furnace equipment
   e. c. and d.

4

Professional Conduct, Ethics, and Standards of Practice

STANDARDS OF PRACTICE

Learning Objectives

1. Learn the principles of honesty and diligence which must be practiced to build and maintain the public's trust in home inspectors.
2. Recognize the importance of complete independence from influences which could compromise the interests of the client.
3. Understand the scope of a visual home inspection, as well as specified limitations.
4. Be aware of the obligations borne by inspectors in regard to reporting requirements.

The magnitude of the responsibility borne by home inspectors imposes the need for extraordinarily high personal integrity. Inspectors must always maintain exemplary standards of professionalism, independence, and fairness. An inspector must protect and promote the interests of his client to the best of his ability at all times. No hint of impropriety can be allowed to exist.

Business should be conducted in a manner which will assure the client of the inspector's independence from outside influences that might compromise his ability to render fair and impartial opinions. Each inspector must consider it his duty to protect the public against fraud, misrepresentation, and unethical practices. For these reasons, no inspector should perform repairs on any property he has inspected, and commissions or finder's fees must never be exchanged without full disclosure to all parties. If an inspector has knowledge of a violation of law regarding inspection practices, he is duty-bound to report such violation to the appropriate state regulatory body.

In the interests of his client and his profession, the inspector should endeavor to continuously increase his level of knowledge regarding existing and developing structural and mechanical systems found in residential real estate. In fact, there is a trend toward mandatory continuing education courses as a prerequisite for annual license renewal in several states.

All advertising or promotional messages distributed or broadcast by real estate inspectors should carry the name of the inspector or his assumed (business) name, and any license identification required for such activity. In states where sponsorship is required for apprentice-level inspectors, the name and license identification of the sponsoring inspector should also appear, as well as a statement describing that relationship.

In those states which regulate the profession, each inspector candidate must consult with the appropriate governing body for specific details regarding eligibility, educational and testing requirements, and other licensing standards. Rules regarding these topics, as well as guidelines prescribing the minimum scope and depth of real estate inspections will be set forth in the language of the provisions adopted by each state's legislature.

Most real estate inspection trade associations maintain proprietary doctrines which spell out the standards of practice to which members are bound. A comparison of the most comprehensive rules promulgated by the various governmental and private bodies will clearly reveal the emergence of a universal common thread in the fabric of home inspection guidelines.

The following is a comprehensive sampling of the developing standards, in language only slightly altered from that found within those Standards of Practice rules prescribed by the most progressive state and industry groups. This sampling is for educational purposes only, and all practicing home inspectors are advised to learn and abide by the rules and laws governing the industry in their respective states.

Standards of Practice

The standards of practice established herein are the minimum levels of inspection required for the accessible parts, components, and systems typically found in improvements to real property. Basic inspection excludes detached structures, decks, docks, and fences. The inspection is of conditions which are present and visible at the time of inspection. All mechanical and electrical equipment, systems, and appliances are operated in normal modes and operating ranges at the time of the inspection.

The inspector must observe, render an opinion, and report which of the parts, components, and systems present in the property have or have not been inspected. The inspector's report must specifically indicate if the inspected parts, components, or systems are not functioning or are in need of repair. The inspector must report on visible existing recognized hazards, and will report as in need of repair any recognized hazard specifically listed herein.

The inspection report must address all of the parts, components, and systems contained herein which can be found in the property being inspected, and inspection items shall be reported in the same order. The inspector may, however, use a form of report which is arranged differently if use of the differing form is required by an agency of the federal government or by a client who buys or sells real property in the due course of business.

All written inspection reports must contain the name and license number, if applicable, of the inspector. The inspector may provide a higher level of inspection performance than required herein, and may inspect parts, components, and systems in addition to those described herein.

These standards do not apply to parts, components, or systems other than those specifically described here. They also do not apply to conditions other than those specifically described here, such as environmental conditions, presence of toxic or hazardous wastes or substances, presence of termites or other wood destroying insects or organisms, compliance with codes, ordinances, statutes, or restrictions, or to the efficiency, quality, or durability of any item inspected.

An inspector shall exclude from the inspection any part, component, or system which the inspector is not competent or qualified to inspect. An inspector may also exclude any item from inspection which is inaccessible, which cannot be inspected due to circumstances beyond the control of the inspector, or which the client has agreed should not be inspected. Upon exclusion from inspection of any part, component, or system other than one the client has agreed should not be inspected, the inspector shall advise the client of the exclusion at the earliest practicable time, and confirm the exclusion in the written report.

Structural Systems

In regard to foundations, grading, and drainage, the inspector shall:

Identify the type of foundation (examples: slab on grade, or pier and beam).

Inspect the foundation, related structural components, and any visible slab surfaces.

Inspect any crawlspace areas to determine the general condition of foundation components found there, and report the method used to observe the crawlspace area when it is not entered due to inaccessibility or hazardous conditions, or when access or visibility is limited.

Render an opinion regarding the performance of the foundation.

Inspect for the presence of adequate crawlspace ventilation.

Observe the conditions or symptoms which may indicate the possibility of water penetration, such as improper grading or plumbing leaks.

Observe and report conditions which may adversely affect foundation performance, such as water ponding, soil erosion, or the presence of tree roots.

Observe the general condition of gutter and downspout systems

Specific limitations for foundations, grading, and drainage.

Inspectors are not required to enter crawlspace areas where headroom is less than 18 inches, or where the inspector reasonably determines that conditions are potentially hazardous to health or safety.

In regard to roof covering, structure, and attic, the inspector shall:

Report the method used to inspect roof coverings if the inspector reasonably determines that conditions are unsafe, or that damage to the roof or covering may result from foot traffic.

Identify the type of roof covering, and inspect its visible components and their condition (excepting the remaining life expectancy of the roof covering).

Inspect the general condition of flashings, skylights, and other roof penetrations.

Enter attic spaces, except where inadequate access or hazardous conditions exist as reasonably determined by the inspector. If attic access is not attained, report the method used to inspect.

Observe and report the approximate depth of insulation where visible.

Observe for the presence of adequate attic space ventilation.

Inspect, where accessible, the condition of roof structure and sheathing, including evidence of moisture penetration.

In regard to exterior walls, doors, and windows, the inspector shall:

Observe deficiencies of exterior walls as related to structural performance and water penetration.

PROFESSIONAL CONDUCT, ETHICS, AND STANDARDS OF PRACTICE

Observe and report the condition and operation of exterior doors, including garage doors.

Inspect the condition of windows and exterior doors to determine whether glazing is present and undamaged.

Inspect insulated glass windows for fogging or other evidence of broken seals.

Observe the presence and condition of window and door screens.

Inspect burglar bars or grates for functional egress in appropriate areas.

Operate all windows at burglar bar locations in sleeping rooms, and a random sampling of other accessible windows.

Inspect for the presence of safety glass at required locations.

Specific limitations for exterior walls, doors, and windows:

Inspectors are not required to report the condition or presence of storm windows or doors, awnings, shutters, locks, latches, or other security devices or systems.

Inspectors are not required to determine the condition of paints, stains, or other surface coatings (except where defects in such surface coatings create vulnerability to water or other damage).

Inspectors are not required to determine the presence, extent, or type of insulation or vapor barriers within the exterior walls.

In regard to interior walls, doors, ceilings, and floors, the inspector shall:

Observe deficiencies in the surfaces of walls, ceilings and floors as they relate to structural performance or water penetration.

Inspect operation of accessible doors.

Inspect steps, stairways, balconies, and railings.

Specific limitations for interior walls, doors, ceilings, and floors:

Inspectors are not required to determine the condition of floor, wall, or ceiling coverings (except as they affect structural performance or water penetration, nor must obvious damage to these coverings be identified).

Inspectors are not required to determine the condition of cabinets, or paints, stains, and other surface coatings.

In regard to fireplace and chimney, the inspector shall:

Inspect the visible components and structure of the chimney and fireplace.

Inspect the interior of the firebox and the visible flue area, excepting the adequacy of the draft or performance of a chimney smoke test.

Inspect the operation of the damper.

Observe for the presence of an adequate non-combustible hearth extension.

Observe the condition of the lintel, hearth and material surrounding the fireplace.

Observe attic penetration of chimney flue, where accessible, for firestopping.

Observe gas valves for function and gas leaks.

Inspect operation of the circulating fan, if present.

Observe for deficiencies in the combustion air vent, if present.

Observe chimney coping, crown or mortar cap, spark arrestor, and rain cap (from best accessible vantage point).

In regard to attached porches, decks, and carports, the inspector shall:

Inspect porches, decks, steps, balconies, and carports for structural performance, including visible footings, joists, deckings, coverings, railings, and attachment points.

Specific limitations for porches, decks, carports:

Inspectors are not required to inspect detached structures, or waterfront structures and equipment, such as docks or piers.

Electrical Systems

In regard to electrical systems, the inspector shall:

Observe service entrance cables for integrity of insulation, drip loop, separation of conductors at weatherhead, and clearances.

Observe that drop, weatherhead, and mast are securely fastened.

Inspect for the presence of a system grounding electrode conductor, and secure connection to the grounding electrode or grounding system.

Inspect all accessible main and sub-panels to ensure that they are secured to the structure and appropriately located.

Inspect for weather tightness, appropriate clearances and accessibility, with inside covers (dead-fronts), in place, and knock-outs filled.

Inspect the type and condition of the wiring in the panels, and the compatibility of overcurrent protectors with the conductor size in use.

Inspect for proper sizing of overcurrent protectors and conductors serving equipment bearing readily visible labels listing power requirements.

Report the absence of appropriate connections and devices related to aluminum or copper wiring.

Observe the presence of required main disconnects

Inspect all accessible receptacles to determine whether power is present, polarity is correct, circuit grounding is present, devices are properly secured to the wall, covers are in place and undamaged, or there is evidence of excessive heat.

Determine, by use of electronic analyzer, that ground fault circuit interrupter devices are properly installed and functioning in bathrooms, garages, within 6 feet of any sink, outdoor locations, and in swimming pool locations. (Absence, improper operation, or improper installation of GFCI devices at required locations must be reported as a recognized hazard).

PROFESSIONAL CONDUCT, ETHICS, AND STANDARDS OF PRACTICE

Operate all wall and appliance switches to determine whether they are operational, there is evidence of arcing or excessive heat, and that they are fastened securely, with covers in place.

Inspect installed fixtures, including lighting devices and ceiling fans, and report their absence or improper operation, or damaged or missing parts.

Observe and report deficiencies of exposed wiring or splices, and the proper use of junction boxes.

Observe and report deficiencies or absence of conduit in appropriate locations, including their secure attachment.

Inspect appliances and electrical gutters for proper bonding.

Observe sub-panels for bonding and grounding.

Observe for the presence of disconnects in appropriate locations.

If aluminum branch circuit wiring is discovered at main or sub-panels, inspect a random sampling of accessible receptacles and switches for approved devices and appropriate connections.

Specific limitations for electrical systems:

Inspectors are not required to determine service capacity amperage or voltage, or to conduct voltage drop calculations.

Inspectors are not required to determine the capacity of the electrical system relative to present or future use.

Inspectors are not required to determine the insurability of the property.

Heating and Cooling Systems

In regard to heating systems, the inspector shall do the following:

Identify the type of heating system and its energy sources.

Operate the system using normal control devices.

Inspect the condition of accessible controls and operating components of the system.

Observe, in gas fired units, the burner and the condition of the burner compartment.

Observe, in gas fired units, the type, condition, draft, and termination of the vent pipe, and its proximity to combustibles.

Observe, in gas fired units, the availability of combustion and draft air, and the presence of forced air in the burner compartment.

Inspect gas burners for flame impingement, uplifting flame, improper flame color, and excessive scale buildup.

Inspect gas branch lines and connectors for proper materials.

Inspect for the presence and proper location of gas shutoff valves, and for gas leaks at the valve.

Determine, in electric furnaces, the operability of the heating elements.

Specific limitations for heating systems.

Full evaluation of heat exchanger integrity requires dismantling of the furnace, and is beyond the scope of a visual inspection.

Accessories, such as humidifiers, air purifiers, motorized dampers, heat reclaimers, electronic filters, and wood burning stoves are not required to be inspected.

Inspectors are not required to determine the efficiency or adequacy of any heating system.

Inspectors are not required to program any digital thermostats or controls.

Inspectors are not required to operate any radiant heaters, steam heat systems, or unvented gas fired heating appliances.

In regard to cooling systems (other than evaporative coolers), the inspector shall do the following:

Identify the type of system and its energy source.

Operate the system using normal control devices (except when the outdoor temperature is less than 60° F).

Inspect for proper performance by measuring the temperature difference between supply air and return air.

Observe for the presence, proper installation, and function of condensate drain lines.

Observe the presence and condition of insulation on refrigerant pipes and primary condensate drain lines.

Inspect condensing units for clearances, air circulation, condition of fins, location, and level elevation above ground surfaces.

In regard to evaporative coolers, the inspector shall:

Operate each motor, and identify each as of the one or two speed variety.

Observe the electrical pigtail connection at the motor.

Inspect the power source in the unit.

Inspect the function of the pump, and the condition of spider tubes, tube clips, and bleeder system.

Observe the water supply line and the condition of the float bracket.

Observe the presence of the required one inch air gap between water discharge (at float), and the water level.

Inspect the fan or blower for rust, corrosion, or other deterioration.

Observe the condition fan belt and pulleys.

Observe the condition of the housing panels, water trays, and roof frame.

Observe and report the condition of the roof jack or other mounting points, and the location of the damper.

Observe the interior registers and supply ducts.

Specific limitations for cooling systems:

Inspectors are not required to measure the pressure of the system refrigerant or determine the presence of refrigerant leaks.

Inspectors are not required to program or operate setback features found in digital thermostats or controls.

In regard to ducts and vents (including dryer vents), the inspector shall do the following:

Observe the condition and routing of ducts and vents where visible and accessible.

Inspect for adequate air flow at all accessible supply registers in the habitable areas of the structure.

Inspect accessible duct fans and filters.

Inspect for improper installation, such as the presence of gas piping, sewer vent piping, or electrical junction boxes inside plenum cavities, or improper sealing.

Inspect for proper materials and condition of the flue system components, and for proper flue termination.

Specific limitations for ducts and vents:

Inspectors are not required to determine air flow efficiency, balance, or capacity, or uniformity of air flow to the various parts of the structure.

Inspectors are not required to determine the types of materials used in insulation, pipe wrapping, ducts, jackets, boilers, or wiring.

Inspectors are not required to operate venting systems unless ambient temperatures and other circumstances are, in the reasonable opinion of the inspector, conducive to safe operation without damage to the equipment.

Inspectors are not required to operate any equipment outside its normal operating range.

Plumbing Systems

In regard to plumbing systems, the inspector shall:

Inspect for the type and condition of all accessible and visible water supply, wastewater, and vent pipes.

Inspect and operate all fixtures and faucets where the flow end of the faucet is not connected to an appliance.

Observe for the presence of back-flow or anti-siphon devices and systems, or air gaps where applicable.

Observe water supply by viewing functional flow in two fixtures, operated simultaneously.

Observe functional drainage at accessible plumbing fixtures.

Observe and report deficiencies in installation and identification of hot and cold faucets.

Operate mechanical drainstops if installed on sinks, lavatories, and tubs.

Inspect commodes for cracks in the ceramic material, proper mounting to the floor, evidence of leaks, and tank component operation.

Observe all accessible supply and drain pipes for evidence of leaks.

Observe existence of visible vent pipe system to the exterior of the structure, and for proper routing and termination of the vent system.

Inspect all shower pans for evidence of leaks.

Operate exterior faucets attached or immediately adjacent to the structure.

Specific limitations for plumbing systems.

Inspectors are not required to operate any main, branch, or shutoff valves.

Inspectors are not required to inspect any system which has been shut down or otherwise secured.

Inspectors are not required to inspect any components which are not visible or accessible.

Inspectors are not required to inspect any exterior plumbing components such as water mains, private sewer systems, water wells, pressure tanks, sprinkler systems, or swimming pools.

Inspectors are not required to inspect fire sprinkler systems.

Inspectors are not required to inspect or operate drain pumps or waste ejector pumps.

Inspectors are not required to inspect the quality or volume of well water, or to determine the potability of any water supply.

Water conditioning equipment, such as water softeners or filter systems are not required to be inspected.

Solar water heating systems are not required to be inspected.

Fee standing appliances are not required to be inspected.

Inspectors are not required to determine the effectiveness of anti-siphon devices at any fixture or system.

Inspectors are not required to observe the system for proper sizing, design, or use of proper materials (except for the presence of dielectric fittings where required).

Inspectors are not required to inspect the gas supply system for leaks.

In regard to water heating equipment, the inspector shall do the following:

Identify the energy source.

Inspect tank and fittings for leaks and corrosion.

Observe and report as hazardous conditions deficiencies regarding the temperature and pressure relief valve piping for 1) gravity drainage, 2) size of drain pipe, 3) material, and 4) termination.

Operate the temperature and pressure relief valve, when of an operable type, if operation will not cause damage to persons or property as reasonably determined by the inspector.

Inspect for broken or missing parts, covers, and controls.

Observe the condition of the burner, flame, and burner compartment, or the operation of electric heating elements and the condition of wiring.

Observe and report materials used for the gas branch line and the connection to the appliance, and inspect for the presence, location, and accessibility of a gas shutoff valve, and for leaks at the valve.

Observe the type of vent pipe and its condition, draft, proximity to combustibles, and its termination point.

Observe for adequate combustion and draft air.

Observe for safe location and installation, including the presence of safety pan and drain where applicable.

Inspect heaters located in a garage (or in a room opening into a garage), for minimum height of ignition sources from the floor (18 inches), and for protection from physical damage.

In regard to hydrotherapy or whirlpool equipment, the inspector shall do the following:
(This heading refers to jet-equipped indoor bathtubs which are filled for each use, as distinguished from spa-tubs which remain filled, heated, and filtered continuously).

Fill the tub and observe its operation.

Inspect for the presence and operation of a GFCI protective circuit.

Inspect for safe location and operation of switches.

Observe under the tub for evidence of leaks if the access cover is available and accessible.

Inspect the movement of the discharge ports and the operation of air intake valves.

Specific limitations for hydrotherapy or whirlpool equipment:
Inspectors are not required to operate or determine the condition of auxiliary components, nor to inspect self-cleaning functions.

Appliances

In regard to dishwashers, the inspector shall do the following:
Inspect the condition of the door gasket, control knobs, and interior parts, including the dish trays, rollers, spray arms, and soap dispenser.

Observe the interior for rust.

Inspect for secure mounting and proper door spring operation.

Observe discharge hose or pipe for condition and the presence of backflow prevention.

Observe for the presence of water leaks.

Operate the unit in normal mode, with the soap dispenser closed, noting that spray arms turn, soap dispenser opens, and drying element operates.

In regard to food waste disposers, the inspector shall:

Inspect the condition of the splashguard, grinding components, and exterior.

Inspect the unit for secure mounting.

Operate the unit, observing for noise, vibration, and evidence of leaks.

In regard to kitchen range exhaust vents, the inspector shall:

Inspect the condition of the filter, vent pipe, and switches.

Operate the blower, observing sound, speed, and vibration levels.

Observe operation of the light switches and lights.

Observe the termination of the vent pipe to an outdoor location when the unit is not of the recirculating type.

In regard to electric or gas ranges, the inspector shall:

Inspect for broken or missing knobs, elements, drip pans, or other parts.

Inspect for operation of the signal lights and elements (or burners), at low and high settings.

Observe and report materials used for the gas branch line and connection to the appliance.

Inspect for the presence, location, and accessibility of a gas shutoff valve, and for leaks at the valve.

In regard to electric or gas ovens, the inspector shall:

Inspect for broken or missing knobs, handles, glass panels, lights, light covers, or other parts.

Inspect the door for gasket condition, tightness of closure, and operation of the latch.

Inspect the oven for secure mounting.

Inspect heating elements and thermostat sensor for proper support.

Observe the operation of the heating elements or the lighting, operation, and condition of the flame.

Inspect the operation of the clock, timer, thermostat, and door springs.

Measure the accuracy of the oven thermostat, set at 350° F, against an oven thermometer of known accuracy, reporting differences greater than 25° F.

In regard to built-in microwave cooking equipment, the inspector shall do the following:

Inspect for broken or missing knobs, handles, glass panels, or other parts.

Inspect the condition of the door and seal.

Observe the oven operation by heating a container of water (or with other test equipment as reasonably determined by the inspector.

Observe the operation of the cooklight.

In regard to trash compactors, the inspector shall do the following:

Inspect the overall condition of the unit.

Operate the unit, observing noise and vibration levels.

Check the unit for secure mounting.

In regard to other built-in appliances, the inspector shall do the following:

Operate the appliance as practicable while inspecting the overall condition, or note otherwise in the report.

In regard to bathroom exhaust vents and electric heaters, the inspector shall do the following:

Operate the unit, observing sound, speed, and vibration levels.

Observe exhaust vent terminations for proper location and the presence of backdraft dampers

Observe for proper bulb type in heat lamps.

Operate electric bathroom heaters, observing functionality.

In regard to whole-house vacuum systems, the inspector shall do the following:

Inspect the condition of the main unit.

Operate the unit if possible.

Inspect the system from all accessible outlets throughout the house.

Observe visible piping for damage or leaks.

In regard to garage door operators, the inspector shall do the following:

Inspect the condition and operation of the garage door operator.

Operate the door manually, or by an installed automatic door control.

Test the automatic safety reversing system.

In regard to doorbells and chimes, the inspector shall:

Inspect the condition and operation of the unit.

Inspect installation of all visible and accessible parts.

Inspection of optional equipment, systems, parts, components, and attachments.

The inspector may need specialized knowledge or tools to perform the optional inspections listed below. It is the responsibility of the inspector to be properly informed and educated regarding current and safe procedures for inspecting these items. The inspector must determine and report conditions found in optional equipment, systems, parts, components, or attachments by visual observation and operation within normal modes and ranges.

In regard to lawn sprinklers, the inspector shall do the following:

Manually operate all zones or stations, observing water flow or pressure at the circuit heads.

Inspect for evidence of subsurface water leaks.

Inspect for the presence and proper installation of anti-siphon valves, backflow preventers, and system shutoff valves.

Observe the condition and mounting of control boxes and visible wiring.

Observe and report the operation of each zone, its associated valves, spray head patterns, and areas of non-coverage.

Specific limitations for lawn sprinklers:

Inspectors are not required to inspect the automatic function of the timer or control box.

Inspectors are not required to determine the functionality or effectiveness of rain sensors, anti siphon devices, or backflow preventers.

Optional Inspections

In regard to swimming pools, spas, and equipment, the inspector shall do the following:

Determine and identify the type of pool construction.

Note the condition of pool surfaces, identifying cracks or deterioration.

Observe the condition of tile, coping, and decks.

Inspect the condition of slides, steps, diving boards, and other equipment.

Inspect the condition of drains, skimmers, and valves.

Observe the presence, condition, and function of pool lights and ground fault circuit interrupter protection.

Inspect the condition and function of pump motors, controls, sweeps, proper wiring, and circuit protection.

Inspect condition and function of heater, if present, including gas branch line and connector materials.

Inspect for presence of gas shutoff valves, and for gas leaks at the valve.

Observe external grounding of the pump motor, blowers, and other electrical equipment, if visible.

Inspect the condition of the filter tank and pressure gauge, and look for above ground leaks.

Observe the presence and condition of fences, gates, and enclosures.

Specific limitations for swimming pools, spas, and equipment.

Inspectors are not required to dismantle or open any components or lines.

Inspectors are not required to uncover or excavate any lines or concealed components, or to determine the presence of sub-surface leaks.

PROFESSIONAL CONDUCT, ETHICS, AND STANDARDS OF PRACTICE

Inspectors are not required to fill any pool, spa, or hot tub with water.

Inspectors are not required to determine the presence of sub-surface water tables.

Inspectors are not required to inspect ancillary equipment, such as computer controls, covers, chlorinators or other chemical dispensers, or water ionization devices or other conditioners not specifically required by this section.

In regard to outbuildings, the inspector shall do the following:

Inspect the building for structural performance and water penetration.

Observe the building for electrical, plumbing, and HVAC standards, where applicable.

In regard to outdoor cooking equipment, the inspector shall:

Identify the energy source, and operate the unit.

Inspect the condition of control knobs, handles, burner bars, grills, box, rotisserie, if present, and heat diffusion material.

Observe the stability of the unit and pedestal.

Inspect for proper gas branch line and connector materials.

Inspect for the presence and location of gas shutoff valves, and for leaks at the valve.

In regard to private water wells, the inspector shall:

Operate at least two fixtures simultaneously.

Identify the type of pump and storage equipment.

Observe and determine water pressure, flow, and the operation of pressure switches.

Observe the condition of visible and accessible equipment and components.

Inspect for proper wiring and circuit protection.

Observe the condition of the well head, as well as the drainage at the well head site.

Recommend, perform, or arrange to have performed a coliform analysis.

Specific limitations for private water wells:

Inspectors are not required to open, uncover, or remove the pump, heads, screens, lines, or other system components

Inspectors are not required to determine water quality or potability, or the reliability of the water supply or source.

Inspectors are not required to locate or verify underground water leaks.

In regard to individual private sewage systems (septic systems), the inspector shall do the following:

Report the observed condition of the accessible or visible components of the system.

Operate plumbing fixtures to observe functional flow.

Walk over the area of tanks and fields or beds to identify, by visual and olfactory means, evidence of effluent seepage or flow at the surface of the ground.

Inspect for areas of inadequate site drainage.

Observe system proximity, if known, to water wells, underground cisterns, water supply lines, streams, ponds, lakes, sharp slopes or breaks, easement and property lines, soil absorption systems, swimming pools, and sprinkler systems.

Inspect the operation of the system.

Observe the presence of access to tanks.

Determine the type of system, if possible, and the location of the drain field.

Verify the operation of aerators, dosing pumps, and proper wiring when such equipment is present.

Specific limitations for private sewage systems (septic systems):

Inspectors are not required to excavate or uncover the system or its components.

Inspectors are not required to determine the size, adequacy, or efficiency of the system.

Inspectors are not required to determine the type of construction used unless it can be readily known.

In regard to built-in security and fire protection equipment, the inspector shall do the following:

Determine the type of security system, and the location of monitoring devices and control boxes.

Inspect and note the existence of point-of-entry, motion, infra-red, or other detection devices.

Note the existence of external alarm, battery back-up, and telephone interconnect.

Determine whether the system is of the local alarm or centrally monitored configuration.

Randomly test the system for operation, if possible.

Determine the type and location of fire detection sensors.

Note whether sensors are smoke, heat, or ionization detectors.

Review Questions - Professional Conduct, Ethics, and Standards of Practice

(circle the letter next to the best answer for each question)

1. Business should be conducted in a manner which:
   a. maintains maximum profitability to the inspector
   b. assures the client of the inspector's independence from outside influences
   c. presents a neat and clean appearance
   d. compromises the inspector's ability to render fair and impartial opinions
   e. minimizes confrontation with the seller's representative

2. All advertising distributed by real estate inspectors must include:
   a. the name of the inspector or his assumed name
   b. a table of prices and charges
   c. the inspector's license number
   d. all of the above
   e. a. and c.

3. Regarding scope and depth of real estate inspections, an inspector must first adhere to all rules:
   a. found within the language of the trade associations with which he is affiliated
   b. set forth in the language of the provisions adopted by his state's legislature
   c. dictated by his corporate partnership agreement
   d. agreed to, in writing, by the client
   e. imposed by the Federal Housing Authority

4. During inspection, mechanical and electrical equipment, systems, and appliances are:
   a. beyond the scope of a visual inspection
   b. only operated in normal modes and operating ranges
   c. operated at their limit capacity
   d. tested for the presence of dedicated GFCI protective circuits
   e. none of the above

5. The inspector is required to render a written report in a format dictated by the governing state:
   a. in all cases
   b. unless a different format is required by an agency of the federal government
   c. unless a different format is required by a client who buys or sells property in the due course of the client's business
   d. unless the inspector provides a higher level of inspection performance than required
   e. b. and c.

6. Inspectors are usually required to:
   a. inspect for the presence of toxic or hazardous wastes
   b. inspect for code compliance
   c. inspect for the efficiency of heating and air conditioning systems
   d. inspect items which are inaccessible
   e. none of the above

7. The inspection of foundation, grading, and drainage does *not* require observations regarding:
   a. crawlspace areas
   b. crawlspace ventilation
   c. nearby tree roots
   d. lead paint
   e. gutters and downspouts

8. Roof inspection always requires:
   a. walking on the roof
   b. identification of the roof covering material
   c. projecting and reporting the remaining life expectancy of the roof covering
   d. a. and b.
   e. b. and c.

9. Inspectors should report the approximate depth of attic insulation:
   a. whenever the attic space cannot be entered for inspection
   b. whenever inadequate insulation is suspected
   c. whenever attic ventilation is excessive
   d. whenever the insulation is visible
   e. none of the above

10. Inspectors are *not* required to report:
    a. damaged or missing glass panes in window frames
    b. fogging or other evidence of broken seals in insulated windows
    c. burglar bars or grates at bedroom windows which interfere with egress
    d. the absence of storm doors
    e. the absence of window screens

11. Inspectors are required to inspect:
    a. operation of doors
    b. operation of awnings
    c. operation of shutters
    d. the condition of paints or stains
    e. the condition of cabinets

12. During inspection of a fireplace, inspectors look for:
    a. adequacy of flue drafting
    b. presence and adequacy of a non-combustible hearth extension
    c. presence and condition of coping or crown flashing, spark arrestor, and rain cap
    d. all of the above
    e. b. and c.

13. During electrical inspections:
    a. integrity of service entrance cables and insulation are observed
    b. the presence or absence of a system grounding electrode is observed
    c. inspection is made for the compatibility of overcurrent protectors with wire sizes in use
    d. all of the above
    e. a. and b.

REVIEW QUESTIONS 179

14. Electrical receptacles are *not* inspected for:
    a. correct polarity
    b. circuit grounding
    c. evidence of excess heat
    d. correct voltage
    e. broken cover plates

15. GFCI protection is *not* required for receptacles:
    a. at all bathroom locations
    b. at garage locations
    c. within 6 feet of sinks
    d. within 5 feet of furnace blower locations
    e. at outdoor locations

16. Inspectors are *not* required to:
    a. determine the operability of heating elements in electric furnaces
    b. observe the type, condition, draft, and termination of gas furnace flues
    c. inspect gas furnace burners for scale buildup
    d. fully evaluate the integrity of the heat exchanger in gas fired furnaces
    e. inspect for proper gas branch line and connector materials at gas appliances

17. Inspectors are required to:
    a. observe for the presence and condition of insulation on air conditioner vapor lines and primary condensate drain lines
    b. operate air conditioner systems (when the outdoor temperature *is* below 60° F)
    c. inspect air conditioner condensing units for the condition of fins
    d. all of the above
    e. a. and c.

18. Inspectors are *not* required to:
    a. measure the pressure of air conditioner system refrigerant
    b. determine the presence of refrigerant leaks
    c. report adequacy of air conditioner capacity as related to dwelling square footage
    d. all of the above
    e. a. and c.

19. During plumbing system inspection, observations must be made regarding:
    a. type and condition of accessible and visible supply pipes
    b. *exterior* plumbing components such as water mains, private sewers, and water wells
    c. free standing appliances
    d. the effectiveness of anti-siphon devices
    e. the proper operation of main, branch, and shutoff valves

20. Inspectors must observe:
    a. functional water flow at 2 plumbing fixtures operated simultaneously
    b. functional drainage at accessible plumbing fixtures
    c. plumbing vent system termination
    d. all of the above
    e. a. and b.

21. Hazardous conditions related to a drain line serving a temperature-and-pressure relief valve installed in a water heater do *not* include:
    a. a drain line with a threaded discharge end
    b. a drain line sloped to prevent positive gravity drain
    c. a drain line of 3/8 inch diameter pipe
    d. a drain line with a full-bore shutoff valve installed near its termination
    e. none of the above

22. One item that is *not* important to inspection of a gas fired water heater is:
    a. height above the garage floor
    b. availability of combustion and draft air
    c. verification of GFCI circuit protection
    d. condition of the flame
    e. presence of a gas shutoff valve

23. Inspectors are *not* required to:
    a. fill whirlpool equipment
    b. look under a hydrotherapy tub if an access panel is not provided
    c. inspect the movement of whirlpool discharge ports
    d. verify the presence and operation of a GFCI protective device serving a whirlpool tub
    e. look for safe location and operation of electric switches serving a whirlpool tub

24. Inspection of built-in dishwashers does *not* include:
    a. condition of door gaskets
    b. operation of soap dispenser doors
    c. condition of dish tray rollers
    d. presence of discharge hose backflow prevention
    e. none of the above

25. Inspection of a built-in dishwasher includes:
    a. operation of the unit
    b. observation of adequate water supply line size
    c. reporting drain flow capacity
    d. determination of heated water temperature adequacy
    e. a. and c.

26. In regard to ovens and ranges, the inspector:
    a. disregards the operation of signal lights
    b. is not obligated to check for gas leaks
    c. uses an oven thermometer to measure oven temperature accuracy
    d. operates a representative sampling of rangetop burners
    e. observes and reports a level transition between rangetop and adjacent countertop

27. While inspecting lawn sprinkler systems, inspectors are required to observe and report:
    a. the operation of each zone
    b. spray head patterns
    c. the functionality of lawn sprinkler rain sensors
    d. all of the above
    e. a. and b.

REVIEW QUESTIONS

28. While inspecting swimming pools, inspectors are *not* required to:
    a. identify the type of swimming pool construction
    b. inspect diving boards
    c. determine the presence of subsurface leaks
    d. inspect the function of pool water heaters
    e. inspect the condition of pool skimmers

29. In regard to outdoor cooking equipment, inspectors are *not* required to :
    a. operate fuel-burning equipment
    b. inspect heat diffusion material
    c. report minor outdoor gas leaks
    d. attempt to identify the materials used for gas connectors
    e. none of the above

30. Private water well inspection includes:
    a. removal of the pump cover
    b. a determination of the future reliability of the water supply
    c. verification of the existence of underground water leaks
    d. identification of the pump type
    e. verification of the efficiency of aerators

5

Forms, Marketing and Contracts

Section 5 is intended to provide a practical guide to the business of home inspection. Here you can see examples of real inspection documents, just as they appear in use. Marketing and other business tips are included as well. Interested readers can get a feel for the nuts and bolts of home inspection contract legalese from the very carefully worded consulting contract found here.

THE HOME INSPECTION FIELD FORM

Every inspector will find that daily use of a complete and familiar field form will render better results in the field and easier transposition of field notes into a report document. The field form serves as a convenient reminder, to help avoid inspection omissions, and as a reference to specifications, standards, and codes relating to every phase of the inspection. Once the inspection is completed, field notes are already arranged in blocks of data which mirror the sequencing found within the reporting format.

The standardized inspection parameters found within the following field form can be updated or changed at any time for continued relevance in any venue or geographical region. Inspectors bound to adopt a reporting format significantly different from the one depicted herein would be well advised to reorganize this field form to coordinate with the scope and sequence of the report form to be used.

Permission is granted to the purchaser of this book by the author and publisher to duplicate this field form only for inspection purposes. The sale or other wholesale dissemination of this material without the express written permission of the author and publisher is prohibited.

HOME INSPECTION FIELD FORM

SUBJECT   CLIENT   CTL #

ADDRESS _____ NAME_____ DATE _____

FOUNDATIONS

Pier & Beam and Basement Foundations

foundation material _____ poured - block
girders & joists support - notches intact
girders & joists twist-sag-split - rot - pests - deterioration
excessive mildew or musty odor
water penetration or efflorescence
ducts - wiring - plumbing - properly supported
plumbing supply or drains leaking
subfloor level - solid
cracks @ beamwall
concrete - mortar - blocks crumbling
beamwall exposure 3", proper grading
sump pump - condition - wiring - operation (basement wells drain)

Slab-On-Grade and Screeded Slab

cracks @ perimeter grade beam wall
visible slab floor surface cracks
cable ports sealed
exposure above finish grade 8-wood/6-brick
evidence of repair
evidence of water - pest penetration
foundation floors level
1st floor tile cracking patterns

screeded slab subfloor venting
   to outdoors is not permitted

Pier & Beam

venting 1/150 inc w/in 3' ea corner
(1/1500 ok w/ vapor barrier)
vapor barrier intact
access opening > 18x24
(30x30 w equipt present)
Min headroom 18" (code) 24" (access std)
HVAC ducts @ crawlspace insulated - supported
debris - ponding - erosion - pests - hazards
underfloor insulation present - secure - v/ barrier up
piers tipping - sinking - supporting girders
girders > 12" to ground - shims missing or dislodged
dryer - range - bath vents terminate @ crawlspace

All Foundations

soil shrinking from foundation
ridge not level - rafters pulling from ridge boards
all trees > 5" from foundation
cracking pattern - fresh paint @ mortar
brick freshly painted
exterior trim @ windows - doors - frieze board racked
addition slab pulling away from original foundation
masonry steps pulling away from foundation
masonry f/ place or chimney pulling away from house
wallboard/corn bead stress cracks - pucker - wrinkle - buckle
windows, doors, cabinets operate - align - close - latch - racked
striker plates moved to align w/ latches

Foundation Performance Conclusions

no - little - some - excessive - evidence found of differential settlement

```
[  ] electronic foundation level measurements taken.  Notes:




```

[ ] SATISFACTORILY PERFORMING   [ ] IN NEED OF REPAIR

© 2002 Richard L. Burgess. All Rights Reserved
Procor Edison Publications

Grading & Drainage

grading @ foundation >1" in first 8' - <5" in first 8'
>3" pier & beam perim wall exposure, 8" to wood siding, 6" to brick
evidence of water penetration into structure
drainage provision @ garden or retaining walls
catch basins drain below inlets
trees cause vulnerability to excessive transpiration

gutters & leaders

drain too close to foundation
securely attached
proper slope
wood/fascia rot or damaged
rust - sagging
splashblocks present or req'd

Roof Covering   Inspection method: [ ] walk roof   [ ] laddertop   [ ] ground w/ binoculars

trees overhanging	roof sagging	flue / vent caps	chimney mortar/coping
flashing, skirts, boots	turbines spin freely		spark arrestor & rain cap
valleys intact	skylites		cricket/saddle req'd if 30" to ridge

composition
(17 yr life)

wavy deck - >33% (4 in 12) or >17% (2 in 12) ok w/ self or hand sealed & 2 felt layers - drip edge
missing - broken - nail pops - hail - granule loss - puffy - curled - brittle - springy - leaks
(composition over wood original - special drip edge/flashing considerations, esp at gable & rake)

wood shingle
(25 yr life)

direct sunlight - >4 in 12 pitch - missing - loose - ev of repairs - split - curled - weathered
cracked - soft - damaged - exposed nails - seams staggered - leaks - algae

wood shake
(25 yr life)

felt visible from outside - >4 in 12 pitch - shakes visible inside - missing - split - algae
damaged - ev of repairs - cracks - soft - exposed nails - seams staggered - leaks

tile,
slate &
asbestos

adequate bracing/support, esp for re-roof - cracked - broken - missing -
flashing @ chimney - mastic @ hips & ridge - birdstops (Spanish tile)
rust streaks @ nails - felt - flashings - leaks

built-up roof
(BUR)
(10 -20 yr life)

ponding - sagging - blisters - aggregate missing or loose - fishmouth
seams visible - alligator - penetrations flashed & cap flashed - gravel guard
soft deck - asphalt flowing (> 0 in 12) - drains - vegetation - leaks

metal

bent - gable fit - ev of repair - hips & ridges well fit - cap flashing at chimney nailed/caulked
flashings sealed - 1" weep holes at vent pipes and turbine flashings - leaks

Roof Structure and Attic   Inspection method: [ ] entry   [ ] laddertop   [ ] floor below   [ ] other

access 22" x 30" min req'd   average depth of insulation _____   (B flue clrnc found @ ea appliance)
ventilation 1/150 of floor area (1/300 ok if 80% is high)
framing or other structural members cut - split - cracked - detached - warped - rotted - damaged - missing - loose - knots
bearing walls notched <25% - bored <40%   non-bearing walls notched <40% - bored <60%
roof decking stained - rotted - moisture penetration - delamination - sagging - cracked - joist splices supported
truss web members or chord cut or missing - gusset plates secure & undamaged
firestops @ all ceiling passthroughs - vents - pipes - ducts - chimneys (inc 2" min clrnc to combustibles)
recessed light fixtures clearance ½" to combustibles, 3" to insulation (unless otherwise listed)   4504.8

© 2002 Richard L. Burgess. All Rights Reserved
Procor Edison Publications

Walls (Interior and Exterior)

Interior wall surfaces - stress - buckling - rippling - stained - bubbled - bowed - water penetration
interior 4x8 paneling lacks gypsum board backing
attached garage walls of fire-rated material (gypsum)
exterior "synthetic stucco", provide consumer alert
exterior wood surfaces rotted - cracked - detached - missing - damaged - loose - buckling - knots - water penetration
exterior brick weep holes - separation of mortar or caulk - pattern cracks - spalling - damage - exp joints caulked - leaks

Ceilings and Floors (Including Stairs and Balconies)

ceilings stressed - buckling - rippled - stained - sagging - water penetration
floors uneven - cracked - weak - "bounce" - creaking - stained - damaged - rotted - water penetration

steps - max rise 7 ¾ "- min tread 10" - max allowable difference 3/8 "
stairways min stair and landing width 36".   min headroom 6'8" (spiral 6'6")
balcony guardrail >36" ht req'd w drop of >30"
stair handrails req'd w 3 or more risers - 30" to 38" ht from nosing (min ht @ open side of stairs 34")
handrails must be "grippable" (x-section 1¼ to 2 inches) or (4 to 6¼ inches circumference)
handrail min 1½ inch from wall - shall "return" to wall
baluster spacing maximum 4 inches (6 inches @ bottom, measured from tread)

Doors (Interior and Exterior)

operation (not over landing or stairs) - max entry door stepdown 8¼ " - max interior door stepdown 1½" - fit - damage
rot - veneer - cracks - glass - lock/latch - hardware - weatherstrip - water penetration - racking - strike plates moved
entry door from attached garage fire rated - sealed - 3 inch curb - self closing
if attached garage has attic access, door must be present
sliding (patio) doors roll - lock - latch - screens - weather seal - damage - racking - water penetration
overhead garage door hardware - springs - damage - rot - rust - finger joints - hinges - tracks - glass - sagging

Windows

bedroom emergency egress min 20" w x 24" h (5.7 sf) <44" to floor & no-tool egress @ burglar bars & wdw function ok
glazing bead present & undamaged - caulk - evidence of water penetration - presence & cond of screens
insulated panes fogging - moisture - cracks - other evidence of broken seals
window @ bottom of staircase min ht 36" (or guardrail)
safety glass label @ doors (& sidelights & wdws w/in 24"), bottom of stair, <18" from flr & >9sq ft, (w/ >4" openings),
@ shower enclosures

Fireplace and Chimney

visible components and structure including lintel (back of facebrick sealed @ lintel)
firebox / firebrick - mortar - visible flue interior / lining - creosote / rain damage
operation of damper - hold open device req'd w gas served fireplace - outside combustion air
non-combustible, visually distinguishable hearth extension 16" f x 8"s (if opening >6sf, must be 20" f x 12"s)
flue clearance from combustibles 2" (1" if exterior chim) - termination 2' higher than x w/in 10' - 3' min from passthrough
gas shutoff valve w/in 4' of outlet, same room - (recommend glass firescreen to improve safety and heating efficiency)
mortar cap / coping - spark arrestor - rain cap

© 2002 Richard L. Burgess. All Rights Reserved
Procor Edison Publications

WALLS • CEILINGS & FLOORS • STAIRS • DOORS • WINDOWS • FIREPLACE & CHIMNEY

Attached Porches, Decks, Carports, (and their steps and balconies)

inspected for structural performance as to visible footings, joists,
deckings, railings, and attachment points, including drainage, water
penetration, damage, & applicable mechanical systems

Electrical Systems (Service Entrance and Panels)

SE cable insulation - drip loop - separation of conductors @ W/head

Main breaker amperage

minimum overhead clearance @ walkway 10' - driveway 12' - roadway 18'
SE cables clear to roof 3' if pitch >4 in 12 - 8' if pitch <4 in 12 - (18" @ eaves)

service riser >3' req's bracing or guy wires   4104.5

_____

service drop, W/head, mast securely fastened

branches or other dangers present

Service entrance cable

grounding electrode present and secure

main and sub panels securely fastened & weather-tight

AWG #_____

evidence of water penetration or corrosion

[ ]Aluminum   [ ]Copper

sub panels bonded and grounded

dead fronts in place - knockouts filled

MB & SE conductors

no panels in bathroom, toilet room, clothes closets   3905.1

compatible   Y   N

panels clear to openable windows, doors, balconies 3'

svc personnel clearance @ panel 36"f x 30"w

breakers & fuses permanently labeled for ampacity

> 6 throws for full off

no double-wired breakers - 240v breakers bridged

requires main breaker

evidence of arcing at busbars

test GFCI breakers, re-set

any conductors show evidence of burning, scorching, damage, oxidation, disconnected (or loose)

100a / 240v (3 wire) min if 6 or more 2-wire branch circuits present   4102.1
60a / 240v (3 wire) is min safe service, max 6 branch circuits
less than 60a - or - 120v-only (2 wire) service is reported as "Inadequate"

branch circuit wiring is   [ ] copper   [ ] aluminum-(brkrs labeled CU/AL ok)   [ ]combination
brkr/fuse vs conductor OK if oversized by 5 amps (up to 50 amps) or 10 amps (50 - 125 amps) in dedicated circuits only

---

Copper and aluminum **Service Entrance** conductor size chart & breaker/fuse rating compatibility   (w/ scale illustrations)

AWG	copper	aluminum
4	100 a	na
2	125 a	100 a
1	150 a	110 a
1/0	175 a	125 a
2/0	200 a	150 a
3/0	225 a	175 a
4/0	250 a	200 a
250kcmil	300 a	225 a
300kcmil		250 a
350kcmil	350 a	300 a

#4   #2   #1   #1/0   #2/0   #3/0

© 2002 Richard L. Burgess. All Rights Reserved
Procor Edison Publications

Electrical (service entrance and panels) con't

Cable labeling and usage

TW	(moisture resistant thermoplastic) for general use	NM	for dry indoor use only
NMC	for indoor damp & above ground outdoor use	UF	(waterproof) for outdoor & underground use
RW	(moisture resistant) for general wet locations	RH	(heat resistant) for general use
RH-RW / RHW	(moisture & heat resistant) general & wet loc.	RU	for general use
THW	(moisture & heat resistant thermoplastic) for general & wet locations		
BX	(metal sheathed / armored cable) special use & where code required		

Typical sizing of overcurrent protectors and conductors for listed equipment, each requiring dedicated circuits

Equipment	Voltage	AWG	Amperage	Equipment	Voltage	AWG	Amperage
kitchen range	240	6	50	built-in oven	240	8	40
cooktop	240	8	40	water heater	240	10	30
clothes dryer	240	8	40	food freezer	120	12	20
BI dishwasher	120	12	20	disposer	120	12	20
trash compactor	120	12	20	bathrm heater	120	12	20
furnace motor	120	12	20	well pump	120	12	20

copper and aluminum **branch circuit** conductor size chart & breaker/fuse rating compatibility (w/ scale illustrations)
(15 & 20 amp switches and receptacle devices w/ aluminum wire must be labeled CO/ALR if pigtailing is absent)

AWG	copper	aluminum
14	15 a	na
12	20 a	15 a
10	30 a	25 a
8	40 a	30 a
6	55-60 a	40 a
4	70 a	55-60 a
2	95-100 a	75-80 a
1	110 a	85-90 a
1/0	125 a	100 a
2/0	145-150 a	115-125 a

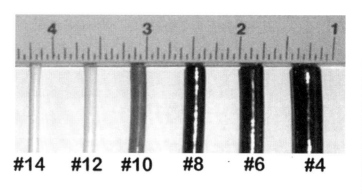

Branch Circuits (Connected Devices & Fixtures)

Aluminum branch circuit wiring - pre- '71 *15 & 20 amp switches & receptacles* were not marked if intended for copper only. If intended for copper or aluminum they were marked CU/AL. Since '71 NEC forbids use of aluminum wire with the CU/AL devices. ONLY DEVICES LABELED CO/ALR ARE ACCEPTABLE FOR ALUMINUM WIRING w/out PIGTAILS. NO STAB-BACK DEVICES ARE APPROVED FOR ALUMINUM. INSPECT FOR LOOSE, BURNED, OR OXIDIZED AL WIRING.

GFCI req @ all receptacles: bathroom, outdoor, garage, countertop, < 6' of any sink, @ crawlspace, unfinished basement.
GFCI circuits req @ swimming pool & spa tub pump motors, lights & receptacles.
GFCI receptacle Exceptions: not readily accessible, intended for permanent appliance or sump pump use, laundry room.
"Absence, improper installation, or improper operation of GFCI devices is a recognized hazard"

© 2002 Richard L. Burgess. All Rights Reserved
Procor Edison Publications

Electrical - Branch circuits - connected devices and fixtures, con't

all splices in j-box - no exposed wires - no wires on ground @ crawlspace - no unprotected wiring w/in 3' of attic access
conduit absent - securely fastened
appliances & electrical gutters bonded
(knob & tube wiring - fused neutral hazard? - System ground present? - integrity of visible insulation & porcelain knobs)

receptacles - power present - polarity - grounding - arcing - heat - secure - damage - covers
2-slot (ungrounded) receptacles @ bathroom or sink locations w/out secured & functional grounding pigtail is "hazardous"
convenience receptacles req'd @ HVAC locations
outdoor receptacles must be weatherproof, (even while in use if not cover-protected)
no appliance cords under rugs or thru walls, ceilings, cabinets, or doorways
no cord-connected (or pendent style) fixtures w/in 3' (horizontal) or 8' (vertical) from flood rim of tubs

wall & appliance switches operational - evidence of arcing - excessive heat - securely fastened - covers - on when up

fixtures, lighting devices, fans

operational - missing - not supported by wires - (attic vent fan functional)
all fluorescent (& recessed incandescent) closet fixtures located >6" from shelf space
surface mount incandescent closet fixtures located 12" from shelf space & must be enclosed

Heating, Ventilation, and Air Conditioning Systems
Heating Equipment

	UNIT 1	UNIT 2	UNIT 3	UNIT 4

Type: forced air - hot water - steam
     gravity/convective / resistance
     other

Energy: nat gas - LP gas - oil
     coal - electric - other

condition of controls - master shutoff present
blowers / belts clean - secure - quiet
blower compartment sealed
filter provided - clean?
thermostat level - secure - damaged
bi-metal dirty - mercury bulb cracked

     If blower fails to operate for "on" check indoor unit disconnect & access panel safety switch

© 2002 Richard L. Burgess. All Rights Reserved
Procor Edison Publications

190

Gas furnace	UNIT 1	UNIT 2	UNIT 3	UNIT 4

proper support & clearances
pilot light - color - adjustment - thermocouple
wires burned or damaged
gas leaks - (esp. at gas control valve & fittings)
burner condition (corrosion - scaling - rust)
heat exchanger scale - holes - rust
flame impingement - uplifting - color - drawdown - dance
tarry black soot @ registers - exchanger failure?

vent type - min 3 inch diameter - condition (2104)
vent - 1 inch to combustibles - 5 feet vertical ht from collar (exc induced draft)
vent terminates 2 feet above roof (1 ft ok if pitch < 6 in 12)
vent terminates 2 feet above any vertical surface w/in 8 ft
approved vent cap
no sgl wall connector in concealed/unoccupied/attic space
vent req's 4 inch thimble @ passthroughs
min ¼ inch rise in 1 foot slope
power vent starts at call for heat
SPILLAGE @ DRAFT DIVERTER

If burners fail to ignite, check thermostat set to "heat", disconnect switch, gas shutoff valve, manual re-sets

availabiltiy of combustion & draft air
independent blower control working
blower noise and vibration
no short cycling w full demand
gas branch shutoff valve w/in 6 feet (leaks)
gas branch line black iron/steel (or stainless) (2605.1)
Connector epoxy coat or stainless, 3 ft max (no brass)
no copper or connectors through wall, floor, ceiling

Condensing furnaces (Thermostat advance not more than 3 degrees above room temperature).

requires induced draft blower - exhaust must be dedicated
plastic pipe to top of masonry chimney
no rusty pipe at attic or roof

requires condensate drain provision (inc proper floor drain if hole-in-slab)

Electric furnaces	UNIT 1	UNIT 2	UNIT 3	UNIT 4

wires burned or disconnected
proper support
blower begins quickly
amperage to each element (allow for sequencers)

If electric furnace conductors are inaccessible, perform temperature differential check at supply / return.
1 element/ 15-20°F; 2 elements/ 25-30°F; >2 elements/ 25-40°F

© 2002 Richard L. Burgess. All Rights Reserved
Procor Edison Publications

FURNACES (CON'T)

7

Oil furnace & boiler   UNIT 1   UNIT 2   UNIT 3

      Homeowner is responsible for environmental concerns related to underground oil tanks

holes evident in combustion chamber
burner head burned off
heat exchanger shows excess carbon or scale
fuel tank damaged - seeping - secured - gauge present
indoor fuel tank > 7 feet from burner - outside fill provision
oil line damaged - loose - broken - (vulnerable)
oil line filter & shutoff provided
barometric damper & combustion air blower ok
oil burner motor operates
independent blower control

Hot water & steam

boiler leaking
relief valves and pressure gauges present
steam system req water level gauge (full - empty ?)
boiler drafting properly
circulating pump operates - no leaks @ shaft seal
expansion tank properly located and supported
equipment room ventilation adequate

```
┌─────────────────────────────────────────────────────────────────┐
│                                                                   │
│                                                                   │
│                                                                   │
│                                                                   │
└─────────────────────────────────────────────────────────────────┘
```

Heat pump   (NOTE: Hybrid heat pump/gas furnace systems will be encountered)

Call for cool, check as A/C.   Not to be operated in cooling mode if outdoor temperature is below 60 degrees.
Call for heat.   Not to be operated in heating mode if outdoor temperature is above 80 degrees.

                          UNIT 1   UNIT 2   UNIT 3   UNIT 4
outdoor & indoor units functioning
(check disconnects - thermostat set to "heat")
indoor unit vapor line should be hot at "heat" setting

set thermostat to "emergency heat", provide call for heat
only auxiliary strips should heat

      Cooling check verifies compressor. Operate heat pump only long enough to verify reversing
      valve. Thermostat set to "emergency heat" locks out compressor to allow auxiliary heat check.

```
┌─────────────────────────────────────────────────────────────────┐
│                                                                   │
│                                                                   │
└─────────────────────────────────────────────────────────────────┘
```

Cooling equipment

      Approx 525 sq. ft. of living space (+ or - 100 sq. ft. depending on type of const) per ton (12,000 btu/hr)
          Window units maximum allowable cord length 10 ft., no extensions.
type: refrigeration - heat pump   UNIT 1   UNIT 2   UNIT 3   UNIT 4
      evaporative - absorption

© 2002 Richard L. Burgess. All Rights Reserved
Procor Edison Publications

192

Cooling equipment (con't)   UNIT 1   UNIT 2   UNIT 3   UNIT 4

supply / return air temperature differential (15 - 20) @ registers & plenum

<u>primary condensate drain lines</u>
¾ " dia - slope - condition - insulation 1st 12 ft - trapped
termination outside - flr drain - plmbg fxtr
sump - sealed vent stack where permitted.

<u>secondary condensate drain lines & pan</u>
¾ " dia - slope - condition - conspicuous loc / dripping / pan secure

<u>indoor unit (evaporator)</u>
shutoff
secure mounting - proper mat'l of feet in safety pan - case corroded
insulation @ suction line
suction line frosted over (low refrig or restricted airflow?)
coil frosted over (low refrig or restricted airflow?)

<u>outdoor unit (condenser)</u>
clearance - air circ - debris - foliage - fins - shutoff
location - level - elevation - damage - leaks - wiring
fan blades damaged - rusted - motor bearings/noise
short cycle
kinks in refrigerant lines - bubbles in sight glass
coil blows warm - suction line cool - liquid line warm or ambient

If blower, condenser fan, and compressor are inoperable, check thermostat for "cool", both disconnects, & breaker.

<u>Evaporative coolers</u>   UNIT 1   UNIT 2   UNIT 3

identification as 1 or 2 speed
electrical pigtail conn @ motor secure
pump - spider tubes - tube clips - bleeder system
water supply line & float bracket
backflow prevention - 1" airgap between discharge (@ float) & water level
blower \ squirrel cage - damage - rust - deterioration - corrosion - deposits
panels - trays - housing - roof frame - jacks (support)
operating sound - vibration

Ducts & vents

materials - condition - routing
all A/C ducts insulated @ unconditioned areas
good flow @ all registers
no gas pipes - plumbing vents - Romex - or J-boxes inside plenum
(wire ok to run short dimension thru stud-joist cavity used as plenum)
plenums properly sealed (X-section 72 sq in per ton A/C)

© 2002 Richard L. Burgess. All Rights Reserved
Procor Edison Publications

193

Plumbing supply system & fixtures   [ ]copper   [ ]plastic   [ ]ferrous   [ ]lead   [ ]brass   [ ]combo

sinks	kitch	Mbath 1	bath 2	bath 3	bath 4	bath 5	bar	other
veg sprayer low pressure - disconn - leak								
faucets or swing spout leak @ stems								
stops broken - drips when off								
sink chipped - damaged - rusted - cracked								
supply connections under sink leaking - corroded								
damaged caused by leaks								
undersink shutoffs present - undamaged - leaks								
1 inch air gap provided - flow rate - hot / cold								
strainers - waterhammer								

bathtub / shower
tub cracked - chipped - damaged - rusted - leaks
tiles loose - damaged - missing - grout maint req'd
shower walls soft or damaged - safety glass label
plumbing loose in walls - handles damaged/missing
stops broken - leak @ stem - drip when off
diverter works
1 inch air gap provided - flow rate - hot / cold
strainers - waterhammer - corrosion

separate shower
32"x32" min (3210.1) - dam 2-9 inches h (3211.1)
tiles loose - damaged - missing - grout maint req'd
leaks at pan (walls/carpet/crwlspace) - walls soft or damaged - safety glass label
plumbing loose in walls - handles damaged or missing
stops broken - leak @ stem - drip when off
flow rate - hot / cold - strainers - waterhammer - corrosion

commodes
30"w x 21"f clearance (307.2) - caulk to floor
cracks - secure mounting @ flr & tank - leaks - rust
fill & flush valves - shutoff - evidence of wax seal failure

hoseblbs
handles damaged or missing - drips when off or @ stem
loose - corrosion - anti-siphon devices

laundry supply
handles damaged or missing - drips when off or @ stem
loose - corrosion - evidence of leaks @ sheetrock / subfloor
stops -hot / cold

Drains, wastes, vents   Type: [ ]plastic   [ ]brass   [ ]iron   [ ]other   [ ]combo

vents: min 1 ¼" dia - term >6" above passthru - term >12" from vertical surfaces - term 2' higher than or 5' horiz
          to openings - term >3' from property line - no term in attic or crawlspace - plastic requires paint @ roof

	kitch	Mbath 1	bath 2	bath 3	bath 4	bath 5	bar	other
P trap missing (S trap forbidden & usually not vented)								
traps level - tailpiece max 24" (3101.3)								
epoxy, glue, tape, other makeshift repairs								
leaks or damage caused by leaks								
drain slowly - drainstops functioning								

© 2002 Richard L. Burgess. All Rights Reserved
Procor Edison Publications

PLUMBING SUPPLY & DRAINS   10

194

Water heating equipment UNIT 1 UNIT 2 UNIT 3

capacity - date of mfr - energy source
dip tube notice ('93-'96 Smith - Bradford White - State - Rheem - Amer Water Htr)
full bore valve at cold inlet - connections reversed
leaks or corrosion @ tank & fittings
dielectric fittings in use - sacrificial anode present
T&P valve ¾" - no trap, threads, or reduction - outside & safe exhaust - gravity drain
broken / missing parts, covers, controls
safety pan & drain and permanent stair or ladder @ attic locations
18" up & damage protection @ garage locations
(electric heater) elements operate - condition of wiring - in-sight disconnect (4601.7)

gas water heaters
not located in bedroom, bathroom, or so accessible (except direct vent)
support & clearances (nominally 6" top & sides, 18" front, see labeling)
adequate combustion & draft air
gas branch line black iron/steel or stainless - no leaks (esp @ gas valve)
gas shutoff w/in 6 ft - connector epoxy or stainless, (no brass)
pilot color - height - thermocouple fully engulfed
burner & compartment rust - scale - corrosion
flame color
vent type - min 3 inch diameter - condition (2104)
vent 1 inch to combustibles - 5 feet vertical height from collar
vent terminates 2 feet above roof (1 ft ok if pitch < 6 in 12)
vent terminates 2 feet above any vertical surface w/in 8 ft
approved vent cap
no sgl wall connector in concealed/unoccupied/attic space
flues req 4 inch thimble @ passthroughs
min ¼ inch rise in 1 foot slope
SPILLAGE @ DRAFT DIVERTER

Hydro-therapy equipment

operation - jet ports move ok - air intakes adjust - leaks
pump provides pressure & aeration
electric timer >5' from flood rim
GFCI protective circuit present
disconnect present (plug ok)

Appliances

dishwasher
door gasket - secure mounting - trays - racks - rollers - rust - door springs
latch - decor panels - skirts - soap door - heating elements
discharge hose backflow prevention - hose ahead of disposer inlet
overflow float switch - cord 36" to 48" & not vulnerable to phys damage (or conduit attachment)
noise - vibration - leaks

food waste disposer
splash guard - grinding components - case - mounting - noise/vibration - leaks
cord 18" to 36" & not vulnerable to phys damage (or conduit attachment)

© 2002 Richard L. Burgess. All Rights Reserved
Procor Edison Publications

WATER HEATER • SPA TUB • DISHWASHER • DISPOSER 11

range hood
light & fan switches - noise - speed - vibration - filter
smooth single wall steel / stainless / copper
not to terminate @ attic or crawlspace - requires backdraft damper (1802.1)

range / oven / cooktop
broken or missing knobs - elements - drip pans - panels
signal lights - elements/burners
report (gas) branch line material (iron/steel)
report connector material (epoxy/stainless) (no brass) vulnerable to phys damage?
shutoff w/in 6' - max conn length 3' (range or dryer max 6') no leaks
burners min 24" to upper cabinets (1804.1)
pilots - gas tunnels - lighting ease - electric service

oven
broken or missing knobs - handles - glass panels - lights & covers
door gasket - close tight - door springs - latch - mounting - anti tip
elements/burners & thermostat sensor securely supported
operation - lighting - flame condition - (gas) shutoff w/in 6' - no leaks
thermostat accuracy +/- 25 deg @ 350 deg
clock - timer

microwave cooking equipment (built-in)
broken or missing knobs - handles - glass panels
secure mounting - cooklight - clock/timer - heat water
condition of door seals (leak detector [y] [n] results_____)

trash compactor
general condition - mounting - drawer operation & latch - controls
deodorant spray - operation - noise - vibration - cord 36" to 48" - ram works

bathroom exhaust fans and heaters
sound - speed vibration - airflow - mounting
no exhaust to attic or crawlspace - exterior termination requires backflow damper
(heaters) secure mounting - proximity to combustibles or danger (injury) zones - operate (electric)

whole house vacuum system
general condition of main unit - suction @ ea outlet, no leaks - elec svc - switches & controls - exhaust location

garage door operators
operation - secure mounting - auto reverse - manual lock hold open device - release catch & cord
1/4 hp req w/ 8' door - 1/3 hp req w/ 16' door - test radio remote controllers if available

doorbell & chimes
condition of visible parts (incl transformer) - operation @ all pushbuttons

dryer vents
exhaust outdoors - rigid metal (no screwthru) - <25' run (- bends) - damper/rain hood
no flexi hose in concealed locations - terminate >3' from property line

other built-in appliances / notes

© 2002 Richard L. Burgess. All Rights Reserved
Procor Edison Publications

RANGE HOOD • RANGE/OVEN/COOKTOP • M/W OVEN • COMPACTOR
BATHFANS • CTRL VAC • GAR DR OPENER • CHIME • DRYER VENT

lawn sprinklers

make & model of controller - # stations - condition & mounting of controller, wiring, visible components
shutoff valve and anti-siphon device (backflow preventer, higher than highest spray head) present
manual operation of each zone/station
report ea zone's operation - coverage (& non-coverage) areas - evidence of surface leaks - flow/pressure @ ea head

swimming pools & equipment

type of construction

Minimum pool dimension for safe dive-board or platform - (depth 9' for horizontal distance of 18')-(trade)
condition of pool surfaces, (cracks, deterioration, level) - (caution: painted f/glass hides repairs)
condition of tiles - copings - decks - slope -drainage
condition of slides - steps - diving boards - etc
condition of drains - skimmers - valves - (skimmer & liner should not be cracked)
presence, condition, function of pool lights & GFCI
condition & function of pump motors - controls - sweeps - (bubbles indicate leak on suction side)
proper wiring & circuit protection
condition & function of heater, (inc gas line & conn mat'ls, shutoff valve, leaks)
observe external grounding of pump motor, blowers, etc (if visible)
cond of filter tank, pressure gauge, above ground leaks (all filters req press gauge)
presence & cond of fences, gates, enclosures (self close - swing out - 48"h - 2" @ bottom)
overhead wire clearance 22' (14' dive board/platform) ok-n (or >10' horiz from pool walls)

spas
proper wiring & circuit protection
pump - filter - heater - jets - blower oper properly
leaks @ pump strainer or shaft
vibration - noise
filter pressure gauge present
leaks @ filter or connections

© 2002 Richard L. Burgess. All Rights Reserved
Procor Edison Publications

Swimming Pool & Equipment (con't.)

<u>general — electrical</u>

all 120v circuits & equipt must be GFCI
all 240v circuits separate & grounded {& GFCI if pool/spa was built later than 1999, (1999 NEC @ 680-bd)}
corded equip max cord length 3' w #12 gd   NEC   680-7
1 GFI receptacle req <6'6" high, >10' & <20' fr water   680-6a2
no receptacles <10' fr water - wall switches must be >5' fr water   680-6a2
pump equip not permitted < 5' fr pool, if less than 10', twistlock recep & GFI req   680-6a1

<u>lighting outlets</u>
no lighting <5' horiz to water unless >12' above   680-6b1
All lights GFCI if <10' from water   680-6b2
(existing secure fixtures ok <5' horiz if >5' vert & GFCI)   680-6b1
(indoor pool) lights over water min 7'6" h, GFCI, enclosed   680-6b1

<u>grounding</u>
bond all metal <5' from pool w #8 insul gd conductor   680-22a
PVC to underwater lights req #8 insul gd conductor   680-20b1

<u>underwater lighting</u>
Listed for pool, GFCI   680-20a1
min 18" below normal water level   680-20a3
J-boxes min 8" above water, 4" above deck   680-b5
wet niche fixture bonded, secured to shell w locking
         device requiring tool for removal   680-20b3
PVC to shell req #8 insulated copper term @ fixture, potted   680-20b1

<u>hot tubs & spas</u>
bond all metal w/in 5 'w threaded conduit, #8 copper or
         metal to metal on common frame   680-40
In-sight disconnect required   CABO   4601.7
GFCI receptacle required >5', <10' fr inside spa wall   680-41a1
all receptacles w/in 10' must be GFCI   680-41a2
no receptacles <5' fr inside spa wall   680-41a1
light fixture if < 7'6" above water requires GFCI   680-41b1
Wall switches must be >5' from water   680-41c

Outbuildings
structural performance & water penetration - compliance w/ electrical, plumbing, HVAC standards as in primary structure

Outdoor Cooking Equipment   report energy source_____
condition of controls - handles - burner bars - grills - case - rotisserie - heat diffuser - mounting >24" to combustibles branch line
black iron or galv steel (galv steel must be factory wrapped for underground use)
connector epoxy or stainless, (no brass) - shutoff valve <3' - flexi hose <15' and listed & labeled for gas use

Gas Lines
Gas lines are only inspected at points of use, where readily accessible.
Full scientific evaluation of gas service supply system performance is beyond the scope of a visual inspection. odor of gas at meter
or gas fittings & control valves @:furnace - water heater - range/oven - fireplace - BBQ - coach lite

© 2002 Richard L. Burgess. All Rights Reserved
Procor Edison Publications

Water Wells   "Scope of evaluation of private wells during visual inspection is limited."
"Recommend all private wells be tested regularly for coliform, bacteria,
hardness, chemicals, and debris"

type of pump_____   type of storage arrangement_____
(submersible-deep, jet-shallow or deep, piston-motor always above, but piston assembly may be in-well)

operation of at least 2 fixtures simultaneously	ok-n
pressure switches cycle normally	ok-n
general condition of visible & accessible equipt. & components	ok-n
wiring & circuit protection	ok-n
condition of well head inc drainage	ok-n

pressure settings normally 20-60 psi.   *air absorption causes waterlogging & therefore shortcycling*

Septic System   report observed condition of accessible or visible components

operation and functional flow @ plumbing	ok-n
evidence of effluent seepage @ surface near tanks, fields, pits or beds	ok-n
is there adequate site drainage?	ok-n

if known, proximity to wells, cisterns, water supply lines, streams, ponds, lakes, sharp slopes or breaks, easement lines, property lines, soil absorption systems, swimming pools, sprinkler systems, foundation walls.

Minimum Safe Distances for Septic System Components

From	To:	Septic tank	Soil AbsorptionSys	Water Tight Sewer Pipe
water wells		50' *	100' **	20'
underground cisterns		50' *	100' **	20'
pump suction pipes		50' *	100' **	20'
public water supply lines		5'	10'	5'
streams, ponds, lakes		50' *	75'	20'
foundation walls (struct)		5'	15	0
property lines		10'	10'	0

*if influent & effluent lines are constructed w solvent weld or watertight sewer pipe, holding or septic tanks
designed for submergence (concrete, reinforced, or equal) may be w/in 20' of ponds, cisterns or water wells.
**minimum distance from public water wells to soil absorption system is 150'.

---

operation of system components	ok-n
presence of visible access to tanks	ok-n

location of drainfield, if known:
operation of aerators, dosing pumps, if present & visible   ok-n
proper wiring

Security Systems
type of system: perimeter - interior traps - video - intrusion/fire/medical (fire: smoke - heat - ionization - combo)
hard wired - RF - combo - key/keypad - monitored - battery backup
location of control panels - keypads - sensors - sirens - interconnects

---

Fire Protection Equipment   (smoke - heat - ionization - combo)   functional alarm operation tested? [y] [n]
"...one (detector) in each bedroom and one in each hall that leads to a bedroom", minimum one per floor.

© 2002 Richard L. Burgess. All Rights Reserved
Procor Edison Publications

SAMPLE REPORT FORM

Regarding the use of report forms, each inspector must follow exactly the rules which apply in his state. The following is a reprint of an actual inspection report written by this author in June of 2000. The subject property was a 10 year old lakefront home, with just under 5200 square feet of living space. The actual inspection took about 5 hours. Drive time and report writing added about 3 hours to that. As reflected in the body of the report, the client hired a swimming pool specialist and a pest control licensee in addition to this inspector.

This inspection was performed under rules set forth by the Texas Real Estate Commission, which also promulgates the report form.

PROPERTY INSPECTION REPORT

Prepared for: INSPECTION CLIENT _____
(Name of Client)

Concerning: SAMPLE ADDRESS _____
(Address or Other Identification of Inspected Property)

By: RICHARD BURGESS (TREC 4615) _____ 00-00-00
(Name and License Number of Inspector) (Date)

_____
(Name, License Number and Signature of Sponsoring Inspector, if required)

The inspection of the property listed above must be performed in compliance with the Texas Real Estate Commission (TREC).

The inspection is of conditions which are present and visible at the time of the inspection, and all of the equipment is operated in normal modes. The inspector must indicate which items are in need of repair or are not functioning and will report on all applicable items required by TREC rules.

This report is intended to provide you with information concerning the condition of the property at the time of inspection. Please read the report carefully. If any item is unclear, you should request the inspector to provide clarification.

It is recommended that you obtain as much history as is available concerning this property. This historical information may include copies of any seller's disclosures, previous inspection or engineering reports, reports performed for or by relocation companies, municipal inspection departments, lenders, insurers, and appraisers. You should attempt to determine whether repairs, renovation, remodeling, additions, or other such activities have taken place at this property.

Property conditions change with time and use. Since this report is provided for the specific benefit of the client(s), secondary readers of this information should hire a licensed inspector to perform an inspection to meet their specific needs and to obtain current information concerning this property.

ADDITIONAL INFORMATION PROVIDED BY INSPECTOR

This inspection has not been of a formal, destructive, or engineering type. All components were judged indirectly by the visible condition of the surfaces open to view, without moving any item which may have been blocking the view. The inspector did not employ any instruments to aid in the inspection, disassemble any component, (such as would be required for full evaluation of the integrity of a heat exchanger), conduct destructive or environmental testing, or remove wall or floor coverings to detect hidden damage unless otherwise noted in the report. The visual inspection method employed will generally produce a competent first-impression assessment of the apparent condition of the inspection items and components, provided refurbishing or repairs have not been performed which might mask the visible distress patterns which would be produced by defects. Because the inspection procedure is visual only, and was not intended to be diagnostic or technically exhaustive, an inherent residual risk remains that undiscovered problems may exist or develop. This report is an opinion of apparent performance, and not engineering fact. *No guarantee or warranty exists that all defects have been found, nor that PRO-TEX Property inspections will pay for the repair of any defects not discovered.*

Any unresolved dispute regarding this inspection shall be submitted to the BBB for binding arbitration. Both parties waive their right to bring suit in court. Acceptance of and payment for this inspection document is an agreement by the client to all the terms, conditions, and limitations found herein.

PRO-TEX PROPERTY INSPECTIONS – XXXX MAIN ST SUITE 100, HOUSTON, TX 77077   PH: 281-XXX-XXXX
Building codes, environmental conditions, design adequacy, efficiency, value, & habitability are beyond the scope of this inspection.

Promulgated by the Texas Real Estate Commission (TREC) P.O. Box 12188, Austin, TX 78711-2188, 1-800-250-8732 or (512) 459-6544 (http:\\www.trec.state.tx.us) REI 7A-0

Report Identification: Address / Client Name / inv #0725   Page 2 of 7 plus 3 addendum pages

Additional pages may be attached to this report. Read them very carefully. This report may not be complete without the attachments. If an item is present in the property but is not inspected, the "NI" column will be checked and an explanation is necessary. Comments may be provided by the inspector whether or not an item is deemed in need of repair.

I = Inspected   NI = Not Inspected   NP = Not Present   R = Not Functioning or In Need of Repair

I	NI	NP	R	Inspection Item

I. STRUCTURAL SYSTEMS

■ ☐ ☐ ☐   **A. Foundations** (If all crawl space areas are not inspected, provide an explanation.)
Comments (An opinion on performance is mandatory.):

All soils compress, and all foundations are subject to settlement. When settlement is slight, uniform, or accommodated in the design, it is of little concern. When a foundation settles unevenly, (differential settlement), it introduces stresses which can weaken the building.

Foundations may have been installed out-of-level, but factors other than an out-of-level condition are good indicators of subsequent foundation movement. These include visible cracks at the foundation's perimeter grade beam or floor planes, window and door frames which are out of square, roof rafters detaching from ridgeboard nailing points, and interior or exterior walls and ceilings which display signs of stress deflection or cracking.

Evidence found supports the opinion that foundation performance is satisfactory, as intended by design. That evidence includes: 1. The absence of cracks at visible portions of the foundation's perimeter grade beam faces and interior tile floor surfaces, 2. The absence of significant racking at door frames, 3. Secure attachment of rafters at ridgeboard nailing points, 4. The absence of significant stress deflection at interior and exterior wall surfaces. 5. Departure from dead-level of the foundation's horizontal floor plane measuring well within normal range. (See addendum pages 1 and 2)

Stress or shrinkage cracks of the type found at the garage floor, (tightly closed, with no evidence of differential settlement), are common. The steel cable tendons as used in this slab generally can help to provide the required strength or stiffness for satisfactory foundation performance, even in the presence of moderately compromised monolithic integrity. This foundation does appear to be satisfactorily performing at this time. (Note: The builder of this home is known to often install piers below the slab at the time of construction, a practice which yields generally superior slab-on-grade performance. It is impossible to determine whether this home was so built without consulting appropriate records).

This is not an engineering report, but is only an opinion based on observation of conditions known to be related to foundation performance, using the knowledge and experience of the inspector.

Report Identification: Address / Client Name / inv #0725   Page 3 of 7 plus 3 addendum pages

I = Inspected   NI = Not Inspected   NP = Not Present   R = Not Functioning or In Need of Repair

I	NI	NP	R	Inspection Item

☐ ☐ ☐ ■ **B. Grading and Drainage**
Comments: Downspouts require splashblocks to prevent soil erosion and the accumulation of standing water at foundation wall locations.

☐ ☐ ☐ ■ **C. Roof Covering** (If the roof is inaccessible, report the method used to inspect.)
Comments: Inspected from ground level with binoculars. Covering is composition shingles in generally good condition. Tree branches in direct contact with roof components at the east corner should be trimmed well back.

■ ☐ ☐ ☐ **D. Roof Structure and Attic** (If the attic is inaccessible, report the method used to inspect.)
Comments: Insulation at attic floor averages 10-12 inches in depth with good Coverage.

■ ☐ ☐ ☐ **E. Walls (Interior and Exterior)**
Comments: Exterior "stucco" finish at front entry area was not positively identified by this inspector as natural or synthetic. The manufacturer of a synthetic stucco known as EIFS has been the target of class-action litigation for moisture-related problems, especially when the product is installed over wood framing. It is recommended that the client obtain written disclosure from the builder or seller regarding the type of stucco in use. More information can be found at www.eifsinfo.com   See addendum page 3.

(Note: Exterior trim paint at the SE staircase window is peeling slightly).

☐ ☐ ☐ ■ **F. Ceilings and Floors**
Comments: Riser (height) dimensions of the stairs at the garage entry door (into the east hall) differ by more than the maximum allowable 3/8 inch, a tripping hazard. Step-down at the wood-floored foyer is not visually distinguishable from the living room flooring, a tripping hazard. (See comments regarding cracks in garage floor at **Foundations**).

☐ ☐ ☐ ■ **G. Doors (Interior and Exterior)**
Comments: Top latch hardware components are missing at French doors in the kitchen. Garage entry doors into living spaces lack the self-closing mechanisms required by some building codes.

☐ ☐ ☐ ■ **H. Windows**
Comments: Exterior caulk repairs are needed. Limestone sill at NW garage window is installed with reverse slope, creating vulnerability to water penetration into the wall cavity. No evidence of water penetration was found.

☐ ☐ ☐ ■ **I. Fireplace / Chimney**
Comments: Permanent hold-open device at damper, required with gas log-set in place, is absent. The installation of a glass firescreen is recommended to improve safety and heating efficiency.

Report Identification: Address / Client Name / inv #0725   Page 4 of 7 plus 3 addendum pages

I = Inspected   NI = Not Inspected   NP = Not Present   R = Not Functioning or In Need of Repair

I	NI	NP	R	Inspection item

☐ ☐ ☐ ■   **J. Porches, Decks and Carports (Attached)**
Comments: Baluster spacing at rear deck is greater than the maximum permitted 4 inches, a hazard to small children.

II. ELECTRICAL SYSTEMS

☐ ☐ ☐ ■   **A. Service Entrance and Panels**
Comments: Main breaker is 200 amps. Service entrance is #4/0 AWG aluminum cable, compatible with breaker rating up through 200 amps. Auxiliary panel (sub-panel) knock-outs do not fully enclose breakers, exposing electrified interior panel components, a shock hazard. Service cables serving sub-panel enter main panel box without the required protective grommet, a hazardous condition. (Note: Pool-related equipment was not inspected, by agreement).

☐ ☐ ☐ ■   **B. Branch Circuits - Connected Devices and Fixtures** (Report as in need of repair the lack of ground fault circuit protection where required.):
Comments: Branch circuit wiring is copper. GFCI device serving indoor spa-tub is wired with a faulty ground connection. Absence, improper operation, or improper installation of GFCI devices at required locations is a recognized hazard.

Both receptacles in the laundry room and the receptacle at the SE wall of the gameroom are also wired with faulty ground connections. All 4 receptacles at master bathroom sinks are loose in the wall. High-voltage (outdoor) wire splices serving the front yard garden light transformer are not enclosed within a junction box as required.

Pool-related equipment was not inspected.

III. HEATING, VENTILATION AND AIR CONDITIONING SYSTEMS

■ ☐ ☐ ☐   **A. Heating Equipment**
Type and Energy Source: Zoned (3) gas fired forced air furnaces with induced draft venting and electronic pilots.
Comments: Although no significant rust or scale was visible at burner or heat exchanger areas, full evaluation of heat exchanger integrity requires dismantling of the furnaces, and is beyond the scope of this visual inspection.

☐ ☐ ☐ ■   **B. Cooling Equipment**
Type and Energy Source: Zoned (3) electric refrigeration / forced air systems.
Comments: <u>For south (attic) unit</u>: Suction (refrigerant) line insulation is missing for first 12 inches from evaporator case, and the resulting condensation is dripping onto the attic floor. <u>For north and middle (attic) units</u>: Secondary condensate (safety pan) drain lines are not routed for continuous positive

Report Identification: Address / Client Name / inv #0725   Page 5 of 7 plus 3 addendum pages

I = Inspected   NI = Not Inspected   NP = Not Present   R = Not Functioning or In Need of Repair

I	NI	NP	R	Inspection Item

Cooling Equipment, con't

gravity drain as required. <u>For NE (outdoor) condensing unit</u>: Electrical conduit is installed so as to be vulnerable to water penetration at the wall-side. <u>For SW (outdoor) condensing unit</u>:   Electrical; conduit lacks the required "drip loop" configuration, and its termination at the condenser case is not properly secured. Supply/return air temperature differential was within normal range for all 3 zones.

■ ☐ ☐ ☐ **C. Ducts and Vents**
Comments:

IV. PLUMBING SYSTEM

☐ ☐ ☐ ■ **A. Water Supply System and Fixtures**
Comments: Supply lines are copper. Tankless "instant" heater at kitchen sink did not deliver water flow. Commode at center powder room is inadequately secured to the floor. Tank at East powder room commode is inadequately secured in place on the bowl. Shower enclosure at east 2nd floor guest bathroom requires grout repairs to prevent water penetration into the wall cavity. Outdoor faucets lack the required anti-siphon devices.

☐ ☐ ☐ ■ **B. Drains, Wastes, Vents**
Comments: Drain stopper at center 2nd floor guest bathroom sink is not functioning.

☐ ☐ ☐ ■ **C. Water Heating Equipment** (Report as in need of repair those conditions specifically listed as recognized hazards by TREC rules.)
Energy Source: Two 50 gallon gas fired heaters were manufactured in '94.
Comments: Appliance gas-control valve at east (attic) unit is leaking gas, a hazardous condition.

■ ☐ ☐ ☐ **D. Hydro-Therapy Equipment**
Comments: See comments regarding GFCI protective device at **Branch Circuits**.

V. APPLIANCES

☐ ☐ ☐ ■ **A. Dishwasher**
Comments: No provision for the prevention of discharge-hose backflow is present. Springs do not adequately support the weight of the door.

■ ☐ ☐ ☐ **B. Food Waste Disposer**
Comments:

Report Identification: Address / Client Name / inv #0725   Page 6 of 7 plus 3 addendum pages

I = Inspected   NI = Not Inspected   NP = Not Present   R = Not Functioning or In Need of Repair

I	NI	NP	R	Inspection Item

■ ☐ ☐ ☐ **C. Range Hood**
Comments:

■ ☐ ☐ ☐ **D. Ranges / Ovens / Cooktops**
Comments:

■ ☐ ☐ ☐ **E. Microwave Cooking Equipment**
Comments:

☐ ☐ ■ ☐ **F. Trash Compactor**
Comments:

☐ ☐ ☐ ■ **G. Bathroom Exhaust Fans**
Comments: Fans at 2nd floor exhaust into the attic space, an improper location. All bathroom fans must exhaust to an outdoor location.

☐ ☐ ■ ☐ **H. Whole House Vacuum Systems**
Comments:

☐ ☐ ☐ ■ **I. Garage Door Operators**
Comments: Driveway gate motor linkage is damaged. Gate does not operate.

■ ☐ ☐ ☐ **J. Door Bell and Chimes**
Comments:

☐ ☐ ☐ ■ **K. Dryer Vents**
Comments: Dryer exhausts into the garage, an improper location.

☐ ■ ☐ ☐ **L. Other Built-in Appliances**
Comments:

Report Identification: Address / Client Name / inv #0725   Page 7 of 7 plus 3 addendum pages

I = Inspected   NI = Not Inspected   NP = Not Present   R = Not Functioning or In Need of Repair

I	NI	NP	R	Inspection Item

VI. OPTIONAL SYSTEMS

☐ ☐ ☐ ■   **A. Lawn Sprinklers**

Comments: Control panel is 9-station XXX brand. Timer functions were not tested. Low-voltage electrical conduit at NW garage wall is damaged. Anti-siphon backflow preventer and main system water shutoff are present as required.

Station 1 serves front lawn & gardens *(sprays across front entry walk and public walkway).*
Station 2 serves front lawn & gardens
Station 3 serves front lawn
Station 4 serves front lawn
Station 5 serves SE property line *(2 pop-up heads inadequately deployed).*
Station 6 serves east yard.
Station 7 serves pool-area lawn and flower beds *(1 pop-up head inadequately deployed).*
Station 8 serves lawn & flower beds at north pool area *(1 head soaks north bedroom window).*
Station 9 serves east side lawn & flower beds

☐ ■ ☐ ☐   **B. Swimming Pools and Equipment**

Comments: Pool-related equipment was not inspected, by agreement.

☐ ☐ ☐ ■   **E. Gas Lines**

Comments: Gas lines were only inspected at points of use, where readily accessible. Persistent odor of gas was noted at front entry porch, in area of gas-fired coach lights. Exact source of gas odor was not determined. See comments regarding gas leak at **Water Heating Equipment**.

☐ ■ ☐ ☐   **H. Security Systems**

Comments: Functional alarm operation was not tested, by agreement.

☐ ■ ☐ ☐   **I. Fire Protection Equipment**

Comments: Smoke alarms were found at all required locations. Functional alarm operation was not tested.

PRO-TEX PROPERTY INSPECTIONS / RICHARD BURGESS / 281-XXX-XXXX
XXXXX MAIN STREET, SUITE 100, HOUSTON, TEXAS 77077
TREC PROFESSIONAL REAL ESTATE INSPECTOR LICENSE 4615
www.protexusa.com

PRO-TEX PROPERTY INSPECTIONS
XXXXX MAIN STREET, SUITE 100
HOUSTON, TX 77077
281-XXX-XXXX
www.protexusa.com

ALL SOILS COMPRESS, AND ALL FOUNDATIONS ARE SUBJECT TO SETTLEMENT. WHEN SETTLEMENT IS SLIGHT, UNIFORM, OR ANTICIPATED IN THE DESIGN, IT IS OF LITTLE CONCERN. WHEN A FOUNDATION SETTLES UNEVENLY, (DIFFERENTIAL SETTLEMENT), IT INTRODUCES STRESSES WHICH CAN WEAKEN THE BUILDING. THE PRO-TEX COMPUTERIZED FOUNDATION PERFORMANCE ANALYSIS IS A MEASURE OF THE FOUNDATION'S DEVIATION FROM DEAD-LEVEL.

FOUNDATIONS MAY HAVE BEEN INSTALLED OUT OF LEVEL, BUT FACTORS OTHER THAN AN OUT-OF-LEVEL CONDITION ARE GOOD INDICATORS OF SUBSEQUENT FOUNDATION MOVEMENT. THESE INCLUDE **1)** VISIBLE CRACKS IN THE FOUNDATION PERIMETER GRADE BEAM OR FLOOR PLANE, **2)** WINDOWS AND DOOR FRAMES WHICH ARE OUT OF SQUARE, **3)** ROOF RAFTERS DETACHING FROM RIDGE BOARDS, AND **4)** INTERIOR OR EXTERIOR WALLS WHICH DISPLAY SIGNS OF STRESS DEFLECTION.

ANY SUCH CONDITIONS FOUND WILL BE NOTED HERE, AS WELL AS A DIAGRAM OF THE FOUNDATION, WITH VALUES FOR LEVEL OBTAINED WITH STANLEY COMPU-LEVEL EQUIPMENT OR EQUIVALENT. THE CENTER OF THE STRUCTURE IS MARKED "Z" FOR ZERO AS A REFERENCE POINT. PLUS (+) OR MINUS (-) VALUES ARE IN INCHES ABOVE OR BELOW ZERO.

 ALTHOUGH EVERY EFFORT HAS BEEN MADE TO ASSURE ACCURACY, RELIANCE UPON THE INFORMATION CONTAINED HEREIN IS WITH THE UNDERSTANDING THAT NO LIABILITY IS BORNE BY RICHARD BURGESS, PRO-TEX PROPERTY INSPECTIONS, OR ITS ASSIGNS, ASSOCIATES, EMPLOYEES, OR SUBCONTRACTORS.

CLIENT NAME __CLIENT__ ADDRESS _____

PHONE (H)_____ PHONE (W)_____ PHONE (ALT)_____

SUBJECT PROPERTY ADDRESS __123 FIRST ST__

DATE OF ANALYSIS __xx-xx-xx__ PROP DESCR __2 STORY SLAB w/ ATT GARAGE__

PRO-TEX PROPERTY INSPECTIONS

compass
NORTH

CLIENT NAME SAMPLE CLIENT

SUBJECT PROPERTY ADDRESS 123 FIRST ST

THE CENTER OF THE STRUCTURE IS MARKED "Z" FOR ZERO AS A REFERENCE POINT.
PLUS (+) OR MINUS (-) VALUES ARE IN INCHES ABOVE OR BELOW ZERO.

VALUES INDICATED HAVE BEEN ADJUSTED TO COMPENSATE FOR FLOOR COVERINGS.

DIAGRAM NOT TO SCALE

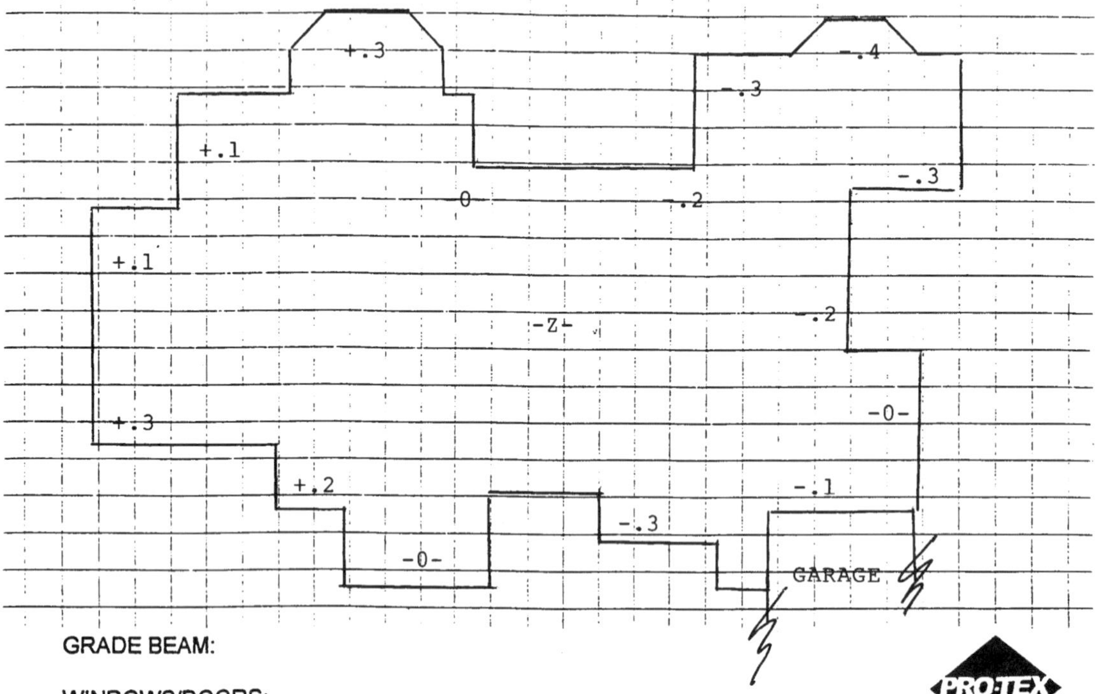

GRADE BEAM:

WINDOWS/DOORS:

FLOOR SURFACE:

RAFTER-TO-RIDGEBOARD: SEE TEXT

INTERIOR / EXTERIOR WALLS:

PRO-TEX PROPERTY INSPECTIONS
www.protexusa.com

TECHNICIAN'S COMMENTS:

SEE TEXT

PRO-TEX PROPERTY INSPECTIONS, HOUSTON, TEXAS / *Level Check* Division

ADDENDUM
Page 2 of 3

THIS DOCUMENT IS ADDENDUM **PAGE 3 OF 3** OF INSPECTION REPORT #0725
BY PROTEX PROPERTY INSPECTIONS OF HOUSTON, TX

LOOPER, REED, MARK & McGRAW
INCORPORATED
ATTORNEYS
1300 POST OAK BOULEVARD, SUITE 2000
HOUSTON, TEXAS 77056
713.986.7000
FAX 713.986.7100

OTHER OFFICES:
DALLAS, TEXAS

Not Certified by the Texas Board of Legal Specialization

July 12, 1999

In March "Dateline NBC" aired a consumer report called: "Is your home crumbling around you?" **If your home is finished with "synthetic stucco,"** also known as Exterior Insulation and Finishing System (EIFS), your home may have serious moisture penetration problems, and as a result, **your home may be rotting from the inside out -- AND YOU MAY BE ABLE TO RECOVER DAMAGES.**

What is EIFS? EIFS is a multi-layered finishing "system" and normally consists of a finish coat, base coat, fiberglass mesh, and insulating foamboard, all of which is adhered to plywood or another substrate on the exterior of your home. EIFS looks very much like stucco, and thus it is often called "synthetic stucco."

What is the potential problem? It is twofold. First, water and moisture may be able to penetrate the exterior of your home (EIFS) through windows, doors, joints, cracks and other places. Second, the moisture may not be able to get out. Typically, EIFS is designed and applied to be water tight and thus it does not allow moisture, even a small amount, to escape.

What is the result? Water may be trapped inside your home behind EIFS, and if this occurs, the moisture may cause the framing to deteriorate or rot very quickly, which may lead to a loss of structural integrity or the "stucco" pulling away from the home. The moisture may also cause mildew and fungus, as well as noticeable streaks on the outside of the walls.

How do you know if you have EIFS or a moisture problem? We will have an EIFS inspector test your home for excess moisture levels, <u>at our expense</u>, if you agree to hire us on a contingent fee basis. If the test shows that your home has been damaged as a result of moisture penetration, we will seek to recover damages on your behalf. In such event, our firm will pay for any reasonable costs involved (including costs of a lawsuit), and we will only be reimbursed for such costs, including the test, if we obtain a recovery or benefit on your behalf. For more information, call Scott Funk, an attorney at Looper, Reed, Mark & McGraw, at (713) 986-7171, or see http://www.lrmmeifs.com.

Very truly yours,

Looper, Reed, Mark & McGraw

ADDENDUM
Page 3 of 3

Marketing and Other Business

Marketing is an essential part of every business, and a home inspection service is no exception. Building a customer base is the one core activity that virtually all businesses have in common. Conventional wisdom dictates that when customers are given great service, they will return again and again as loyal customers. In the home inspection business, though, even the most satisfied and loyal clients won't call back until the time of their next home purchase, possibly several years out. Additionally, many of those purchases will be outside of the region serviced by the familiar and trusted inspector. This leaves the work to another inspector, perhaps in a distant city.

For this reason, it becomes imperative that inspectors implement a targeted and carefully orchestrated marketing plan, which begins with asking each client for referrals. This can be done informally, at the time of inspection, or as part of an organized follow-up plan that includes a phone call, mail contact, or both. In any case, clients are best served by the inspector who initiates follow-up contact for the purpose of explanation or clarification regarding conditions described in the report document.

Local networking clubs are a good source of new business. Most clubs meet once or twice per month at a restaurant or other public gathering place. Generally speaking, members are there solely to exchange business related conversation. Making important new business friends under such circumstances does not require polished salesmanship, and can, in fact, be enjoyable. Club members not only rely upon each other for a direct exchange of commerce, but also for recommendations and referrals of an unlimited variety. A steady stream of business can come of it. Membership in a property owner's association is also useful. Local homeowners who have regular contact with an inspector in this venue are quite likely to choose him when the time comes to purchase a home.

The vast majority of home buyers enlist the services of a real estate agent to guide them. Just a few years ago, in the absence of special contracts, both a listing agent and an agent bringing a buyer to a seller, (known as the sub-agent), were legally bound to act, at all times, in the best interest of the seller, (according to the most common language of the real estate laws). Recently, though, a change in the legal relationship between parties in many states provides for representation of the buyer's interests by the (buyer's) agent.

This is a significant change which better protects the buyer in home purchases. In the course of their work, buyer's agents are often put in the position of selecting or recommending a home inspector. While some brokerages discourage this practice to limit broker liability in the case of dispute, the best buyer's agents freely recommend or select an inspector for the client. Knowledgeable, thorough, and reliable home inspectors can expect to gain the trust of good real estate agents through repeated contact. In this arena, good work is appreciated, and can help to fill the inspector's calendar.

Few brokerage offices allow free access to the agents for face-to-face solicitation, but a direct mail campaign intended to keep agents abreast of the latest prices, rules, and details of the individual inspector's work can be productive. An invitation to a Realtor's party, sponsored by an inspector, can add considerably to the good will. Joining the local Board of Realtors, or writing a continuing column for their newsletter is another marketing strategy which should not be overlooked.

Print advertising can be useful only if it can be inexpensively placed in local publications which will reach the inspector's target audience, the home buyer. Don't overlook homeowner's association newsletters, local real estate periodicals (placed at grocery stores for free distribution), and the proprietary booklets given by individual brokerages to potential customers. Advertisements placed here are often low in cost, and can be quite productive. Yellow pages and newspaper advertising are more costly, and so may not bring the return needed to make them viable. Experimentation and imagination are the keys to finding what works best in carefully budgeted print advertising.

First impressions are very important, not just to clients, but also to Realtors, sellers, neighbors, and casual observers. Inspectors are consultants, and should present themselves in a professional manner at all times, with quality business cards, sales brochures, invoices, fax cover sheets, web sites, and truck signage. It is best to keep it all clear, neat, and simple. Professional trade associations can be useful both for the continuing educational opportunities they offer and the prestige of membership, as announced within your marketing materials through the authorized use of their logos.

Where to spend marketing dollars is a decision which must be made with great care. Opinions vary widely in regard to the optimum rate of marketing expenditures, but 10% to 15% of projected revenues would not be out of line, especially for a new inspector breaking into the market.

One very important and potentially productive marketing tool that cannot be overlooked is the Internet. The cost of web site production and hosting is very low compared with other advertising media, and may well be more productive. Programs are available which allow an average computer user to create stunningly professional sites, but priority placement within the major search engines is of critical importance if the site is to be found amongst its competitors by a potential client. Priority of rank is left to the discretion of those who manage the search engines, and each search engine has a different and complicated formula for ranking, a formula which remains a total mystery to most users. Professional attention by an experienced Internet expert can optimize web site ranking within most search engines. This could represent either a one-time charge or a monthly fee. With some care in assembling the appropriate materials, and consultation with a very good web site master, this author gives credit to www.protexusa.com for generating 40% of his 2001 inspection volume.

Home inspection customers invariably find themselves racing against the clock, with purchase agreements signed and only limited time remaining to address structural and mechanical conditions. They have no time for unanswered phones or delays in scheduling. Many inspectors are sole proprietors, who personally handle all aspects of their business, often from an "office" vehicle. In such cases, it is prudent to be close to a pager and cell phone at all times. In circumstances where an assistant is available at a central office location, that individual should be well schooled in all aspects of the business, to answer questions intelligently and schedule appointments accurately.

Some inspectors delegate the task of transposing field notes into the report document. This practice allows the inspector more time in the field, perhaps resulting in higher revenues, but it can quickly lead to errors and ambiguities within the report document unless there is perfect coordination and understanding between inspector and assistant.

A recent trend has been to create the report document by laptop computer at the inspection site, and to deliver it into the hands of the client before leaving. Although this may be an efficient use of the inspector's time, it increases the potential for friction between the parties, fueled, perhaps, by idle time and the inspector's findings. Most inspectors advise the client briefly of the most significant adverse conditions found, then generate the report document in an office setting where building codes and other materials are readily available for reference. Delivery of the document can be by fax, e-mail, overnight carrier, messenger, regular mail, or any other method desired by the client. In all cases, it is advisable to issue the invoice and collect payment at the time of inspection.

Inspectors may bear considerable liability in two significant ways. Any damage done to the subject property while performing an inspection could cost the inspector the price of repairs. A sink left unattended which overflows, for example, or a ceiling panel accidentally stepped on from the attic space can leave the inspector no satisfactory option but to pay up. Secondly, failure to perform up to standard can result in a demand by the client for repairs to an overlooked inspection item.

Liability insurance and errors & omissions insurance are available from many insurance companies to cover such situations. Some government agencies, lenders, investors, or other clients require proof of such insurance coverage from their inspectors. Others do not. Each inspector must be aware of the regulations governing his activities and assess his own overall needs. Some professional trade associations offer special rates for such insurance to their members.

Consulting Contracts

Regulation of real estate inspection commerce will vary somewhat from state to state. Each inspector must learn and abide by the rules and laws governing the state in which he operates. Fortunately, much of the language found in the regulations developing within the various state bodies has evolved from a common parentage, as regulators continuously seek to adopt provisions which have demonstrated success.

An inspector may require a signed agreement or contract before each inspection begins, regardless of whether this is required by law in his state. Such an agreement serves to reduce misunderstanding and subsequent problems between inspector and client. Where no formal pre-inspection agreement is executed, the terms, conditions, scope, disclaimers, and limitations should be clearly spelled out within the report document.

The following sample Consulting Services Agreement was developed by a Texas attorney for use by real estate inspectors. It is presented here for educational purposes only. This document deals with many of the legal issues which are likely require attention by every home inspector.

The author, publisher, and all other parties and contributors to this book disclaim responsibility for the use of or reliance upon any of its contents, and recommend that every reader seek competent legal advice regarding all points of law.

Consulting Services Agreement

THIS AGREEMENT is made on _____, in the year _____, between _____("Inspector"), State License #_____, and _____("the Client"). The purpose of this writing is to describe all of the terms of this agreement, including a description of the professional consulting services that the Inspector has agreed to perform for the Client, what the client will pay in exchange for those services, and the contractual rights and obligations to which the Inspector and Client have agreed.

Nature and Scope of Services

On _____, in the year _____, at ____:00 __.m., or at such other time and date that the client and Inspector may agree, the Inspector or a representative of the Inspector, will provide only the following professional consulting services to the Client: observing and rendering opinions as to the visible accessible parts, components, and systems of the residential building located at _____, City of _____, (State)____, excluding detached structures, decks, docks, and fences, and excluding the items described below in this Agreement. All mechanical and electrical equipment, systems, and appliances will be operated , for the purposes of the inspection, in normal modes and operating ranges. The inspector shall only opine as to whether the accessible parts, components, and systems, which are included in this inspection, are functioning at the time of the inspection, or whether these parts, components, and systems are in need of repair at the time of the inspection.

Because the consulting services the Inspector has agreed to provide the Client are limited to making observations and providing written subjective opinions of a limited nature, the Inspector cannot and does not agree to be responsible or liable for (1) any defects in the residential building inspected; (2) the failure to observe or provide opinions with respect to any part, component, or system of the residential building that is not included in the inspection as provided in the Agreement; (3) the failure to observe or provide opinions with respect to any defects that cannot be visually observed; or (4) defects which become apparent after the time and date of the inspection, commonly referred to as "latent defects", or the failure to observe or provide opinions regarding such latent defects. Also the inspector DOES NOT AGREE TO MAKE , AND DOES NOT MAKE ANY WARRANTIES, EXPRESS OR IMPLIED, AS TO THE CONSULTING SERVICES PROVIDED THE CLIENT, OR ANY WARRANTIES, EXPRESS OR IMPLIED, AS TO THE PARTS, COMPONENTS, OR SYSTEMS INCLUDED IN THE INSPECTION PROVIDED FOR BY THIS AGREEMENT. Additionally, the inspector cannot and does not agree to be responsible or liable for any decision whether or not to purchase the residential building inspected, or any decision whether or not to make any repairs to the residential building or its parts, components, or systems. Further, because this is an Agreement between only the Client and the Inspector, the Inspector does not agree to provide these services for anyone other than the Client, or for the benefit of anyone other than the Client. Accordingly, no one other than the Client should rely on the observations and opinions provided by the Inspector, and the Inspector cannot be responsible or liable for any such "third party" reliance. Finally, in the event that the Inspector opines that certain parts, components, or systems are in need of repair, the Inspector recommends that the Client properly complete those repairs prior to any purchase of the residential building, and to request that the inspector once again inspect the repaired parts, components, or systems to determine if such items are then performing the function for which intended, or whether they are in need of further repair.

The Report

After the inspection, the Inspector will provide the Client with a writing reflecting the opinions of the Inspector as to whether parts, components, and systems included in the inspection are performing the function for which they are intended, or whether they are in need of repair. Additionally, the Inspector's report will include his observations of any visible, recognized hazards existing in the residential building at the time of the inspection.

Items Excluded From the Inspection

In order to make sure that there is no misunderstanding as to the nature and extent of the services the Inspector agrees to provide the Client, the Inspector will not inspect nor provide any opinions regarding any of the following parts, components, systems, or conditions of the residential building inspected:

(a) environmental conditions;

(b) presence of toxic or hazardous wastes or substances;

(c) geological conditions, including the existence or non-existence or proximity of fault lines;

(d) presence of termites or other wood-destroying insects or organisms;

(e) compliance with codes, ordinances, statutes or restrictions, including deed restrictions;

(f) the efficiency, habitability, quality, durability, expected life, future performance, value, or insurability of any part, component, or system inspected;

(g) any condition of any part, component, or system inspected, other than the condition of whether the part, component, or system included in this inspection is functioning or in need of repair at the time of the inspection;

(h) the following miscellaneous items:

*Manufacturer installations	*Gas lines (piping)	*Operation of windows
*Smoke or fire alarms	*Septic tanks or systems	*Central vacuum
*Pools	*Furniture of any kind	*Elevators
*Timer devices	*Photocells	*Driveways & sidewalks
*Recreational appliances	*Heat exchanger	*Wall or ceiling voids
*Damaged wood inside walls	*Intercom systems	*Clothes washer/dryer
*Refrigerator	*Security systems	*Water softeners
*Cesspools	*Wells/springs	*Solar systems
*Outdoor cooking equipment	*Playground equipment	*Tennis courts

*Audio and video equipment, including televisions and stereophonic systems, telephones, answering machines, or related equipment

*Parts, components, or systems covered by carpeting or attic insulation

*Landscape lighting or lawn or garden sprinkler system

*Re-inspection of repairs recommended by the Inspector

No Insurer/Limitation of Liability

The Inspector and the Client agree that the Inspector is not an insurer, and that insurance, if any, may be obtainable through home warranty insurance policies in the marketplace, or manufacturer issued policies; the Inspector and the Client also agree that the fees paid by the client to the Inspector for the professional consulting services provided by the Inspector pursuant to this Agreement, are based solely on the value of the professional consulting services agreed to be provided, and are unrelated to the value of the items, components, and systems being inspected. The client acknowledges that it is impractical and extremely difficult to fix the actual damages, if any, which may result from the failure of the inspector to perform any of the obligations required by this Agreement. The Client understands and agrees that if the Inspector should be found liable for any losses, damages, attorney's fees, costs or expenses, no matter the kind or nature, the Inspectors liability shall be limited to a sum equal to the fees paid by the client to the Inspector for the professional consulting services provided to the Client in accordance with this Agreement. The Client agrees that the Inspector shall not be liable for consequential or incidental damages or losses, except to the extent of the limited damage amount provided for in this paragraph; and THE PROVISIONS OF THIS PARAGRAPH SHALL APPLY IF LOSS OR DAMAGE, IRRESPECTIVE OF CAUSE OR ORIGIN, RESULTS DIRECTLY OR INDIRECTLY TO PERSONS OR PROPERTY, FROM PERFORMANCE OR NON-PERFORMANCE OF THE OBLIGATIONS IMPOSED ON THE INSPECTOR BY THIS AGREEMENT, OR FROM NEGLIGENCE, ACTIVE OR PASSIVE, OF THE INSPECTOR, ITS AGENTS, SERVANTS, ASSIGNS,

OR EMPLOYEES (SUCH AS FAILING TO PROPERLY REPORT THE INSPECTOR'S OPINIONS ON THE CONDITION OF THE VISIBLE ACCESSIBLE PARTS, COMPONENTS, AND SYSTEMS OF THE RESIDENTIAL BUILDING INSPECTED, OR FAILING TO OBSERVE OR OPINE AS TO A PART, COMPONENT, OR SYSTEM WHICH IS IN NEED OF REPAIR AT THE TIME OF THE INSPECTION).

Arbitration Agreement

Additionally, the Inspector and the Client agree that any dispute or controversy which arises out of this Agreement or the consulting services the Inspector provides the Client, shall be resolved by mandatory and binding arbitration administered by the American Arbitration Association ("AAA") in accordance with this arbitration agreement and the commercial arbitration rules of the AAA. Additionally, enforcement of this arbitration agreement shall be governed by federal common law. As authorized by federal common law, we agree that there shall be no less than three arbitrators, all of whom shall be required to conduct the arbitration hearing, and at least one of the arbitrators shall be a licensed professional real estate inspector in this or another state, or a registered professional engineer who is in the business of performing real property inspections in this state.

To the extent that any inconsistency exists between this arbitration agreement and the above referenced law or the commercial rules of the AAA, this arbitration agreement shall control. Also, the Client agrees to act as his own attorney in the decision as to whether to make this arbitration agreement, and as to the terms and conditions of this arbitration agreement. By the Client's signature below, the client expressly acknowledges it is acting as its own attorney in the making of this arbitration agreement. To the extent any state law requires the Client to have independent counsel to advise the Client in the making of this arbitration agreement, the Client expressly waives that right.

Attorney's Fees

Finally, both the Inspector and the Client agree that in the event any dispute or controversy arises as a result of this Agreement, or the consulting services the Inspector provides the client, whoever prevails in that dispute, whether by a net higher money award or otherwise, and whether in an arbitration proceeding, legal proceeding, or other forum or proceeding, shall be entitled to recover all of the prevailing party's reasonable and necessary attorney's fees and costs incurred by that party.

General Provisions

This Agreement and the consulting services which the Inspector agrees to provide the Client, will terminate upon the delivery by the Inspector of its written opinions to the Client. This Agreement contains the only agreement between the Inspector and the Client, and takes the place of any prior understandings or written or oral agreements between the Inspector and the Client regarding the consulting services the Inspector has agreed to provide the client as described above. Also, this Agreement cannot be changed except by execution of another written instrument signed by both the inspector and the Client or their authorized representatives. This Agreement shall be interpreted in accordance with state law, except as provided expressly otherwise herein. Further, in case any part of this Agreement is later determined to be invalid, illegal, or unenforceable, it will not affect any other part of this Agreement, and the remaining valid, legal, and enforceable parts of this Agreement will be interpreted as if the invalid, illegal, or unenforceable part never existed.

Both the Inspector and the Client acknowledge that this written document correctly and completely describes all of the terms of their agreement, by signing their names on the spaces below.

INSPECTOR: **CLIENT:** (acting in its individual capacity and as its own attorney)

By: _____   _____

Name: _____   _____

Title: _____   _____

Reporting Language Samples

The following language samples will help inspectors to provide their clients with clear, informative report documents. Although the primary purpose of the report document is to identify adverse conditions, it is often good to provide a reason why a reported condition is, in fact, adverse. "Soil is too high on foundation wall" takes on more meaning when "...creating vulnerability to water and insect penetration" is added.

Inspectors should be careful, though, about suggesting remedies for adverse conditions. Determination of the precise nature of repairs required within an electric service panel, for example, should be made by a licensed electrician.

Language used by the inspector for the Identification of certain defects may be dictated by a licensing authority. *Some states require the inspector to describe certain conditions as "recognized hazards".* Know and follow the laws of your state.

The following phraseology is not intended to be taken as "The Correct Way" to report conditions found. Inspectors should always seek to find and improve upon the reporting language that they feel will best serve their clients.

Foundations

Evidence found supports the opinion that the subject foundation has experienced excessive settlement of a differential nature, and is not satisfactorily performing the function for which it is intended. Evidence found includes: 1. significant stress deflection and cracks at interior and exterior walls; 2. moderate racking of door and window frames; 3. separation of rafters at ridgeboard nailing points; 4. vertical cracks visible at foundation perimeter grade beam faces; and 5. departure from dead-level of slab floor plane measuring 2.2 inches over 30 horizontal feet.

Stress or shrinkage cracks of the kind found in the subject slab, (fully closed, with no evidence of differential settlement), are common. The steel cable tendons as used in this foundation can generally help to provide the required strength/stiffness for satisfactory foundation performance, even in the presence of moderately compromised monolithic integrity (fractures). This foundation does appear to be satisfactorily performing the function for which it is intended at this time. The structure should be monitored for signs of differential foundation settlement, with corrective measures taken if excessive settlement does occur.

This is not an engineering report, but is only an opinion based on observation of conditions known to be related to foundation performance, using the knowledge and experience of the inspector.

No evidence of the loss of monolithic integrity (fracture) was found at foundation perimeter grade beam faces, garage floor, or interior tile flooring.

Level measurements were obtained using XYZ Brand of measuring equipment.

Girders and joists are in generally deteriorated condition, showing splits, twisting and sagging.

Inadequate crawlspace ventilation is provided. At least 15 square feet of crawlspace vent area is required for adequate ventilation in a single-story 2200 square foot structure. Only 6 square feet of vent area is provided.

Available crawlspace head room is less than the required minimum 18 inches.

Several cinder block piers are crumbling, and 2 piers at north porch area are tipping excessively.

Presence of excessive crawlspace mildew and a strong musty odor are indicative of a high-moisture condition there.

No underfloor insulation is provided as is appropriate for optimum comfort and heating efficiency. The installation of unfaced fiberglass batting is recommended.

The presence of mineral stains, (or efflorescence), which ring the basement walls 2 inches above floor level is indicative of water penetration and/or previous flooding.

Large tree roots at north side of garage have apparently caused foundation damage.

Soil is too high on foundation wall at back yard, creating vulnerability to water and insect penetration.

Grading and Drainage

Void in soil at west foundation wall should be filled and graded to prevent the accumulation of standing water and provide positive runoff away from the structure.

Installation of drain conduit is recommended at front garden downspout to carry water well away from the structure.

Gutter at east side of garage is damaged and sagging.

Soil at rear is of reverse grade, creating vulnerability to the accumulation of standing water at the foundation wall, a condition known to be a factor in foundation failure. Re-grading is required there.

Approximately 75 square feet of standing water has accumulated under the center of the structure. No sump pump was found. Recommend re-grade, fill, and/or install sump pump system to prevent the accumulation of standing water at crawlspace (to help prevent piers from heaving and to reduce vulnerability to pest attraction and premature woodrot at underfloor components).

Roof Covering

Inspected from ground level with binoculars.

Roof was accessed for inspection.

Flat portion of roof was not accessible, and was not visible from inspector's ground level vantage points.

Use of composition shingles with roof pitch of less than 2-in-12 inches, (as found at addition room) is improper, creating vulnerability to wind damage and leaks.

Covering is composition shingles in generally good condition.

Several shingles at east roof plane are torn.

Both turbine vents are rusted, and both fail to turn.

Direct daylight visible from within attic is indicative of improper wood shingle installation, creating vulnerability to leaks.

Wood shingles are split, curled, weather-worn, and soft at various locations, indicating limited remaining service life.

Required cricket (saddle) at intersection of roof and (32 inch wide) fireplace chimney (for water diversion) is absent.

Blistered seams at built-up (flat) roof covering creates vulnerability to leaks.

Tree branches in contact with eaves at NE corner should be trimmed back to prevent structural damage and to limit vulnerability to insect penetration.

5 foot section of drip flashing at rear entry door area is missing.

Rake and frieze boards at north gabled roof are deteriorated and partially detached from structure.

Roof Structure and Attic

Inadequate fireblocking is provided at opening from attic floor into 1st floor wall cavity near the water heater area, a recognized hazard.

Purlin brace at South side in center of structure bears improperly on makeshift support, transferring roof loads (and causing damage) to kitchen ceiling.

Collar tie at west side of attic has detached from its south rafter position.

Several rafters at north side are split, knot-flawed, and water-damaged, causing roof to sag there.

Rafters have separated from their ridgeboard nailing points, a condition normally associated with foundation movement.

Evidence of water penetration and related damage was found at SE roof valley area, (apparently caused by improperly installed valley flashing).

Attic access opening size is inadequate for removal of furnace equipment installed there.

No ventilation or access provisions are present at garage attic as required.

Insulation at attic floor averages only 2 inches in depth, with poor coverage.

Walls (Interior and Exterior)

Stairstep pattern of brick/mortar separation was found at east wall, a condition normally associated with foundation movement.

Weep holes at first course of brick, (required for ventilation of wall cavities), are absent.

Wood-product siding is generally deteriorated, indicating limited remaining service life.

2nd story vertical (exterior) wood trim at NE corner of structure is rotted.

Required wallboard (or other fire-rated material) at (attached) garage walls is absent.

Water damage was found at north master bedroom wall behind master shower enclosure, (where grout and caulk repairs are required to prevent water penetration into the wall cavity).

Wood-paneling at office walls is installed without wallboard backing, indicative of economy-grade construction.

Ceilings and Floors

Water damage was found at ceiling in center 2nd floor bedroom, (evidently caused by condensation dripping from uninsulated A/C drain line at attic).

Minor stress cracks were found at living room ceiling.

Floor at 2nd story north bedroom feels excessively uneven underfoot, a condition which suggests the failure of joists and other subfloor components there.

Floor tile cracks (in a pattern normally associated with foundation fracture) were found at kitchen and breakfast areas.

Bottom stair differs in rise (height) dimension by more than the maximum allowable 3/8-inch, a tripping hazard.

Baluster spacing at staircase guardrail is greater than the maximum allowable 4 inches, a hazard to small children.

Doors

Several interior and exterior door frames were found to be severely racked out-of-square, a condition normally associated with foundation movement.

Weather strip at front entry door is damaged.

Lock/latch hardware at sliding patio door set is not functioning.

Sweep strip at rear entry door scrapes carpet.

Garage entry door into living space lacks the self-closing mechanism required by some building codes for fire safety.

Attic access door in garage is missing, (a fire acceleration hazard).

Garage entry door into living space is not of the fire-rated type as required.

Springs fail to hold the overhead garage door in a fully open position.

Permanent lock hold-open device at overhead garage door, (required with auto-opener), is absent.

Laundry room door is pet-damaged.

Windows

Exterior caulk repairs are needed at various locations.

(Exterior) plastic glazing bead is damaged/deteriorated at south wall windows.

(Exterior) brick sills at front living room windows are installed with reverse slope, creating vulnerability to water penetration.

Screens are damaged or missing at several locations.

Glass pane at gameroom window is broken.

Presence of burglar bars which require tools for emergency egress is hazardous at bedroom window locations.

Fogging found between insulated (double) window panes throughout the structure is indicative of failed seals, a condition which can only be remedied by sash replacement.

Evidence of water penetration was found at south master bedroom window sill.

Lock mechanism at south living room window is broken.

No safety-glass identification label was found at breakfast room window panes, (which are required to be of the safety glass type when less than 18 inches from the floor and larger than 9 square feet).

Evidence of leaks (water staining) was found at hallway skylight shaft.

Fireplace and Chimney

(Non-combustible) hearth extends less than the required minimum 16 inches to the front of the firebox.

The required provision for the introduction of outside combustion air was not found.

Gas branch line to fireplace is of PVC plastic, a material not approved for this purpose.

Firebox brick requires mortar repairs.

Permanent hold-open device at damper, required with gas log set installed, is absent.

Required rain cap and spark arrestor (at chimney top) are missing.

(Chimney top) mortar cap is deteriorated, creating vulnerability to premature deterioration of the structural brick chimney.

Excessive creosote build-up was found at flue and firebox. Cleaning is required.

(Metal) flue provides less than the required minimum 2 inches of clearance to (combustible) roof deck at roof passthrough.

Service Entrance and Panels

Main breaker is 150 amps. Service entrance is 1/0 AWG aluminum cable, which is only compatible with breaker rating up through 125 amps. Conductor/breaker incompatibility is a recognized hazard.

Service panel location in (master) bathroom is no longer permitted.

Overhead clearance at entrance cables (above driveway) is less than the required minimum 12 feet.

Mast is inadequately secured in place at its south wall mounting straps.

Bottom left cover-plate securing screw makes contact with (and has slightly damaged) the enclosed service entrance cable insulation.

System grounding conductor is loose at grounding rod clamp.

Several breaker knockouts remain unfilled.

Two 20 amp breakers are double-wired.

240 volt breaker set serving dryer circuit is not bridged as required.

Several breakers are not permanently labeled for ampacity as required.

Branch Circuits, Connected Devices, and Fixtures

Aluminum branch circuit wiring was found connected to a sampling of devices inspected which were labeled "for copper use only".

Required GFCI protection is absent at both receptacles within 6 feet of the bar sink.

2-slot (ungrounded) receptacles without secured-pigtail grounding adapter at guest bathroom is hazardous.

Use of light-duty appliance cord (routed under rear entry door threshold) for permanent connection to garage light fixtures is an improper use of material.

Electric cord serving food disposer is too long, requiring a length of 18-36 inches for code compliance.

Pendant style (hanging) light fixture installed above guest tub is hazardous.

Soot and evidence of electrical arcing was found at indoor receptacle to right of the rear entry door.

Light fixtures in bedroom closets lack the required protective globes or covers.

All south wall receptacles in office are wired with reversed hot/neutral connections.

Open junction box was found at family room ceiling (with exposed wire ends).

Required nearby electric service shutoff at (outdoor) A/C condensing unit is absent.

Heating Equipment

Heating equipment provided: Zoned (2) gas fired forced air furnaces with induced draft venting and electronic pilots.

High voltage wiring enters the north (attic) furnace case without the required cable clamp or protective grommet.

Furnace blower causes excessive vibration while operating.

Odor of gas at shutoff valve near west (attic) furnace is indicative of a leak condition.

Although no excessive rust or scale was found at heat exchanger or burner areas, full evaluation of heat exchanger integrity requires dismantling of the furnace, and is beyond the scope of this visual inspection.

Flue provides less than the required minimum 1 inch clearance to (combustible) roof deck at roof passthrough.

Fabricated aluminum flue connector at (attic) furnace is not an approved material.

Required flue termination cap is missing.

Furnace short-cycles at full heat demand.

Use of PVC pipe for gas branch line to furnace is not permitted.

Use of bare brass gas connector at furnace is not permitted, and is known to be hazardous.

Condensing furnace condensate discharge location at basement floor, without plumbed floor drain, is not permitted.

1 (of 3) electric furnace heating elements failed to operate.

(Oil) burner head is burned off, and the heat exchanger shows excessive carbon/scale buildup.

Oil tank has no fuel gauge, and the oil line to the boiler has no filter or shutoff valve as required.

Water circulating pump leaks at its shaft seal.

Outdoor heat pump unit failed to operate at thermostatic call for heat in normal heating mode.

Cooling Equipment

Cooling equipment provided: Electric refrigeration / forced air.

Supply/return air temperature differential at 1st floor zone was below normal range, at 12°F. as measured at supply registers and return plenum. Normal range is 15-20° F.

Primary condensate drain line lacks the required insulation at attic location.

Secondary condensate drain line at attic space is not sloped for positive gravity drain as required.

Safety pan in attic is full of water and its drain line is continuously dripping, a condition normally associated with a blocked primary drain system.

Evaporator coil is frosted over, possibly caused by airflow restriction at filter, which is fully clogged.

Bubbles in sight glass at outdoor liquid line is a condition indicative of low refrigerant charge.

No attempt to operate cooling system was made due to the possibility of damage when outdoor temperature is below 60° F.

Evaporative cooler motor is of the two-speed type. Pigtail connections at motor are excessively corroded.

Ducts and Vents

Duct serving north bedroom is crushed at its attic location.

Ductwork insulation wrap is generally deteriorated at all attic locations.

Low airflow was noted at west guest bedroom supply register. Balancing damper adjustments may be required for optimum comfort there.

Gas branch line and plastic plumbing vent routed within return air plenum is not permitted, creating a fire acceleration and toxicity hazard.

Return air plenum is inadequately sealed, drawing unconditioned air from wall cavities and attic space, and introducing it into the living space.

Water Supply System and Fixtures

Faucet at kitchen sink leaks at its stem when on.

Vegetable sprayer hose is disconnected under kitchen sink.

Undersink shutoff valves at master bathroom are leaking, causing water damage to sink cabinet floor.

Waterhammer (banging pipes) at kitchen ceiling area is produced during use of kitchen sink faucets, a condition normally associated with inadequately secured pipes.

Shower diverter at guest tub spout is not functioning.

Walls behind master shower tile are soft, indicating water penetration and damage.

Hot (left) and cold (right) faucet connections at powder room sink are reversed.

Commode at north guest bathroom is inadequately secured in place, and the required bowl-to-floor caulk is absent.

Porcelain finish at guest tub is chipped.

Evidence of wax seal failure was found at powder room commode.

Tile grout/caulk repairs are required at guest shower enclosure.

Faucet handles at laundry area are damaged, with sharp, rusty edges.

Outdoor faucets lack the required anti-siphon devices.

Drains, Wastes, Vents

Drum traps found at both bathtubs are not of a currently approved type, and both show evidence of leaks.

Makeshift repair (duct tape) was found at kitchen sink drain line components.

Plumbing vents provide less than the minimum required 6 inches of height above roof passthrough.

Plastic plumbing vents lack the required paint or covers at rooftop (to protect from ultra-violet deterioration).

Plumbing vent at SE corner of structure terminates in attic space, an improper location.

Drain stopper at guest bathtub is not functioning.

Water Heating Equipment

50 gallon gas fired water heater was manufactured in '99.

Water heater is installed less than the required minimum 18 inches above the main garage floor for fire safety.

No shutoff valve is provided at cold water inlet as required.

Water heater location (in west guest bathroom) is not permitted by current building codes.

Inlet and outlet fittings are excessively corroded.

Temperature-and-pressure relief valve drain line is not routed for positive gravity drain as required, and its discharge location (at shoulder level) is improper and hazardous.

Excessive rust and corrosion were found in the burner compartment.

Gurgling noise during heating cycle is typically caused by mineral build-up inside the tank. Limited remaining service life is indicated.

Appliance gas control valve is leaking.

Flue provides less than the required minimum 5 vertical feet from collar to termination, and the termination cap is not of a currently approved type. Evidence of flue backdraft (spillage) was found at the draft diverter.

Appliance case shows scorching at burner compartment access panel area.

Hydro-Therapy Equipment

Although pump motor operation sounds normal, jets provide no water flow, a condition which may be indicative of a loose pump-to-motor shaft connector.

Leaks were observed at water jet lines (behind decorative skirt) during operation.

Electric timer installed less than 5 feet from tub rim is not an approved location.

Required GFCI protective device is not provided.

Dishwasher

Door gasket is damaged and leaking.

Tub interior is badly rusted.

Appliance is not adequately secured in place.

Discharge hose leaks at its connection to food disposer inlet nipple.

No provision for the prevention of discharge-hose backflow is present.

Discharge hose does not enter drain system ahead of food disposer as is appropriate when disposer is present.

Soap door is damaged.

Springs fail to adequately support door weight.

Food Waste Disposer

Interior of grinding chamber is excessively rusted.

Motor is frozen, and the integral overload breaker fails to reset.

Pivoting hammer blades are frozen, failing to turn.

Unit vibrates excessively in operation.

Case is rusted and leaking at bottom.

Range Hood

Recirculating type, does not exhaust outdoors.

Exhaust discharges into garage, an improper location.

12-foot section of accordion aluminum vent material (in attic) is not approved for this use.

Fan did not respond to switch.

Filters are missing.

Although blower motor sounds normal, failure to provide airflow indicates blockage, improper installation, or other need for repair.

Ranges - Ovens - Cooktops

2 of 4 gas control knobs at cooktop are missing

Use of bare brass gas connector (at range location) is not approved.

Left front electric element at cooktop failed to heat, and both signal lights are not functioning.

Electric bake element at bottom of oven failed to function.

Thermostat sensor is inadequately secured in its mounting clips.

Oven door hinges are damaged, causing improper door fit.

Oven door does not fully open due to interference with adjacent cabinet handle.

Oven reached only 275 degrees at 350 degree setting after 15 minutes operating time.

Microwave Cooking Equipment

Door latch is damaged.

Cooklight failed to function during testing.

Timer control knob is broken.

Glass front panel is cracked.

Trash Compactor

Excessive noise and vibration were noted during operation.

Although motor sounds were normal, ram actuation could not be confirmed, (appliance failed to crush a rolled newspaper for testing).

Unit is inadequately secured in place, and drawer operation is very rough.

Control buttons are loose.

Bathroom Exhaust Fans and Heaters

Fans exhaust into attic space, an improper location.

Fan at guest bathroom failed to respond to wall switch.

Backdraft damper louvers at West wall are damaged.

Gas fired heaters of the type provided at bathroom locations are no longer approved for use, and their use is known to be generally hazardous. No attempt to operate was made by the inspector.

Aluminum gas branch line serving gas heater at master bathroom is not an approved use of material.

Whole House Vacuum Systems

No suction was evident at 2nd floor inlet receptacles.

Main inlet hose at (garage) canister is crushed.

Start sensor at laundry room inlet receptacle is malfunctioning, motor fails to start when hose is inserted there.

High voltage connections at canister are not enclosed in a junction box as required.

Garage Door Operators

Auto-reverse safety mechanism is not functioning.

Permanent hold-open device at manual lock mechanism, (required with auto-opener present), is absent.

Door release catch at traveler attachment is not functioning.

Radio remote control functions were not tested.

Doorbell and Chimes

Button housing hangs from its wires at front door area.

Push button is deteriorated.

Chime housing at west hallway is inadequately secured to wall.

Dryer Vents

Vent improperly exhausts into attic space.

Flexi-hose routed through attic space is an improper use of materials. Rigid smooth-wall vent pipe is required in concealed locations.

Vent pipe is disconnected in attic space.

Vent termination cap (rain hood) is fully clogged with lint, restricting airflow.

Required backdraft damper door at vent termination location is absent.

Swimming Pools and Equipment

Pool water is in a stagnant condition, restricting proper inspection of interior surfaces and components.

Required safety equipment, (life ring with rope or shepherd's crook) is absent from pool area.

Pool's interior plaster surfaces are excessively abrasive, a condition which is typically caused by prolonged PH levels that are too high (acidic). Interior is in need of re-surfacing.

Fiberglass spa body appears to have been damaged by the use of abrasive cleansers or sanding, as evidenced by dull appearance and scratch patterns, (a condition which increases vulnerability to the formation and growth of surface algae).

Pool is out-of-level. Shallow end is ¾ inch higher than the deep end, as determined by observation and measurement of water-line at deck and coping. Concrete deck and coping stones show no corresponding displacement or cracks, indicating that this out-of-level condition may have been created at the time of pool installation.

Verification of the presence and proper function of a hydrostatic relief valve is beyond the scope of this visual inspection.

Anchor hardware at diving board pedestal is excessively corroded, a hazardous condition.

Pool is too shallow to provide safe use of the diving board. Removal of the diving board is recommended.

No ladder or other means of assisted egress is provided at the deep end as required.

Coping stones are not properly sealed at the concrete decking.

Deformation of the pool wall shape at its east side appears to be caused by the rotting of several wooden buttresses there. Rotted wooden buttresses require replacement to restore original design strength.

Discharge line from the cartridge filter leaks.

Anti-siphon device at pool-water supply faucet is located less than the required minimum 12 inches above the pool deck (to properly protect potable water supply from contamination by pool-water).

There are bubbles in the water at the return outlets, a condition which is normally indicative of a leak at the suction side of the pipe system, (as all points of intake for this pump are well below the waterline).

Pump/filter pipe components are not labeled to indicate function.

Spa blower vibrates excessively.

Leaf basket at the surface skimmer in the shallow end is damaged, and the weir gate required there is missing.

Adjustable eyeball inserts at 2 of 6 hydrojets in the spa are missing, limiting flow-direction adjustments and creating improper flow balance.

Pool heater shows excessive external corrosion at its case bottom, a condition caused by direct soil contact at its mounting location.

Required pressure gauge at cartridge filter canister is missing, and the gauge tap there has been plugged.

Hose for the automatic cleaning equipment, (which has been repaired with duct tape in several places), still leaks. Replacement is needed.

Required GFCI protective device serving the in-water pool light failed to trip at induced ground fault as required. Improper operation of GFCI devices at required locations is a recognized hazard. Device must be replaced.

Spa heater is not electrically bonded with other pool equipment as required.

Springs at the self-closing mechanism serving the pool barrier fence gate fail to provide enough force for positive gate latching.

Wood-Destroying Insects

The services of a pest control licensee for inspection regarding the presence of insects and related damage is advised.

Wood pile at East side of structure and rotted tree root at rear entry door area are conditions conducive to termite and other insect attraction.

Active termite nest was found in soil at NE corner of structure.

Termite damage was found at rafters in NE side of attic.

Carpenter ant infestation was found at various locations throughout the structure.

Evidence of termite activity was found at west living room interior wallboard.

Private Water Wells

The scope of evaluation for private wells in a non-invasive visual inspection is limited.

Private water wells should be regularly tested for coliform, bacteria, water hardness, chemical contamination, and debris.

40-amp breaker serves the pump motor, which is labeled for use only with breakers rated at 20 amps, (a condition called overfusing).

Tank pressure gauge fluctuates during non-demand periods, normally indicating a leak condition.

Required pressure relief valve at storage tank is absent.

Poor drainage grading was found at the well head area, causing the accumulation of standing water and creating vulnerability to well-water contamination.

Piston type pump provided is old, rusted, obsolete.

Pump short-cycles, which can be caused by a condition known as waterlogging, usually remedied by draining the tank to permit the re-introduction of air into the bladder.

Tank pressure reading at its integral gauge is 80-psi, well above the maximum 40-psi design pressure limit stated on the equipment manufacturer's label.

Septic Systems

All private septic systems require periodic maintenance and performance evaluation by qualified personnel.

Drain flow rate is too low throughout the structure.

Excessive effluent seepage, unusually green vegetation, and the strong odor at the leaching field area are normally indicative of a clogged leaching field. Installation of a new leaching field may be required.

Soil absorption field provides less than the required minimum 5 foot distance to the North foundation wall of the main dwelling.

Access portal to septic tank was not found.

Building is served by a simple cesspool collection pit, which is no longer approved for new construction. The replacement of a malfunctioning cesspool with a modern septic system (or hookup to the municipal sewer system) may be required by local building authorities.

Lawn Sprinklers

Control panel is ABC model 6 with 6 stations or zones.

Station 1, serving front lawn, sprays across public walkway and front entry porch.

Spray head at SE corner wets living room window, causing water penetration and related damage at interior sill.

Several pop-up heads at west property line failed to fully deploy.

Evidence of underground leak (percolating puddle) was found at curb area near driveway apron.

Control panel is inadequately secured in place.

Required anti-siphon device (backflow preventer) is absent.

System water shutoff valve leaks at its stem.

No sprinkler coverage is provided at east side yard.

Outdoor Cooking Equipment

Location of permanently installed cooking equipment, providing only 6 inches of clearance from grille to wood siding at patio area, is hazardous.

Pedestal base is damaged, unit is unsteady.

Gas control knobs are damaged.

Igniter wire is detached at burner area sparking tip.

Interior is badly rusted.

Burner bar is burned through, requires replacement.

Cooking grate is missing.

Gas Lines

Gas lines were only inspected at points of use, where readily accessible. Full scientific evaluation of gas supply system performance is beyond the scope of this visual inspection.

Odor of gas at the (outdoor) gas meter area is indicative of a leak condition there.

Bare brass gas connector in use at furnace area is not permitted, and is known to be hazardous.

Security Systems

Control code was not available to inspector. Functional operation was not tested.

Main control panel is XYZ brand with battery backup. 2 keypads are provided, located at front entry foyer and laundry room.

System is a hardwired perimeter intrusion detection system, using magnetic switches at doors and windows, plus one interior infra-red motion detector at the east hall. A telephone interconnect is included. A local external siren is mounted in the attic. Electrical connections at the siren were found detached.

System annunciator failed to sound when the rear entry door was opened.

Windows at vulnerable 2nd floor locations were not wired for intrusion detection.

Reference to equipment manufacturer's data and consultation with equipment owner are advised for operating details.

Fire Protection Equipment

3 smoke alarms were found. Functional alarm operation was not tested. Recommend installation of additional units, yielding one in each bedroom and one in each hall that leads to a bedroom, including at least one per floor.

Smoke alarm at master bedroom failed to sound when its test button was pressed.

Smoke alarm at 2nd floor hall sounded continuously during inspection, in the apparent absence of detectable smoke.

Smoke alarms were found at all required locations. Each responded normally to function testing.

GLOSSARY

A

aerator (fitting) - a device installed at faucets which serves to introduce air into a water stream.

ambient temperature - in any given area, the temperature of the surrounding air.

ampacity - the current-carrying capacity of a wire or cable, expressed in amperes.

ampere - a measure of electrical current. An electromotive force of 1 volt acting across a resistance of 1 ohm results in a current flow of 1 ampere.

aquafer - a formation of gravel, rock, or sand which provides water to springs or wells.

asphalt - a tar-like substance made of a variety of bitumen, naturally occurring or obtained by evaporating petroleum.

AWG - American Wire Gauge.

B

base flashing - the upturned edges of a watertight membrane on a roof.

batten - a strip of wood.

beam pocket - an opening in any structural component intended to receive one or more girders or beams.

bearing wall - a structural wall designed to carry a load.

bi-metallic strip - an element formed of two bonded metals with dissimilar coefficients of thermal expansion, designed to mechanically bend or curl under changing temperatures.

bitumen - mineral pitch or any material obtained as asphaltic residue in the distillation of coal tar, wood tar, petroleum, etc., or occurring as natural asphalt.

brick ledge - that portion of a foundation upon which the first course of brick is installed.

bus bar - a heavy, rigid conductor which serves as a common connection between the electric power source and the load circuits inside a service panel.

C

CABO - Council of American Building Officials.

calcium carbonate - A white chalky substance often found at the evaporation line of pools and spas.

cap flashing - (counterflashing) a sheetmetal strip which covers the top edge of base flashing to prevent water from entering.

cavitation - The introduction and rapid collapse of air bubbles. (Within a pump housing, this condition causes a sound like marbles churning within the housing.)

cesspool - an excavation in the earth which receives and retains drainage and sewage from a building.

chord - a component of a truss which acts as a rafter (upper chord) or joist (lower chord).

cohesive soil - fine-grained soil which, by molecular forces of attraction, stick together when wet and hold together when dry.

collar beam - (collar tie) a horizontal framing member which spans two opposing rafters.

condensate - liquid formed by the condensation of a vapor.

conduit - a tube, pipe, or channel used for protecting or conveying wiring or water.

convection - gravity-caused heat transmission by the movement of air, due to the density differences between air currents of differing temperatures.

coping - 1. a protective cap or cover for masonry structures, installed to prevent water penetration. 2. The ribbon-like edge of material (usually masonry) around the perimeter of an in-ground pool (or spa) installed to prevent surface-splash and rainwater from draining into the pool (or spa).

corner bead - a vertical molding used to protect the convex angle of two intersecting walls.

counterflashing - see cap flashing.

crawlspace - an unfinished accessible space below the first floor of a building with no basement.

creosote - a combustible and acidic by-product of wood fires, also obtained by distilling coal tar for use as a wood preservative.

cricket - a saddle-shaped projection on a sloping roof installed to divert water around a chimney or other obstacle.

cross-connection - a condition which permits connection between a potable water supply system and a drain or wastewater system.

D

deadfront - a service or sub panel cover plate which encloses the electrically energized parts.

diatomaceous earth - A fine powder derived from the porous opaline shells of diatoms, sometimes used as a medium within pool and spa filters.

dielectric fitting - an adapter with a non-metallic contact surface used to connect pipes of dissimilar metals in a water supply system, in order to prevent galvanic corrosion.

differential settlement - uneven sinking of a structure's foundation.

GLOSSARY

dip tube - a pipe within a water heater which delivers inlet water to the bottom of the tank for heating.

dope - (plumber's dope, pipe dope) a lubricating and sealing compound used in making a pipe joint.

downwarping - the sinking of the perimeter of a foundation relative to the center.

downspout (leader) - a vertical pipe used to carry water from a roof drain or gutter to ground level.

dosing pump - (ejector pump) a pump within a sewage collection tank for transfer to another location.

draft diverter - a device fitted to a flue to prevent downdrafts, and to admit draft air for aiding in the evacuation of gasses.

drip flashing - an "L" shaped metal strip which extends beyond a roof edge to direct rainwater away from the structure.

drip loop - a sag in an electric cable or conduit to prevent water from entering at its ends.

E

efflorescence - a deposit of white salts caused by the leaching of moisture through a masonry component.

ejector pump - see dosing pump.

electrolysis - see galvanic corrosion.

erosion - the carrying away of soil by flowing water.

F

fascia - (board) an eaves fascia. a board nailed across rafter ends, sometimes supporting gutters.

ferrous - having iron content.

fireblocking (firestops) - a material which fills construction cavities to impede the spread of fire.

flashing - sheet metal or other material installed to block water penetration at construction seams.

frieze board - a horizontal band of decorative material at the top of an exterior wall, just below the eaves.

G

gable - the triangular portion at the top of a wall with a double sloping roof.

galvanic corrosion - corrosive breakdown which takes place when dissimilar metals are in contact in the presence of an electrolyte.

girder - a principal horizontal beam which supports concentrated loads.

glazing bead - removable trim which holds glass panes in place at a glazed opening.

grade beam - (interior or perimeter) the below-grade load-bearing part of a foundation system, designed as a beam, which either bears on footings or is self-supporting.

grout - mortar which is poured or troweled into the joints between tiles or other masonry components.

gusset plate - a plate used to connect two or more framing members, especially in a truss roof system.

H

hearth - the floor of a fireplace.

hose bib - (sill cock) an outdoor water faucet.

HVAC - relating to heating, ventilation, and air conditioning.

hydrojet - A spa jet designed to have air injected into its water flow by a mechanical blower.

hydrostatic relief valve - A valve (installed at the bottom of an in-ground pool) designed to relieve external ground-water pressure which might cause the pool structure to heave.

I

incandescent lamp - a light bulb in which a filament is energized by electric current to make light.

IRC - International Residential Code.

J

joist - one of a series of parallel horizontal beams used to support floor and ceiling loads.

K

knockout - a scored area in the surface of an electrical outlet box or panel which is removed to accommodate cables, circuit breakers or other electrical devices.

L

lattice - woven strips of any material used for ornamental screening.

leaching field - (absorption field) an array of trenches containing aggregate and distribution pipes through which septic-tank effluent seeps into the surrounding soil.

leader - a downspout.

lintel - a horizontal beam or structural member over an opening which carries the weight of the wall above it.

liquid line - a pipe carrying liquid refrigerant from a condenser to a metering device.

M

milliampere (MA) - 1/1000 of an ampere.

mortar cap - see coping.

N

NEC - National Electric Code.

ni-chrome - metal alloy from which nickel-chromium heating elements are made.

nosing (stair tread) - the horizontal projection of a stair tread beyond the riser.

O

oriented strand board - (OSB) manufactured sheet lumber made of strands or chips of wood glued and pressed together.

P

pane - a flat sheet of glass for glazing windows and doors.

panel box (service panel) - a box, usually containing breakers or fuses, located at the point of entry of electric service conductors.

plenum - an enclosed box or chamber used to aid in the distribution of conditioned air.

promulgated - officially published rules, requirements, laws or decrees.

psi - pounds per square inch, a measure of pressure.

P-trap - a "P" shaped bend in a wastewater pipe designed to seal out sewer gasses.

purlin - a structural member attached horizontally across rafters of a roof structure for strength.

purlin brace - a strut or post supporting a purlin.

R

racking - the movement of structural components out of plumb, often caused by foundation settlement, wind loads, seismic stress, thermal expansion & contraction, or shrinkage.

rafter - one of a series of inclined structural members to which a roof is attached.

rail - one of the horizontal structural members of a door or window frame.

rain cap - a device installed above the opening of a chimney or flue to prevent the entry of rain.

rake board - a board or molding at the sloping edge of a gable.

refractory - any material, especially cement, brick, and concrete capable of withstanding high temperatures.

refrigerant - the medium of heat transfer in a refrigeration system.

ridge board - a horizontal framing member at the apex of a roof which supports the upper ends of the rafters.

ridge brace - a vertical framing member which supports the ridge board.

riser - 1. the vertical face of a stair step 2. a plumbing vent.

run - 1. the width of a single stair tread as measured from front to back. 2. the horizontal distance covered by a flight of stairs.

S

saddle - 1. a cricket. 2. a threshold.

scab - a gusset plate or other flat brace used for bolting, nailing, screwing, or otherwise connecting two framing components.

service entrance - electric service components from the point of utility company supply to the service equipment or service panel.

shim - a thin, often tapered piece of wood, metal or stone which is inserted between structural members to adjust height or clearance.

short cycle - too-frequent sequencing of on-off cycles related to mechanical equipment.

sill plate - the bottom horizontal wall-framing member which is attached to the foundation and serves as a base for the studs.

soil stack - vertical waste pipe which carries the discharge from toilet fixtures.

sole plate - the bottom horizontal wall-framing member which is attached to a sub-floor and serves as a base for the studs.

spud washer - sealing washer used between the tank and bowl in a commode.

stile - one of the vertical structural members of a door or window frame.

strongback - a framing component which spans across the top of joists to connect and reinforce them.

suction line - the vapor line in a refrigeration loop.

sump - a pit, tank, or basin for the collection of liquid waste.

swale - a low area of soil in which excess surface water can flow.

T

terra cotta - unglazed fired clay used as roof or floor tiles.

thermocouple - a device which generates a voltage when heated, used to control fuel burning appliances.

threshold - a door sill.

top plate - the horizontal framing member at the top of a stud wall.

transpiration - the removal and evaporation of soil moisture by trees and other plants.

tread - the horizontal part of a step, including the nosing.

truss - a pre-assembled arrangement of framing members for roof or floor construction.

U
UBC - Uniform Building Code.

V
vapor line - See suction line.

vent skirt - a roof jack, flashing, or boot used to weatherproof a vent pipe at its roof penetration.

vent stack - a drain venting pipe open to the air, installed to prevent vacuum induced siphonage from breaking the water trap seals or interfering with the free flow of wastewater .

venturi jet - A spa jet specially designed to passively draw air, which is then mixed with its water flow.

volt - the unit of electromotive force which results in a current flow of 1 ampere when applied across a resistance of 1 ohm.

W
waterhammer - a banging noise caused by resonating water within supply pipes.

web members - a structural member which joins top and bottom chords in a truss.

weep hole - an opening in a wall or window frame through which excess moisture can escape.

weir gate - A floating gate or door at a pool skimmer inlet, designed to permit water into the skimmer while preventing debris from backwashing out into the pool.

REFERENCES

Books

International Code Council, Inc., *International Residential Code for One- and Two Family Dwellings*, fourth printing. 2000

Council of American Building Officials, *CABO One and Two Family Dwelling Code*, second printing. 1995

Kardon, Redwood, *Code Check, A Field Guide to Building a Safe House,* Revised Edition. The Taunton Press, Inc., 1996

International Conference of Building Officials, *Uniform Building Code (UBC)*, 1994 edition

National Fire Protection Association, *National Electric Code (NEC)*, 1999

Harrison, Henry S., *Houses. The Illustrated Guide to Construction, Design & Systems*, second edition. Dearborn Financial Printing, 1992

Ching, Francis D.K., *Building Construction Illustrated*, second edition. Van Nostrand Reinhold, New York, 1991

Black & Decker, *The Complete Photo Guide to Home Repair*, Creative Publishing international, 1999

Moore, H.B. Ph.D., *Wood Inhabiting Insects in Houses: Their Identification, Biology, Prevention and Control*, US Department of Housing and Urban Development, Washington D.C. 1979

Becker, Norman PE, *The Complete Book of Home Inspection*, second edition. TAB Books / McGraw-Hill, Inc., 1993

Burgess, Russell W., *Real Estate Home Inspection, Mastering the Profession*, second edition. Dearborn Financial Publishing, 1994

Harris, Cyril M. ed., *Dictionary of Architecture and Construction*, second edition. McGraw-Hill, 1993

CETC Unlimited, Inc., *Heating, Ventilation & Air Conditioning,* CE HI 007, 1997

Jacobus, Charles J. and Harwood, Bruce, *Texas Real Estate*, fifth edition. Prentice Hall, 1991

Taylor, Charles H., *Everything You Always Wanted to Know About Pool Care*, revised edition. Service Industry Publications, 1994

Perry Homes, *Construction Training Program, Phase II Manual*, Perry Homes, 1998

Periodicals

National Association of Property Inspectors, *Property Inspector News*, Vol 8 no. 2 – vol.10 no. 1. Rudy Linares, Real Estate Law Institute, Inc. 2000-2002

American Society of Construction Analysts, *A.S.C.A News*, George Szontagh, Gary Lemley, 1999-2002

Online sources

Pillar to Post, Information Series Bulletins, <www.pillartopost.com>, 2000-2001

Government documents

Texas Real Estate Commission, Austin, TX, Provisions of the Real Estate License Act, 535.227-535.231, 01 September 2000

US Federal Housing Administration, Washington, D.C., Division of HUD, Guidelines

Structural Pest Control Board of TX, Austin, 2000 Law and Regulations, Article 135B-6, Rules and Regulations, sections 4,5,10

Non-print sources

Richard Sewing, instruction, Houston Community College System Technology Center, Building Construction, 1998, Inspection Techniques, 1998

"Is Your Home Crumbling Around You?", Dateline, NBC Television, March 1999

Attorneys

Thomas A. Lukesetich, Atty.

Looper, Reed & McGuire, Attys.

L.J. Meyer, Atty.

PROCOR EDISON PUBLICATIONS CONTACT AND SERVICE INFORMATION

BOOK ORDERING

Professional Home Inspection Results $69.95

252 pages, 58 illustrations

To order, please visit our order fulfillment website page at:
www.procoredison.com

Also see our discount program for approved education providers
and other re-sellers at our website.
Questions? Call 1-800-724-2630

REVIEW QUESTION ANSWER KEYS
100 QUESTION FINAL EXAMINATION AND ANSWER KEY

for *Professional Home Inspection Results*

(Available only to education providers)

Phone: 1-800-724-2630

For additional information: www.procoredison.com

CONTINUING EDUCATION COURSE LICENSING AGREEMENTS

Education providers can obtain reproduction rights to individual modified chapters of *Professional Home Inspection Results* for the administration of continuing education courses. Procor Edison can assist you with course customization. Modest royalties are paid Procor Edison on a per-course-delivery basis.

Phone: 1-800-724-2630

For additional information: www.procoredison.com

Richard Lee Burgess

About the Author

Richard Burgess was raised in the New Jersey home built by his father. Through his school years, Richard was exposed to various construction trades during summer breaks, working at jobs including framing, concrete, cabinetry, roofing, and tiling. After purchasing his first home, he extensively remodeled bathrooms and kitchen, replaced staircases and doors, added porches, and re-designed the central heating and air conditioning systems.

Over time, he intensified his interest in the trades, completing several courses related to building construction and inspection techniques. In 1989, Richard moved to Houston, where he earned Texas' highest real estate inspector's license. During 1993 and 1994, he carried pre-sale inspection responsibilities for one of Houston's largest builders.

Since that time, Richard set out to develop his property inspection business, Pro-Tex Property Inspections. In 2001, Pro-Tex' inspection volume was over 275 home inspections.

On the premise that formal inspection would soon become an integral part of virtually every residential real estate transaction, the need for a complete source of reference became abundantly evident. Richard set out to fill that need. He worked tirelessly over a 4 year period to bring you this book, Professional Home Inspection Results. His goal was to bring aspiring and practicing home inspectors a complete understanding of the requirements of this most rewarding career.

READER SURVEY AND CONTRIBUTION

In order to provide the most accurate, complete, clear, and useful text possible, we need to know what you think. Your input is an essential part of our ongoing effort to maintain the highest standards. Please find the copy of this evaluation form provided online at www.procoredison.com and send it on to us. We promise to read and consider *every* comment submitted for inclusion in the next edition. Thank you!

PROFESSIONAL HOME INSPECTION RESULTS, 1st edition
Reader Survey & Contribution

your name   address   phone

course name   company name & address

email address   lic. classification / lic. # / expiration date

This course was part of a   ☐ self-study program   ☐ classroom study   ☐ correspondence course
Completion of this course took approximately how many hours? _____

Reader's comments: (Please circle one rating number per category)

Rating category:	Excellent	Good	Average	Fair	Poor
Text Organization	5	4	3	2	1
Relevance	5	4	3	2	1
Value of Content	5	4	3	2	1
Clearly Written	5	4	3	2	1
Subject Coverage	5	4	3	2	1

you found the material to be generally (circle one) -too complicated- -too simplistic- -about right-
you found the material to be generally (circle one) -not very useful- -somewhat useful- -very useful-
you found the material to be generally (circle one) -incomplete- -mostly complete- -very complete-

The book's fulfillment of its purpose is (circle one)   -poor-   -fair-   -good-   -very good-

The most useful part of this course:

The most difficult part of this course:

Changes you would like to see:

Errors or omissions you have found:

Additional comments:

Notes